$12.95

ASTROLOGY IN MODERN LANGUAGE

D1189185

THE ZODIAC

the zodiac is the belt of space surrounding the earth

ASTROLOGY IN MODERN LANGUAGE

Richard Vaughan

CRCS PUBLICATIONS
P.O. Box 1460
Sebastopol, CA 95473
USA

Library of Congress Cataloging-in-Publication Data

Vaughan, Richard B. (Richard Blackmore), 1916-
    Astrology in modern language.

    1. Astrology. I. Title.
BF1708.1.V38 1985   133.5   85-28074

SECOND PAPERBACK EDITION
INTERNATIONAL STANDARD BOOK NUMBER: 0-916360-50-4

Published simultaneously in the United States and Canada by:
CRCS Publications
Distributed in the United States and internationally by
CRCS Publications
(Write for current list of worldwide distributors.)
Cover Design: Image & lettering both by Rebecca Wilson

Contents

Chapter 1

WHAT IS A HOROSCOPE?

A horoscope is an astrological map of the heavens keyed to the time and place of a specific birth.

First, think of the earth as a circle or ball that rotates on its axis, making a complete turn (360°) approximately once every twenty-four hours. Then think of space as a fixed frame of reference that is arbitrarily divided into twelve equal segments of 30° each. If you were to place a mark on the circumference rim of the earth, this point would, as the earth turns, pass through all 360 points in space every twenty-four hours.

We call the twelve equal areas of space the signs of the zodiac. They follow each other in the following order: Aries, Taurus, Gemini, Cancer, Leo, Virgo, Libra, Scorpio, Sagittarius, Capricorn, Aquarius, Pisces. Each sign has special characteristics that mark and distinguish it from the others. They could be thought of as WEATHER CONDITIONS IN THE SKY.

In setting up the astrological map for the birth of a native we divide the circle into twelve sections (but not necessarily equal sections) depending on the longitude and latitude of birthplace. These areas are called houses. Each house defines a SPECIFIC AREA OF HUMAN EXPERIENCE in the affairs of the native. The first house concerns the native's personal identity. The second house deals with the native's earning power or source of supply. The third house concerns the native's thoughts or sense of communication, etc.

Since the circle, which is divided into twelve areas of experience, is rotating at the rate of one degree every four minutes, each area of experience passes through each of the twelve zodiacal areas of space (weather condition) during a twenty-four-hour period. There are various theories in astrology on how to divide the houses and assign the zodiacal areas of space. The system that is used in this book and is the most generally used in American and British astrological circles is known as the TROPICAL zodiac and the PLACIDUS house system. The questions that immediately arise are: How can there be more than one system, and which one is correct?

Astrology is more of an art than an exact science. In fact, by many standards it is not considered a science at all. Astrology is a system of symbolic values that is related to certain astronomical facts.

Historically, astrology preceded astronomy and the science of astronomy grew out of astrology. The symbolic values of astrology are today generally ignored and disputed by modern astronomers. While the astronomers feel that astrology cannot be proved in astronomical terms, at the same time they cannot disprove astrology. They can ignore it—pretend it doesn't exist—but they cannot disprove it.

The possibility that any set of symbols has value as it relates to human affairs happens to be something that one is constitutionally prepared to accept or utterly reject.

Astrology is in much the same position as religion. Either you concede that it has spiritual value or you do not. Religion cannot be proved or disproved. It is a matter of feeling—having faith in spiritual values—and not of knowing in a rational sense.

People who believe in astrology come to regard it as their religion because it is based on spiritual concepts. This is probably why mention of astrology tends to stir up fundamental controversy and why orthodox religions tend to be dead set against it.*

It is perhaps significant that astrology should once again gain in popularity just as the hold of religious organizations is being reexamined by many people.

Referring again to astrology as a system of symbolic values rather than facts, the evidence of truth or communication of knowledge comes from what the symbol SUGGESTS to the reader rather than what it is in a factual sense.

First, the reader has to have some familiarity with the nature of the symbols and the ways in which these symbols can be organized.

*Ed. Note: Not all astrologers regard astrology as their religion, and in fact quite a few people now use it for stock market analysis, commodity trading, weather predicting, etc. Many professionals in the healing arts and helping professions find it tremendously useful for a quicker understanding of their patients, even though they themselves do not consider

But there is no single reference in the symbol itself, nor is there any one set organization in which these symbols can be arranged.

That is why it is possible to have a number of astrological systems all of which may be equally valid in application. An astrologer may be more ideally suited to one set of suggestions than to another. The various answers (or reactions) should tend to substantiate and correlate one another, but the methods used to obtain these answers may widely differ.

This is a particularly difficult point to get across to people who are drawn to astrology yet require assurances from one definite system or a completely rational (as opposed to intuitive) explanation for things.

There is a similarity to the Rorschach inkblot tests used in psychological testing. The inkblot is a symbol. There is no exact category which this inkblot represents to the exclusion of other possibilities. The value of these symbols for testing is in the response of the viewer—what he sees in the inkblot. It is considered that certain psychological types tend to see similar objects in the inkblots, thus creating so-called normal reactions and variations from normal reactions. The purpose of the test is to discover variations from the normal rather than to confirm the normal.

The horoscope map, in addition to house areas and spatial designators called signs, also contains a third symbol—the planets (including the Sun and Moon, which are technically luminaries, not planets, but for convenience we will henceforth refer to them as planets).

While the houses of the horoscope identify areas of experience and the signs set the stage under which these areas of experience will operate, the planets act as symbols of force or the focus of attention bringing the other two elements together. There are two primary ways in which these three elements (houses, signs, planets) relate to each other.

One is through the "natural order" of relationships called RULER-SHIPS. The sign of Aries is considered, because of its nature, the natural sign of the first house. And Aries is focused or controlled by its natural planetary ruler, Mars. Each sign is naturally related to a specific area of experience, and each planet is naturally related to a specific sign.

At the present time science has confirmed the existence only of ten planets in our solar system. Since we have twelve house sections of the horoscope, two planets are said to rule two houses. Mercury

<hr>

it their religion. A survey of astrologers some years ago showed that considerably over 50% of them held very strong (and often unorthodox) spiritual values, but most would acknowledge that their faith in astrology developed after its accuracy and usefulness proved itself in experience.

rules both Gemini and Virgo, and Venus rules both Taurus and Libra. Most astrologers believe that there are two more planets yet to be discovered (or located) and that one of these will rule Virgo and the other Libra.

The other way in which the three elements relate is through their spatial distance, measured from each other by degrees. Planets at SPECIFIC DISTANCE POINTS from each other are said to be in ASPECT.

Thus the horoscope is a map showing the houses, signs and planets, and these elements relate to each other through natural RULERSHIPS AND ASPECTS.

The only way to master horoscope interpretation is to learn exactly what each house represents (and what it does not) and what characterizes each sign of the zodiac (and what does not) and the nature of each planet (and what it is not). Then become aware of how these elements relate to one another AND FIND WHAT THIS SUGGESTS TO YOU.

Thinking astrologically is similar to a challenge in LOGIC. If one premise is present and another condition is also present and certain other factors are introduced, the conclusion is THE WEIGHT OF PROBABILITY. You have to retain all the factors in mind so as to be conscious of their character IN COMBINATION.

One astrologer's reaction can be superior to another's, depending on the contribution that his particular talents can make to the picture or synthesis. We are not all equally gifted with understanding, analysis, intuition, synthesis and judgment. And we may also be subconsciously drawn to or focused on one particular pattern. We are dealing here with a complex picture that has a number of possibilities.

Nevertheless, there is a BASIC PATTERN or overall trend or COMMANDING JUDGMENT that can be seen AFTER ONE HAS LEARNED A TECHNIQUE.

Astrology is neither one exact system nor an exact science in the ordinary use of that term, even though it uses factors and measurements of a mathematical nature.

To interpret astrology is really an art, and no matter what others may tell you, IT REQUIRES INTUITION. I do not feel that you can develop a sense of intuition IF YOU ARE NOT BORN WITH IT. All these things, of course, show in your own horoscope.

The birth map is considered the NATAL HOROSCOPE. It is supposed to show all that is possible for the native to accomplish in this life, and it also shows what the native cannot achieve. The natal horoscope is considered a PROMISE. Nothing can happen that is not promised at birth. If the probability of a violent death is not in the natal horoscope, then the native will not have a violent death. If the probability of an important inheritance is denied in the natal horoscope, then the native will never enjoy such an inheritance. If the native's natal horoscope shows tempestuous relationships with children, then the native will always experience such relationships with children.*

Naturally the native would like to know WHEN certain things are likely to happen. This is perhaps the most hazardous element in horoscope reading. Many astrologers get themselves out on a limb in making exact predictions. Other astrologers have been extremely gifted in picking things out of the horoscope that have proved to be right.

Some astrologers do not actually approve of predicting future events of a personal nature. I would say that this is generally because they have no confidence in their ability to do this and they criticize others for trying. No one is 100 percent accurate all the time, but practice and confidence does improve one's "batting average," especially the more removed one is from any personal involvement with the horoscope.

Perhaps one of the most difficult questions to answer in astrology is whether or not the native will win a certain competition. This is because winning or not winning is a relative matter. One can win something in one way and lose in another. Also, life is considered by the astrologer to be primarily a spiritual challenge. Winning or not winning in a physical or material sense is only part of the scene. Many times the native may actually lose in a material sense but gain far more in a spiritual sense.

The probable outcome of the native's WHOLE LIFE PATTERN IS IN THE HOROSCOPE.

I have already mentioned that the astrologer considers life a spiritual challenge. This brings up two related matters: the irrevocability of predestination and reincarnation.

It is my considered position that the more one goes into these matters, the more predestination becomes overwhelmingly convincing. We are also involved with some pattern or form of reincarnation in which a soul or spirit lives on and experiences lessons and challenges on other levels, since the present life pattern is clearly mapped or designed in a specific direction (always implying other lessons and

*Ed. Note: Many experienced professional astrologers would strongly disagree with these statements. Although the opinions of practicing astrologers range from complete fatalism to belief in complete free will, the value of astrology for understanding self, others, and life's

other directions). To me this is inevitable if one is to pursue this matter deeply. However, I was born with a faith and a natural acceptance that this was the order of things. Astrology only proves to my satisfaction that this is so. I do not think that anyone can get very far in astrology if one does not take naturally to this kind of philosophy.

There is a great deal of controversy among astrologers themselves (who supposedly believe in astrology) as to what is implied by "free will" and "predestination." Many astrologers like to excuse themselves and get off the hook by stating that the "stars impel—they do not compel." I consider this an evasion of the ultimate implication upon which their belief is based.

Either your horoscope is your life map or it is not. And the condition of your so-called will is fully delineated in the horoscope. If you are strong in context A and weak in context B then you will characteristically react as weak when confronted with context B. It would be unnatural (and somewhat impossible) for you to do otherwise.

So where does free will come in?

What is known as free will is really a form of self-will, where the individual demands or feels the necessity to consider that his own ego creates both the opportunity and the solution for all that confronts him.

This may be somewhat true on a purely physical or material level. But man is generally considered more than just a physical or material animal. Not all men, unfortunately, but the best of men reflect a spiritual awareness, and it is with this spiritual awareness that astrology concerns itself.

Predestination denies free will. Predestination says that each of us has a purpose in life that can be defined in spiritual terms. This purpose is designed or laid out in advance by a force or spirit larger than our individual egos.

The purpose of our lives is to take what we have been given—our assets and our liabilities (which are also definable qualities in the horoscope)—and meet the challenge of our fate. The probability of this outcome is also predetermined because the measurement of life is the spiritual challenge, not the material achievement. It may seem that we exhibit some free will on material or physical matters, but control over spiritual matters is beyond us.

Very strong, self-willed, materialistic people believe that predestination robs them of the only excuse for living, WHICH THEY LIKE.

patterns is nonetheless the same. As more and more of astrology's medieval superstitions are discarded and as more practitioners acquire training in psychology and counseling, a greater number of astrologers believes that one's attitude toward one's experience and one's cosmic inheritance is absolutely crucial.

They often say, "What point is there in living if you know it all in advance?"

The point is, you only know the spiritual answer in advance—the real purpose for living. You do not know all the material details necessary to resolve the spiritual challenge.

We are not in this life to perform senselessly mechanical functions. It is hoped that we are in this life to accept some kind of spiritual growth.

There are many paths for seeking this knowledge. Astrology is only one such path, but it does offer a rather unique system of CHARACTER ANALYSIS, PREDICTION PROBABILITIES and a TIME SCHEDULE for making this fascinating journey called life.

Chapter 2

HOW TO SET UP A HOROSCOPE

It is very important from the beginning that you have your own horoscope to refer to because this is the only satisfactory way for you to test the validity of anything that is said about astrology. You must convince yourself that it really works. If you don't test it on your own horoscope, then it is all speculative.

You may have a horoscope map (or birth chart) calculated for you by using ACS, P.O. Box 16430, San Diego, CA 92116, or any number of other professional services. Be sure to check them out first since the accuracy of the calculations are crucial, and numerous heavily advertized services are incompetent. For a complete birth chart, you must have the date, place of birth, and exact time. For those with unknown birth times, there is still considerable valuable information you can obtain through astrology. (See Chapter 22.)

The time of birth, generally referred to as clock time, should be exact as possible. Only small allowance on time is possible because every four minutes of clock time accounts for one degree of movement by the earth around the zodiac. Any appreciable error is going to throw the house divisions off and place planets in the wrong houses.

A horoscope map looks like this:

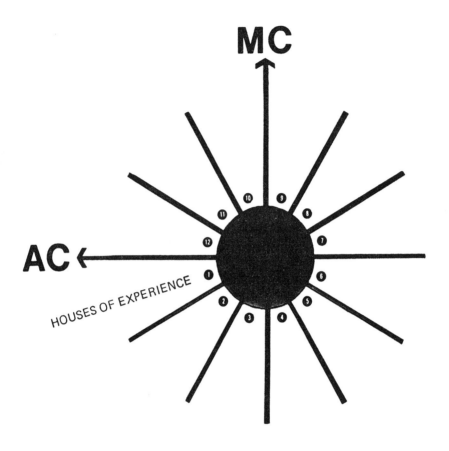

The Sun and planets may be at any position in space (i.e., in any house) at the moment of birth. The horizon of the earth at the place of birth at the moment of birth is indicated by the arrow above pointing to AC (the Ascendant).

The abbreviation AC is used throughout this book for the Ascendant. However, the abbreviation ASC is more commonly used in astrological literature. The *Sign* on the Ascendant is also called "The Rising Sign" since that sign is *rising* over the eastern horizon at the moment of birth.

The abbreviation MC (see above diagram & always found in the upper part of each horoscope) derives from the Latin *medium coeli*, meaning the "middle of heaven", and is generally referred to as the *Midheaven*. It is identical with the 10th house cusp in most house systems.

It is easy to set up a horoscope if you have a certain amount of technical skill. You may feel that you could never read a horoscope because you can't master the mathematics of setting one up. This is not necessarily true. People who are efficient at setting up horoscopes are not always best suited for a penetrating interpretation. Setting up a horoscope tends to be a mechanical skill. Interpreting a horoscope is an intuitive art.

Unfortunately, you will require the use of at least four reference books to calculate your own horoscope. That is why I am only describing in general the steps required for setting up the horoscope.

The house divisions appear as equal since we use printed forms. The actual area, however, is measured in degrees distance from the sign reading on one house line (cusp) to the next.

The houses are always shown in order. The cusp (beginning) of the first house (also known as the ascendant—AC) is the left-hand horizon. The tenth house cusp (also known as the meridian—MC) is always at the top, although it may not actually be at right angles (exactly 90°) to the horizon (AC) on the left.

At the moment of birth (which is calculated for a specific time and place) the tilt of the horizon (the Ascendant of the horoscope) was touching or at that point of space shown by the sign and degree measurement on the first house of the horoscope. *By mathematical relationship this point locates all the other features of the horoscope.*

At this moment of time each of the planets was at a specific point in space measured by the zodiac. This is calculated for noon at point zero degrees Greenwich (which is an observatory near London). This calculation is published annually in *Raphael's Astronomical Ephemeris* and other publications. It is one of the reference books necessary to setting up your horoscope.

Everything in the horoscope is placed by measurement in degrees of the zodiac. The zodiac is the BELT OF SPACE surrounding the earth. It is hypothetically divided into twelve equal segments of 30° each called SIGNS.

Since everything in the universe is in constant movement, the KEY to all measurements in astrology is TIME. That is why it is so important to know the exact time of birth.

The order of the signs around the zodiac is always the same:

ARIES, whose symbol is ♈ , is always opposite LIBRA, whose symbol is ♎

TAURUS	”	♉	”	SCORPIO	”	♏
GEMINI	”	♊	”	SAGITTARIUS	”	♐
CANCER	”	♋	”	CAPRICORN	”	♑
LEO	”	♌	”	AQUARIUS	”	♒
VIRGO	”	♍	”	PISCES	”	♓

Each sign contains exactly 30° (one-twelfth of the circle). The distance from 0° Aries to 15° Taurus is 45°.

SIDEREAL TIME is a BASE TIME FACTOR calculated for noon at zero degrees Greenwich. This is shown for each day of the year in *Raphael's Astronomical Ephemeris*. We must adjust this to the TRUE SIDEREAL TIME for the horoscope according to the actual time and place of birth.

We then trace this sidereal time reading to a set of HOUSE TABLES, where we can read off the measurements by sign and degrees for each of the twelve house divisions of the horoscope.

Once we have identified the area for each house division, we can then insert the planets into the horoscope BY HOUSE according to their own measurements by sign and degree. The planets' positions are calculated for each day at noon zero degrees Greenwich in *Raphael's Astronomical Ephemeris*. A slight adjustment is necessary for time and place of birth.

A complete horoscope would look like this:

This is the horoscope of President Richard M. Nixon.

The emphasis of this book is on how to interpret a horoscope rather than the mechanical know-how of setting one up; and since one needs four reference books with precalculated tables, the reader is referred to the abundance of good astrological textbooks on this subject.

It is realistic to state, however, that 80% of students trying to learn accurate chart calculation from a book will fall into the habit of making numerous errors. Not only does a complete set of calculation books cost over $50 total, but learning how to use them is much easier if one has a competent teacher. Therefore, the best approach for new students of astrology is to find a local teacher with whom you have some rapport. Otherwise, new students are best advised to use the chart calculation service mentioned on page 19; that company also sells very good ephemerides (tables of the planets' positions) for various time periods which enable you to look up where the planets were for any day in the past and where they will be for any future day.

The following general textbooks are recommended to new students for detailed study of chart interpretation:

The Modern Textbook of Astrology by Margaret Hone
All Works by Dane Rudhyar
All Works by Charles Carter
An Astrological Guide to Self-Awareness by Donna Cunningham
Astrology, Psychology and the Four Elements by Stephen Arroyo
Astrology, Karma and Transformation by Stephen Arroyo
Relationships and Life Cycles by Stephen Arroyo
Reincarnation Through the Zodiac by Joan Hodgson
A Journey Through the Birth Chart by Joanne Wickenburg
The Spiral of Life by Joanne Wickenburg
The Art of Chart Interpretation by Tracy Marks
The Planets and Human Behavior by Jeff Mayo

Chapter 3

THE HOUSES OF THE HOROSCOPE

Not only are the houses of the horoscope—their nature and their function—fundamental to the entire structure of astrology, but they should command the highest attention, consideration and study.

THE HOUSES DEFINE THE AREAS OF EXPERIENCE, LOCATE WHERE THE ACTION IS, AND FOCUS THE CONSCIOUS ATTENTION OF THE NATIVE ON THE MATERIAL THAT IS MOST IMPORTANT TO HIM.

The signs of the zodiac serve primarily as units of identity and measurement. That is, by their presence and degree they establish the character and "weather conditions" under which the action will take place (within a specific house area). They set the stage and color the scenery against which the story will unfold.

The planets provide the cast of characters and type of action that will take place. The nature of the action, disclosed by the houses, is more important than the scenery or tempo or weather conditions under which the action takes place (the sign on the house) or the instrumentalities or agents or instigators of the action (the planets).

Each planet is keyed to a specific sign of the zodiac. A planet is said to rule a sign because of an affinity in their natures.

Each sign of the zodiac is keyed to a specific house area of the horoscope also because of an affinity in their natures.

This so-called natural order of relationships is very important in learning TO THINK ASTROLOGICALLY because each contributes to the interpretation of the other. It is also through this chain of meaning that one synthesizes and interprets the individual horoscope.

Oddly enough, most astrologers tend to minimize the importance of the house factor in favor of the aspects that represent the angular relationship between the planets. You will often find astrologers talking exclusively about the angles between planets and saying almost nothing about the house structure, which is the ONLY FRAME OF REFERENCE THROUGH WHICH ANYTHING IN ASTROLOGY CAN MANIFEST ITSELF.

This is one reason why you will find this book on astrology different from most others on the subject. Throughout this presentation I will stress the function of HOUSE EMPHASIS over the importance of aspects between planets.

All the houses figure in some way in the native's total perspective. Each house contributes its influence in the affairs of another house through the affinity of rulerships. The planet that rules the sign on the cusp of the house points (by its house position) to the area of experience by which the affairs of one house "serve" another house. This is a very fundamental FLOW OF COMMAND. By a series of disposals—one house's affairs disposing (taking precedence) over another house's affairs—you can resolve the entire focus in a horoscope to one or more planets and several areas (sometimes just one area) of experience. This disclosure of pattern points out how a particular native will ultimately work out his "final" programs. It does not at the same time preclude independent action in any of the houses.

On examining horoscopes you will find that some houses are unoccupied by planets while other houses have many planets. An unoccupied house means that the native has no real problem or challenges with regard to the affairs of that house. Whatever is called for in the affairs of that house, the native can more or less take in his stride. It would be most unlikely to throw him out of balance or distort his overall perspective.

Any planet in a house immediately signifies that the native will have some conscious concern in that area of experience. This may be either pleasant or difficult, depending on other considerations.

Two or more planets in the house naturally give even more concern to the native over the affairs of that house. Through the chain of command—signs, planets and rulerships—one is able to determine the areas of experience that will occupy the native most and where the greatest concentration of force should ultimately be directed.

Regardless of any other considerations, the most important area of experience TO THE NATIVE is the house that holds the Sun. Since the Sun is the ego-force, this house identifies the focus through which the native must resolve his basic self.

The second most important area of the horoscope is the first house, since this is the FRONT DOOR through which most experience must enter in order to make meaningful contact.

Other houses that command special attention are the house that holds the ruler of the ascendant (first house), since this is the key to daily contacts; the house that holds the ruler of the Sun house, since this is the key which unlocks the native's fate; the house that holds the Moon, since this is the focus of the native's emotional attention; and the tenth house, which identifies the native's conscious ambitions as well as the report card that he will ultimately receive in life.

The house which holds the planet which rules the house under consideration naturally holds the key for the situation according to the nature of the planet itself.

As an initial step in learning astrology one is advised to concentrate first on the meaning of the houses. When one knows what affairs a house contains, one should also realize what affairs it does not include. Ultimately one should be able to fit any subject matter into one of the twelve house areas where it is related.

THE FIRST HOUSE: SIGN OF ARIES ♈ RULING PLANET, MARS ♂

As stated earlier, the tilt of the earth on the left horizon at the moment of birth determines the placement of all the other factors of the horoscope. This point of beginning, the ascendant, shows the rising sign and degree on the horizon at the moment of birth.

It is the FRONT DOOR through which all daily experience enters the life of the native. It has to do with the native's personal appearance and especially the casual impression he creates on superficial contact. In every sense this should be called the native's personality, since this is what shows on the surface. The nature of the first house shows how the native APPEARS TO OTHERS. This is how the world SEES the native, whether the world knows him in other ways or not. Outsiders are attracted to the native by the "sign" on this door. Whatever it says to them is what the world is initially expecting of the native. Naturally this may be at considerable variance with the native's own interests or real or hidden values, but this is something else.

This accounts to a great extent for certain people seeming to be natural sex symbols when in fact they may have no consciousness of sex. It also explains why certain people may indeed be extremely sexy yet seem not to appear so. It is also why some people are forever getting in trouble or attracting trouble through no intention of their own. In short, it accounts for most of the glaring contradictions we find in human behavior.

The first house also deals with personal identity and the sense of individuality and what it means to the native. When the first house is unoccupied, it means that the native's individuality is not a matter of personal and conscious concern. He accepts himself as he is, and there is no identity hangup. He does not have to spend conscious effort trying to develop or resolve personality problems.

If the first house is occupied with one or more planets, then the native is consciously concerned with some aspect of his identity. He has something to resolve on this matter.

The first house is considered to be referring to the general conditions of health and body, while illness and health fixations and such belong to the sixth house.

The first house has a great deal to do with not only the general treatment one usually receives, but also the type of work or kind of job assignments the native attracts. On quick survey the native would be judged best qualified for the tasks related to the sign on the AC. This may not be what the native wants at all, but the public is acting on the outside package and knows nothing of the contents. Life is like that. Packaging gets all the attention (and some of the rewards) and the real substance tends to get left behind.

There is some justification for this because it takes time to unwrap packages, and on the whole few people are interested enough to give more than a cursory reaction to anything besides their own affairs. The sooner people realize this, the better prepared they will be to adjust to the REALITIES of life.

ONE MUST ACCEPT PACKAGING AS A VERY REAL FACTOR IN DAILY LIVING. I think this is important to emphasize because, although it is desirable and an ideal attitude to look beneath the surface of a person for the so-called real man, we should at the same time realize that LIFE IN GENERAL DOESN'T CARE. There is a serious gap between our modern educational values, which stress the total inner man, and the surface reality we find in everyday life. It takes some people a lifetime to get over the impractical gaps that our educational system has helped create.

The reaction factor (of others to us) of the first house cannot be underestimated and should be constantly reexamined. Our natural attitude is focused on other (undoubtedly more meaningful) goals, but the "sign on our theater marquee" is what brings in the audience, whether or not we are prepared for the show they expect.

One system of considerable merit for tying the horoscope to certain key factors is the polarity of the Sun sign and the ascendant sign. There we would find the ego balanced against the image. Another grouping that receives even more attention is the "ego" contrasted or polarized with the "emotions"—Sun sign vs. the Moon sign.*

Naturally, a strong AC gives a strong impression and a weak AC gives an unfortunate impression. One has to work WITH AND AROUND this impression, regardless of any other factor in the horoscope.

The degree to which this surface image fits the rest of the native is important when considering other factors such as a happy life, ultimate chances for satisfaction or success, achieving one's purpose, securing cooperation or attracting opposition, and making something of your life or falling by the wayside.

♈ ARIES as the sign of spring, the beginning of a new cycle of growth, is the natural sign of the first house. The elemental makeup of Aries is FIRE, describing its spirit, and its position is CARDINAL, referring to leadership. Aries is very strong on individuality and a "me first" attitude. Aries is courageous, nervy, pushy, determined, aggressive, resourceful and competitive. Aries is also vain, conceited, opinionated, domineering, impulsive and defensive. Aries is better at starting things than at finishing them. Aries is warmhearted, ardent, sincere, outspoken, enthusiastic, optimistic and well intentioned. Aries also needs encouragement, faith and appreciation. Aries is essentially naïve and trusting but also brave, strong and protective. Aries is an instigator, promoter and pioneer. They make good leaders but poor followers. They can be recklessly unconservative. As might be supposed, as natural ruler of the first house, THEIR GREATEST STRENGTH LIES IN THEIR SENSE OF INDIVIDUALITY.

The reader will note that I do not believe in listing qualities as positive or negative. Such terms are relative to some moral frame of

---

*Perhaps the most outstanding collection of Sun/Moon polarity readings is found in Grant Lewi's excellent book *Heaven Knows What.*

reference according to how others feel one SHOULD ACT. All these above qualities are natural to Aries. The natives of every sign should use ALL THEIR NATURAL RESOURCES to be themselves. I do not want to stress the "don'ts." If one concentrates on being oneself, the "don'ts" tend to take care of themselves.

To caution Aries to stop being part of himself is to discard part of what Aries is. And there is too much balancing out to zero in most astrological commentaries.

If someone is an Aries (Sun in Aries), his ego drive has to win on Aries' terms. There is no choice. If this offends some other sign of the zodiac, that is unfortunate. We are here to fulfill our individual destinies. And if each one will be true to his own qualities, there is no need for interference with another's natural functions. Astrology teaches us that each person is unique.

♂ MARS, the natural ruler of Aries, is the planet of INITI-ATING FORCE. It is the natural energizer in the horoscope. It takes the spirit of Mars to put all the Aries qualities into action. Like Aries, Mars flares up but fizzles out. It does not sustain a constant output of high-voltage energy but generally acts as a trigger or impulser. It is the planet most associated with sex as a physical and biological pas-sion. It is both creative and destructive. When fully aroused, it is invariably violent. Its strength lies in its force and sudden action. It makes war and also love. Mars is said to be hot, moist and volatile, sharp and penetrating. It is ideally designed for getting things done and to hell with the consequences (a typical Aries attitude).

While Aries is the natural ruler of the first house, it may be found in any house in the horoscope. It is only most at home in the first house. Wherever Aries is found in the horoscope, there is where he will show the most individuality, the most resourcefulness and the most "ego resistance," along with all the other Aries characteristics. The same applies to Mars. While Mars is most at home in the first house, directing its energies toward the native and keeping his own individuality in line, Mars can fall anywhere in the horoscope—on any area of experience or interest and under any weather condition (sign of the zodiac). For a discussion of Mars in the horoscope see Chapter 8.

THE SECOND HOUSE: SIGN OF TAURUS ♉ RULING PLANET, VENUS ♀

The second house of the horoscope is concerned with the nature of supply and resources. This is the money house in terms of earnings and what the native acquires through his own labors. It also includes possessions and so-called portable property.

If this house is unoccupied, it means that money and earnings as such are not really a major issue in the native's life. Generally speaking, whatever the native has to do to earn sufficient money is done in due course with no problems.

If the house is occupied by one or more planets, then the native's conscious attention is focused on the necessity and importance of money and possessions. Whether this is a make-or-break factor depends on the signs and planets involved. With planets in the house, the affairs of the houses that these planets rule are also brought to bear on matters of money and supply. These houses are natural contributors to the native's source of earnings. For more detailed treatment see Chapter 10, "The Source of Money in Your Life."

♉ TAURUS is the natural accountant of the zodiac, and it is fitting that Taurus should preside over resources and possessions. Taurus is steady and dependable and enjoys looking after all the comforts that make life easier, more pleasurable and satisfying. The Taurus element is EARTH and mother nature, and its disposition is FIXED and unswerving. Its other qualities are earthy sensitivities, material instincts, fidelity, compulsion, sense of reality and practicality. As one can see, Taurus needs some kind of function to perform, some situation which he can nourish and supply.

THEIR GREATEST STRENGTH LIES IN THEIR PROVISION FOR NOURISHMENT.

♀ The planet VENUS is the natural ruler of Taurus. Venus is the SENTIMENT OF LOVE AND AFFECTION, conservation and comfort. It is known as the lesser benefic. Jupiter of abundance is the greater benefic. Venus is a force that beautifies and makes life attractive and comfortable and smooths over the rough spots. It has a certain fixation and earthy attachment which adjusts or covers over anything that is displeasing or unattractive.

THE THIRD HOUSE: SIGN OF GEMINI ♊ RULING PLANET, MERCURY ☿

The third house is the house of communication. It rules the instrumentalities of thought such as the native's tools for thinking and his thought patterns in general. It is also said to include brothers and sisters, short journeys, the immediate neighborhood, messages, news and all forms of communication or places where thoughts or goods are exchanged such as the market place, shops, and clientele.

If unoccupied, the native (in spite of how it may appear to others) feels no self-consciousness on any of these matters. He responds in due course as expected or in his natural fashion, which can be eccentric but may not seem so to him.

If occupied by one or more planets, then the native is self-conscious and concerned in some way about his own thought processes or need for communication or how to get something across. Difficulties in speech, ease or command of language or characteristics of expression are all shown in the third house.

The houses ruled by the planets in the third house contribute, inspire or influence the native's thinking and sense of communication.

♊   The sign of GEMINI, the messenger, is the natural ruler of the third house. The element of Gemini is AIR (concerned with ideas) and its disposition is MUTABLE (changeable, flexible, and adaptable). Gemini is a mental sign and exhibits a certain surface brilliance. It is said to be alert, suggestive of intellect; to grasp things quickly; to be able to communicate on all levels and switch from one subject to another with ease; to seem to know something about everything; to have a fondness for talking and exchange of news and views. Gemini often provides a link beween one position and another that would otherwise not be possible. It breaks down barriers and puts things on an equal mental footing where we can all communicate. There is a spirit of comradeship and brotherly interest in fellow travelers. Gemini tends to speak his piece and then fly off. The effect is fleeting, transitory, somewhat superficial BUT HIGHLY EFFECTIVE AT THE TIME. Gemini also has a sense of gaiety and a happy-go-lucky quality. Their talk is warmly engrossing at the moment but can be quickly forgotten. Out of sight is out of mind with Gemini. Gemini can be very persuasive. They make good salesmen. Their challenge is to convince others. There is no absolute standard for Gemini, so their truth is highly variable, depending on their mood and what they are trying to sell. They can be charming and captivating, entertaining and lively.

THEIR GREATEST STRENGTH IS EXPRESSION AND COMMUNICATION.

☿   The planet Mercury is the natural ruler of Gemini, and mental Mercury suits it perfectly. Mercury is said to be the quality of the "mind." Mind in this sense is considered the reflector of the inner man (or ego-drive), so Mercury is a mirror or messenger for another (the self).

Natives with a fortunate Mercury are very persuasive and easily draw attention to themselves for their apparent brilliance and ease of expression. They may not be saying anything very profound, but it sounds good.

Mercury is more the packaging or outer dressing of the thought rather than the contents or intent, since Mercury is only the agent or go-between in the mind process. It does not stand on its own and in fact is never very far removed in space from the Sun (ego-drive), being either ahead or behind according to its rate of speed, which varies considerably.

THE FOURTH HOUSE: SIGN OF CANCER ♋ RULING PLANET, MOON ☽

The fourth house (like the first, seventh and tenth) is one of the four angles of the horoscope. These cardinal points, as they are called, are considered leading and prominent. Natives with heavy concentrations of planets in any of the four angular houses are destined to influence their fellow men in some way.

The fourth house is a subjective area. It is concerned with the home, basic security, the parental influence (the mother or the parent most motherly), early upbringing, background, heritage, and it describes the general conditions at the end of life. More abstractly it also defines one's methods, natural technique or pattern of operation by which one approaches the world or conscious goal as defined by its opposite (the tenth house). It is also associated with real estate, fixed or unportable property and elements of value buried in the ground.

The native is naturally touchy about anything that involves his fourth-house affairs, for it threatens his security, home and the ideals of his heritage.

The fourth house is essentially HOW THE NATIVE SEES HIM-SELF—SUBJECTIVELY.

If the house is unoccupied, then the native accepts his background as a matter of course and makes the best of it. There are no unresolved questions in his mind about fourth-house matters.

If, on the other hand, there are one or more planets in the fourth house, then the native's conscious attention is directed toward his background. He has reason to question, doubt and rearrange those matters that give him concern and threaten his security as he sees it. He is also conscious of the functional techniques by which he hopes to gain his conscious goals (shown in the tenth house). Some people are prone to do the wrong thing in terms of what they are seeking.

Others have the most unfortunate liabilities to overcome before they can seem to make any headway in getting what they want. Others suffer immeasurably from early parental influences that leave a permanent scar on the consciousness. All this is shown in the fourth house.

The affairs of the houses ruled by the planets in the fourth house all have bearing and influence and disruptive potential on the security of the fourth house.

♋ CANCER, the symbol of protection, is the natural ruler of the fourth house. Its element is WATER (emotionally fluid) and its position is CARDINAL (a leading influence). Cancer is the maternal sign and its dominant characteristic is motherly (even in men). Cancer possesses great sensitivity, intuition and a native talent for timing, rhythm and harmony.

Timing in every sense of the word is perhaps the greatest gift one can have. There is no point in doing the right thing at the wrong time. Those who have a perfect sense of timing always seem to be at the right spot when the best things are being handed out. Cancer in a prominent place in the horoscope—or a very fortunate Moon—gives this sense of inborn timing. Cancer, no matter what others may think, always knows what is best for himself. And he wants to know what is best for those he loves. This, however, may not always be possible, for each life is an independent matter. Cancer also has a way of turning on and off, which gives him great staying powers. When he senses things are as he likes them, he turns on. And when he doesn't want to see something, he can turn completely off, which saves his delicate sensibilities but also makes him seem strangely cold and hardened, which is out of keeping with what one normally expects from Cancer. But this is the very source of Cancer's strength; otherwise he would be hopelessly dissipated with stimuli of no value.

Cancer is a fruitful and productive sign once it is fertilized. But once fertilized, it can also prove very independent and self-willed. It is more than willing to be receptive and listen to what the other party has to offer and it also has a magnetic power to attract what it needs. This is more than can be said for most of the other signs. The greatest hazard that Cancer has to face is to let its "turned off" (negative) rest periods predominate over its "turned on" (creative) periods. Sometimes Cancer finds it very difficult to feel positive about anything. They can be excessively negative in all directions. The one thing that seems to snap them out of this is—unfortunately because it is so material—to get set on building up a super sense of security. Cancers are great money-makers. They never feel they have enough. They are often plagued with a fear-security and this drives them to fantastic moneymaking. It is said that the best moneymakers in the world are prominent Cancer types (Sun, AC or MC in Cancer). THEIR GREATEST STRENGTH IS PRODUCTIVITY.

  ☾   The mysterious and feminine Moon is the ruler of Cancer. It gives sensitivity, intuition and understanding, but it also gives moods, cycles and unstable attitudes.

It is perhaps somewhat odd that the most unstable and changeable planetary force is the natural ruler of our holiest of holies—the fundamentals of our security. Perhaps there is a good reason for this. Perhaps we associate too much fixed security thinking with matters of the fourth house. Perhaps we should be more fluid, changeable and responsive in our thinking as to exactly where our sense of security comes from.

While the general content of the fourth house is said to be fixed and nonportable assets like real estate, mineral wealth and family heritage, perhaps the REAL SECURITY IS ADAPTABILITY TO CHANGING CONDITIONS AND CAREFUL ATTENTION TO THE RHYTHM AND HARMONY OF TIMING—all qualities of the Moon. The two do not always go together, as evidenced by the changeable and fickle Moon. This lesson also points out that when you can do nothing constructive about a situation, you should tune out, reflect on the matter, and tune in when you feel you can do something. The Moon does this all the time, and so does Cancer.

The Moon as natural ruler of the fourth house also indicates that no one should be so positive or fixed in his attitudes or technique patterns that he turns a deaf ear to the changes and possibilities that are always there for those who look for them.

THE FIFTH HOUSE: SIGN OF LEO ♌ RULING PLANET, SUN ☉

The fifth house is the house of creative self-expression. It also has to do with pleasures, speculation, taking a chance and making romantic love.

IF YOU ARE GOING TO GAMBLE AND WIN, YOU HAD BETTER HAVE A GOOD FIFTH HOUSE: OTHERWISE YOU ARE GAMBLING TO LOSE.

If the house is unoccupied, fifth-house matters tend to play a small role in the native's life. These matters do not have much attraction for the native. He can take them or leave them alone. This does not mean that the native will have no children, love life or enjoy the pleasures of life, but it does mean that the native will not be much affected by them.

If the house is occupied with one or more planets, then the native has a natural interest and/or problems connected with all fifth-house matters. One cannot have a poor fifth-house condition and enjoy some fifth-house matters and not others. All these matters are related in some way and a poor fifth house is reflected in all related matters.

Naturally, the houses ruled by the planets in the fifth house contribute and inspire all fifth-house creativity (art, children, speculation or love). Perhaps it is advisable to mention at this time that there are many kinds of love and they all are expressed differently in various houses.

The love, admiration and esteem for one's parents or heritage is found in the fourth house.

Romantic love as a pleasurable flirtation and the love for one's children or self-created art forms is found in the fifth house. Sex connected with romantic love-making is also a fifth-house matter.

The love for one's duty or obligations in servitude (if this can be considered love) is found in the sixth house.

The love for one's partner AND ENMITY FOR ONE'S OPEN ENEMIES is found in the seventh house.

There is a sensual side of sexuality connected with the "regenerative" effect of sex that treats sex for its own sake and not a part of romantic love-making. This sexuality is found in the eighth house.

The love for God or higher principles is found in the ninth house.

The love for authority and for one who dominates you in some important way—as one's master—is found in the tenth house.

The love for one's friends and the joys of companionships is found in the eleventh house.

The love for the downtrodden, lost and unfortunate is found in the twelfth house. This is a very real and even sexual love for some people.

In fact all love forms as listed above can take on a sexual implication depending on other factors shown in the horoscope.

But love, in the ordinary sense, is the romantic love-making (including sexuality) found in the fifth house. If one's sexuality is related to this kind of love-making, then it is a fifth-house matter.

♌ . LEO the king of beasts is the natural ruler of the fifth house. His element is FIRE (in spirit), and his position is FIXED (unyielding and determined). Leo is the symbol of the king, and it takes all the self-assurance in the world to feel really creative, grand and noble.

Leos tend to be arrogant, self-centered and imperial, but when they feel safe and secure, they can give all their kingdom away in one gracious gesture because it flatters their ego, which is tremendous. The trouble is, their ego needs constant support and nourishment; otherwise they feel very unkingly. In fact a king without a kingdom and subjects to rule is not a king at all. A proper audience is mandatory in order for Leo to come on in kingly fashion. Leos take great risks and will gamble on anything. They can also be childish and peevish and sulky and naughty—just like most children. Their charm and their downfall both stem from the childlike qualities they have. Everything equates to their ego. If their ego is safe and ACKNOWL-EDGED AS DOMINANT, then everything is fine. If not, they feel crushed.

Leo tends to play the game on an all-or-nothing-basis like all gamblers. The trouble is, in real life this can lead to disastrous results. Leos (like children) have a tendency when thwarted to "pack their toys and go home." In life this can mean "lights out." Leos are very suicide-prone. They just cannot accept halfway measures or much of anything that compromises their position as they see it. Leo will seldom tolerate being crossed or bypassed, so to keep on the good side of Leos, you have to cater to them most of the time. This may or may not be a joy, but like it or not, you have to keep it up or Leo will walk right out the door.

Never put your ego ahead of a Leo. Always let Leo think that your ideas were his. Leo has a blindness for the most obvious facts and truths which never seem to bother him. His fondness for creativity and position encourages him to throw everything into the pot and believe it is all true. What Leo makes up or pretends is true is just as real to him as anything else.

THEIR GREATEST STRENGTH IS NOBILITY OF SPIRIT.

● The Sun as the supreme ego is the natural ruler of the fifth house. It feels most at home in this freedom-and pleasure-seeking area, where speculations and gamble are the order of the day. The ego Sun can really shine when all its children look up to it as a respected father image, and at the same time it is unlimited in its generosity to indulge and delight all those who flatter its vanity and support its ego.

THE SIXTH HOUSE: SIGN OF VIRGO ♍ RULING PLANET, MERCURY ☿

The sixth house is the house of responsibility. It represents duty, service, obligations and a sense of indebtedness that either the native owes to others or others owe to him. Thus it is the house of servants and employees and also the native's own role as servant or employee. It is the least "free" area of the horoscope. One feels or senses a bondage which must be worked off. It is also considered to represent sickness and health, whereas the first house represents one's general physical condition. The native's general susceptibility to illness is indicated in the first, but the conditions of illness are reflected in the sixth.

The sixth house is somewhat karmic in nature, as the reason for this sense of obligation or duty or debt to be discharged is somehow linked with associations not obviously on the surface.

♍︎　The sign of VIRGO, the virgin, is the natural ruler of the sixth house. Her element is EARTH (and physical ties) and her position is MUTABLE (supports another or exists only to lend herself to others). Virgo natives are very exacting, precise and detailed. They take great pains with all their undertakings and expect others to do the same. While Virgos are keyed to serving others in some way, they are also very demanding in the quality of service that is due to them. As a mutable sign they contribute the content while others determine the form. They are less effective as leaders, since they naturally look for outside direction. The most difficult experience for Virgos occurs when their contributions (which are made in utmost sincerity) are rejected, downgraded, or unappreciated in the way Virgos feel entitled. Any service that relates to the routine of daily living is a welcome assignment for Virgos. This would include housing, providing a home away from home, food, beverage, health and any kind of order keeping.

THEIR GREATEST STRENGTH IS THEIR PRECISE REFINEMENT.

☿　Mercury, at the moment, is considered the natural ruler of Virgo. However, it is felt that an undiscovered planet is probably more closely related to the exacting nature of Virgo than the mercurial Mercury. Mercury as a mental reflection of a more forceful guiding principle fits Virgo (and the sixth house) well. But there is a deep-seated and compelling force about Virgo that is not wholly explained by just Mercury. Until that planet is discovered, Mercury will continue to rule Virgo. But when a new ruler is discovered, all those natives who have a prominent Virgo will experience fundamental changes. This could affect the reputation of the dead, as well as those living at the time.

THE SEVENTH HOUSE: SIGN OF LIBRA ♎ RULING PLANET, VENUS ♀

The seventh house is the house of other people in the way they relate to the native. Or, more exactly, in the way in which the native sees others. While the first house represents HOW THE NATIVE APPEARS TO OTHERS and the fourth house HOW THE NATIVE SEES HIMSELF, the seventh house represents HOW OTHERS APPEAR TO THE NATIVE. The seventh house represents the general nature of the native's outlook on the world. It represents partnerships of all kinds—marriage, business, etc. It also represents one's open enemies and obvious competitors—those who challenge or assist the native in some way. The first house is all "me." The seventh house is all "they" or the other fellow. It represents the extent to which the native is dependent on others and also the extent to which others help or guide or dominate the native. It does not represent the whole world, but only those whose lives touch the native. It defines the native's audience and who can potentially respond to him as a personality.

If the house is unoccupied, the native is comparatively free of the influence of others in most of his affairs. He does pretty much as he pleases as far as having to consider others or adjust to suit someone else. But it also means that other people are generally not much help to the native. The native must stand on his own feet and generate his own opportunities. When it comes to others, the native can generally take them or leave them alone. The affairs of this house are always related in some way to that area and persons representing it where the planet that rules the sign on the seventh cusp lies.

If there are one or more planets in the seventh house, the native is consciously dependent on others in some respect and other people tend to control his affairs (connected with that planet). The affairs of the houses that these planets rule are also controlled or keyed to others. The native has less to say about any of these matters.

♎ The sign of LIBRA, the balance, is the natural sign of the seventh house. Its element is AIR (based on ideas, ideals and concepts) and its position is cardinal (dominating). Libra is always concerned with other people. It is the most social sign of the zodiac. While usually friendly, gracious and hospitable, Libra can also be argumentive, threatening and revengeful. The seventh house is also the house of open war, and Libra is capable of instigating an all-out war when necessary to restore the balance to the other side of the scales. Whether Libra makes love or war depends on which idea or ideal Libra happens to be pushing at the moment.

Libra, like all cardinal signs, tends to step forward and assume leadership and direction. While Aries originates his own conviction for leadership (based on his personalized individuality), Cancer is motivated for emotional reasons that are generally protective and self-centered. Libra springs into action as a result of an interaction or reaction to someone else. Libra reacts to others on the basis of an idea or ideal which to him seems out of balance and in need of correction. Each cardinal sign is just as convinced of the inherent right of its own position but on different grounds. It is the spirit of the thing to Aries, the feeling of the thing to Cancer, the idea of the thing to Libra, and the practical desirability of the thing to Capricorn (the fourth cardinal sign).

The trigger motivation for Libra is not so much originality (as it would be for Aries) but a reaction or response to other people. This can and does sometimes lead to love and cooperation, but it can also lead to resistance and war. Some Libras are more responsive to resistance than cooperation.

THEIR GREATEST STRENGTH IS THEIR CAPACITY TO RELATE TO OTHERS.

♀ VENUS, the social planet, is said to be the natural ruler of Libra and the seventh house. All the general qualities of Venus (beauty, comforts, feelings of satisfaction, general inducements toward goodwill and emotional rapport) fit well with most of Libra's qualities. But there is another side to Libra that is not too well represented by Venus. Therefore the yet undiscovered planet that some astrologers feel should be assigned to Taurus might better be considered the true ruler of Libra. The nature of Taurus is pretty much a single piece or tempo like Venus. But Libra has a decided gingerlike kick, which is not at all like Venus. Until this planet is discovered, however, Venus will continue to rule Libra.

THE EIGHTH HOUSE: SIGN OF SCORPIO ♏ RULING PLANET, PLUTO ♇

Here we come to one of the mystery areas of the horoscope, which is generally misunderstood by most people, including astrologers. This is probably because of an unpleasant side to all three factors (the eighth house, Scorpio and Pluto), which frightens some people.

First, the eighth house represents a point in time or space where some significant transition or mutation takes place. It therefore represents some crisis or catastrophic event or happening, where one form of something stops or dies and another takes over. This can be a form of rebirth or a devastating revelation to the native. It can be triggered by an event or it can come from within. The eighth house is known as the house of death, and it generally describes the nature of the native's death. But it also describes important changes in the native's life and his reaction to them. Death in the philosophy of astrology is not just an ending where something ceases to be. Death is considered a transition of the spirit in which one form is discarded for another—one form mutates into another. Thus rebirth and death go together.

There may be many points of crisis in the native's life, where one mode of living completely comes to an end and the native is forced to pick up the pieces and carry on in a different way. These things are all shown in the eighth house. The eighth house is also the area of rejuvenation or breathing new life into old forms or how the native has been accustomed to seeing things.

The sexuality of the eighth house is sexual expression for its own sake. The "pickup" value of sex, as evidenced in prostitution (sex without love), is found in the eighth house. Sexuality as a ritual and by-product of states of individual consciousness is a matter of the eighth house. Perversions of sexuality could be a matter of the eighth house but not exclusively. Some people consider any sex that is not associated with creating offspring as some form of perversion. This is, of course, a narrow point of view not realistic or compatible with the whole of nature.

The eighth house is an area that also represents the supplies and resources created by the native in partnership with others. It represents taxation and insurance, and most important, it is the affairs and property of the dead—therefore inheritance through death.

Inheritance that comes to the native as part of his parental background is a matter of the fourth house. The inheritance that comes from the eighth house represents supply not earned by the native as a product of his work efforts. It comes about through a link with another, which may be of a secret or hidden nature. It is also the wealth or resources of the partner, but this may not always come to the native through inheritance.

There is a fiduciary aspect of eighth-house matters in which the native may take care of or hold property in trust for the benefit of another.

If the house is unoccupied, the native generally takes all eighth-house matters in stride. If an emergency arises, the native usually faces it with some degree of appropriate action. The affairs of this house are always related in some way to the area (and the persons representing it) where the planet that rules the sign on the eighth cusp is found. If the house is occupied, eighth-house matters are of some conscious concern to the native. A prominence there makes the native well suited to some form of fiduciary role or of managing the affairs of the dead or providing direction for others in times of crisis. It also gives a talent for discovering or realizing profit or advantage from things or circumstances left for dead by others. This would include dealing in antiques, artifacts, junk, and archaeological findings. The former owner's link to the object has died, and a new link or value is established by the native.

The affairs of another house (or people represented by them), as shown by the sign that the planets in the eighth house rule, contribute to the significance of the native's eighth-house strength.

♏ SCORPIO is the natural ruler of the eighth house. Its element is emotional and its position FIXED (rigidly concentrated). Almost everything about Scorpio is hidden and secretive, and Scorpio wants everything to remain that way as far as his own affairs are concerned. On the other hand, Scorpio has a naïve curiosity about the intimate affairs of everyone else. There is a strong sexual character to most of Scorpios' motivations, although they would be the last to admit it to themselves. They have great powers for rejuvenation and endurance WHEN CALLED UPON, but they often remain in a semidetached state of mind unless some important crisis arises. Scorpios are perhaps at their best when actively engaged in helping others face some momentous crisis. At such times they seem to understand everything, even though they may never have faced such a situation before.

Most of the time Scorpios idle away their time poking into situations that others have given up or discarded for something more obviously lifelike. But Scorpio, with his fixed determination, often turns up hitherto-unsuspected values and rewards in these dead situations. In any event it gives Scorpio secret satisfaction to be able to say, "I told you so." Not all Scorpios are called upon to serve at times of great crisis, but they often are on affairs of less dramatic import. Others seem to sense naturally Scorpios' talents for such emergencies and instinctively turn to them.

THEIR GREATEST STRENGTH IS TO RESTORE NEW LIFE INTO OLD FORMS.

♇   PLUTO, a planet discovery of only recent times, is now considered the real ruler of Scorpio. Pluto's inner nature fits perfectly the dual aspect of Scorpio (before and after change). Before the discovery of Pluto in 1930, Mars the warmaker was considered the ruler of Scorpio. The Mars quality fits perfectly the simple directness of Aries but does not begin to describe fully the limitless depths of the Scorpio nature, half of which is always hidden under the surface.

Pluto is the symbol of revolutionary change. It destroys or wipes out with one hand while it gets ready to build anew with the other. It is always a two-way deal. Revolutionary Pluto is always ready to ring the death bell on old situations in order to make way for an improvement. Most people (including many astrologers) fear Pluto, for they only see the dark side and are naturally reluctant to release the familiar in order to receive something new and different. Change is frequently difficult when it calls for emotional leave-taking. But the thrill of new projects can be very stimulating, creative and constructive. Too often Pluto is thought of only as death—not the life giver as it can be. How much of what anyone enjoys today would be possible without the death of the past on which it stands? The cycle of life and death and then life again is part of nature and always renews itself by natural means. Pluto is the instrumentality of this process.

THE NINTH HOUSE: SIGN OF SAGITTARIUS ♐ RULING PLANET, JUPITER ♃

The ninth house is the house of higher learning. It represents the point at which many thoughts are gathered together and codified into one cause or principle. Thus laws and religions and philosophies are created, as well as all sorts of principles, which in essence represent the thinking of many minds. If the third house is the individual mind, the ninth house is the collective mind after it has been organized.

If the house is unoccupied, the native finds it easy to accept the validity of certain principles or causes or religions because he naturally identifies with some part of them. There is no resistance to higher principles that have been organized or coded by others. He does not reject the conceivability of an ego greater than his own. The affairs of this house are always related in some way to the area or persons representing it where the planet that rules the sign on the ninth cusp is found.

If the house is occupied, the native is concerned with the formulation of or opposition to some aspects of collective thought or

developed principles. The affairs or other areas and the people represented by them contribute to the importance of ninth-house thinking
according to where the signs are that these planets rule.

♐ SAGITTARIUS, the archer, is the natural sign of the ninth
house. His element is MENTAL and his position is MUTABLE and
yielding. He symbolizes the spirit of the law rather than the law
itself. Sagittarians are naturally optimistic, enthusiastic, positive,
self-ordained for their mission, dedicated to their cause, generally
unselfish in their ambition, pure in heart, devotedly loyal, and sus-
tained by faith in the desirability of their cause. They are useful in all
expressions of higher learning, law, religion, philosophy and politics.
They assume that in most respects they are their brother's keeper,
and they know better than he does what is best for him. If he fails
immediately to see the situation in that light, they are gifted with
great faith and endurance to persuade the less fortunate to see their
more enlightened point of view. Naturally they need a cause worthy
of their highest efforts and pure enough in spirit to justify the sacrifices and devotion of which they are capable. While Sagittarians are
mutable in their position, they have a way of reflecting causes or
principles that sometimes are not exactly in keeping with the realities
around them. Sagittarian thinking tends to be up in the clouds rather
than down-to-earth. On the whole Sagittarians are much less effective
during periods of change, when old institutions are being replaced
and the new ones have not yet established themselves sufficiently to
be "obviously right." Since Sagittarians put so much faith in the
power of collective thought, particularly that established by pre-
cedent, they tend to resent the thrust of any individual positions that
challenge them. Sagittarians are not nearly so well prepared for defensive tactics as they are for the circulation of the "right gospel."
They become obstinate when challenged, and their faith can turn to
blind sacrifice. They are at their best when the going is all "up and
up." They can be pitifully ill equipped to strike a meaningful note
when underlying ideas are challenging the principles they originally
fostered or produced. Sagittarians often become a voice out of time
and place, which somehow they are unable to see about themselves.
They do not get along with everybody. They are generally unable to
share the same enthusiasm for causes other than their own and they
can be intolerant of and uncharitable to those who do not share their
convictions.

THEIR GREATEST STRENGTH IS A SELF-GENERATING
FAITH.

♃ JUPITER, the symbol of abundance, is the natural ruler of Sagittarius and the ninth house. Its force is expansion, favors, rewards, honors and a "green light" for more of the same. It generally bestows a feeling of good fortune. As abundance, however, it also leads to overconsumption, overflow and contents that outgrow their form or container. You can have too much of a good thing. The presence of Jupiter anywhere in the horoscope is benevolent, comforting and proof both material and spiritual of the essential rightness of things. As one of the rewards of life—like the dessert—it comes best at the end of the meal rather than during the meatier groundwork.

THE TENTH HOUSE: SIGN OF CAPRICORN ♑ RULING PLANET, SATURN ♄

The tenth house shows the native's conscious ambitions and the material and physical judgment generally imposed on him by the world. It is not the final answer, but it does indicate how the native's life will generally turn out in the eyes of the world. As the conscious goal of the native, the tenth house gathers, solidifies and channels the native's best efforts or the real substance of his inner convictions. This is true, even though the native at any one moment may be too young, immature, confused or secretive to state clearly his real ambitions. There is a certain superficiality about the tenth house, as there is about the first, reflecting the reaction by others to surface images on physical and material matters. As the first house is HOW OTHERS SEE THE NATIVE, the tenth house is HOW OTHERS JUDGE THE NATIVE AFTER HE HAS REACTED IN KEEPING WITH HIS FOURTH- AND SEVENTH-HOUSE CONDITIONS.

If the tenth house is unoccupied, there are no conscious problems of the native on tenth-house matters. The native's ambitions and their probable outcome are more directly related to that area of his affairs or people representing it where the planet that rules the sign on the tenth-house cusp is found.

If the house is occupied, the native has some conscious struggle both to formulate his ambitions and to put them across in the eyes of the world. The affairs of other areas of his life and the people representing them contribute directly to his ambitions and recognition, as shown by the signs that these planets rule.

♑ CAPRICORN, the disciplinarian, is the natural ruler of the tenth house. The element is MATERIAL and physical, and the position is CARDINAL and leading. Capricorns always have their eye on the big chance, which they pursue to the bitter end. Thus Capricorns tend to win ultimately, not through superior talents, but by their persistence. This attitude undoubtedly accounts for more material success in life than any other combination of talents. Capricorns are said to be born old. Their mannerisms are mature from the start, and they sometimes experience pleasure from denying or disciplining themselves in order to achieve some material gain. Their objectives seem to be obviously desirable from a practical point of view, and they are absolutely determined once they make up their minds. They achieve through an endless accumulation of small steps, which eventually relate beautifully to each other. They seem to know what they want from the beginning, and they can always rationalize their position with cold hard facts and logic. A Capricorn has to be convinced beyond the shadow of a doubt because once the die is cast, everything from then on has to work like clockwork. It need not always be just a material goal, but it must have some practical application and at the same time fit in with the accepted standards of which Capricorn feels a part. There is a great deal of vanity and self-acknowledged superiority to Capricorns, which they never question. They are constructive, down-to-earth, self-reliant people whose goals have generally been tested over and over again. Their judgment is usually superior to others, except on themselves. Although they always seem to have set goals, until they are absolutely convinced, they are troubled by self-doubts and insecurity. But even this usually fails to stand in their way because they seldom change. It makes them sour and unhappy, however, as they go about their business.

THEIR GREATEST STRENGTH IS REGULARITY AND CONSISTENCY.

♄ SATURN, the taskmaster, is the natural ruler of Capricorn and the tenth house. The power of Saturn is to boil things down to their bare essentials and then build slowly up from there. Saturn stresses facts, figures, measurements, care, order, discipline, economy, thrift, logic, common sense and TRUTH. People generally dislike the transit passage of Saturn in their horoscope because it brings them down to earth and exposes the truth about what they are doing. Most people are unprepared to face the truth, and they will go to endless means just to escape it. Yet Saturn is never unfair. It calls the shots exactly as they are. If you have been reasonably honest in the game of life, there is nothing to fear from Saturn. The ones who never pay and feel they should get something for nothing are the ones whom Saturn brings to their knees. This happens as Saturn (which takes approximately twenty-eight years to travel once around the horoscope) comes in contact with the vital parts of your horoscope. For further details on this see Chapter 7, "The Cycles of Saturn."

THE ELEVENTH HOUSE: SIGN OF AQUARIUS ♒ RULING PLANET, URANUS ⛢

The eleventh house is the area of honors usually attendant on, or resulting from, tenth-house prominence or judgment. The eleventh is also the house of friendships and hopes and wishes (as opposed to conscious personal goals). The hopes and wishes of the eleventh house are more in the nature of fond desires that are shared and enjoyed in the company of others. A person represented by the eleventh house is usually a good friend—most frequently an old friend—but can also represent a new acquaintance who can immediately fit into a relationship of long-standing familiarity. When friendships extend into a more meaningful relationship, they become matters of seventh-house partnerships. This is particularly important in horary astrology (which sets up horoscopes for asking specific questions) to distinguish friends from persons who are partners in our lives.

If the eleventh house is unoccupied, the native does not consciously feel the need of friendships or, particularly, the need to share his hopes and wishes with others. Such important friendships are valued most for the way in which they contributed to the affairs of his house, where the ruler of the sign on the eleventh house is found.

Those who have a strongly occupied eleventh house always work best within groups or closely united with others in a common purpose. There is a sort of family of interests, which sometimes transcends one's personal family ties.

♒ AQUARIUS, the freedom seeker, is the natural ruler of the eleventh house. Its element is IDEALISTIC and its position is FIXED and concentrated. Actually Aquarians always seem to stand out from the crowd, even though they consider themselves closely involved with group interests. They seem to have some sort of communication (mental or emotional sympathy) that transcends usual ties and therefore gives them a special application of brotherly love. To understand Aquarians fully, one must be prepared for the sense of group identity that they believe in AND the objective detachment that is part of their nature. Aquarian thinking and feeling operates on a rarefied wavelength that gives them not only a feeling of superiority but also an unreal quality because it cannot be tied down or keyed to the general facts at hand. This makes them seem unpredictable, scatterbrained and eccentric. Aquarians have a way of justifying themselves that is most forgivable by those on their wavelength but exasperating to those who are not.

Because of Aquarius' position falling between the tenth and twelfth houses, it is suggested that the real function of Aquarius is to instrument the breakdown and generally prepare us for the possible contrast between the judgment given us by others (evidenced in the tenth house) and the ultimate value structure that lies hidden in the tribal subconscious of our inner self (the twelfth house). The two may be in considerable conflict. Aquarius prepares us for this because its nature is to eliminate the boundaries of our comprehension and give a hint of the infinite or a reality beyond the comprehension of our personal egos. Aquarians do this naturally with everyone they meet. Even in small ways they suggest that there is something more than meets the eye, that there is something indeed beyond our physical realities. Aquarians are often regarded with a great deal of skepticism and charitable indulgence, even by those who enjoy their friendship. The Aquarian loyalty seems related or bound to things beyond what we pretend to know. Aquarians can be charmingly friendly with most people but are not very close to anyone in particular.

THEIR GREATEST STRENGTH IS THEIR CONVICTION TO ACT INDEPENDENTLY.

♅ URANUS, the unpredictable, is the natural ruler of Aquarius and the eleventh house. Uranus is the only planetary force that can dislodge the death grip of Saturn. The essence of Uranus is its erratic behavior. Its virtue and its vice is its talent for sudden and unexpected deviations from any system of regularity. This deviation is upsetting to those who are unprepared for it. But it is only through such "breaks in pattern" that new angles of insight are created, which eventually make possible changes and improvements. If we never ventured from a fixed pattern, we would never change, grow or develop. The presence of the Uranus effect is usually accompanied by tension, apprehension and a desire to burst forth or escape from a situation that suddenly seems confining and intolerable. The force of Uranus is to set things free. Sometimes it does this by placing a bomb under the present situation, forcing the participants to reassemble themselves in a new pattern. The Uranian force is usually not welcome, although it is effective and generally constructive. The pulse or tempo of Uranus is anything but a steady flow of energy. It builds up tensions, explodes, and then subsides until it generates new energy for another blowup. Uranus often blows away cobwebs from outworn conditions that have gone unnoticed or been taken for granted. The Uranian aim is for freedom—freedom so that elements can regroup themselves in new ways. New allegiances can be formed and new patterns developed. Uranian people have a natural sense of "extended vision," WHICH IS THE TRUE SPIRIT OF THE SO-CALLED AQUARIAN AGE. They see far beyond what most people are concerned with. That is why Uranus and Aquarians are generally out of step with those immediately surrounding them.

THE TWELFTH HOUSE: SIGN OF PISCES ♓ RULING PLANET, NEPTUNE ♆

The twelfth house is the final key to everything that has gone before. It is the accumulated subconscious, which abstracts meaning from the past and builds a foundation into the future. It is the residuum of ultimate values. The twelfth house is the end of the road where we find ourselves after having passed through all the other phases of living. As the end of everything (prior to suggesting a new beginning in another cycle) it holds the secrets of life and the hidden or subconscious motivations of any life that may follow. It also holds the secrets of past lives that may have preceded this one. Obviously, it is the least-understood area of the horoscope and, understandably, the area most frightening to ordinary mortals.

The twelfth house is not the house of death. The substance of the subconscious, even though hidden, is every bit a part of life as are the conscious points of focus in our daily lives. The fourth house is said to symbolize the grave or end of physical matter. Just as it represents the heritage or background of the native, it also represents or describes the general conditions at the close of the native's life. The native's actual death—passing from one state to another—is described by the conditions of the eighth house.

In the twelfth house we have the essence of the native's final confrontation or final summation of all his values. After his individuality is created (shown in the first house), molded into form, method or pattern (shown in the fourth house), joined with (or renounced by) others (shown in the seventh house), judged and labeled (shown in the tenth house), we come to the point where the native faces his own subconscious—the warehouse of all his consciousness. This is where the native faces himself in his entirety and must JUDGE HIMSELF.

Small wonder that most people would prefer not to consider the implications of their twelfth house. To some it is their undoing, their downfall, their incarceration, their prison. These all are states of mind or terms generally used to describe the twelfth house. It is connected with institutions of correction, hospitals, jails, secluded spots and private hells. It is usually termed an area of disappointment, failure, catastrophe, loneliness, abandonment, rejection and despair. This is because most people tend to live exclusively in a materialistic world based only on material values. They seem utterly unprepared to see their naked spirit devoid of material or physical considerations. Yet as naked they entered the world, naked will they depart. This is the implication of the twelfth house.

Far from the area of darkness and horror that usually describes the twelfth house, there is a richness of the spirit—providing one has the capacity for spiritual awareness. Whether we like it or not, life has a way of forcing this awareness upon us because it is part of the full cycle of human experience. Exactly how one confronts this part of life is described by the condition of the twelfth house.

If unoccupied, the native is generally not consciously confronted with the implications of twelfth-house values. He may be consciously aware of them, but he accepts them and works within the framework they provide. He does not live in fear of the secrets hidden there. In fact a subconscious reliance on these hidden values contributes greatly to the function of that area in life and to relationships with the people related to it, shown by the location of the planet that rules the sign of the twelfth house.

If the twelfth house is occupied, the native of course has some actual business in the affairs of this house. This may be either what it may mean to himself, or what he can do to help others on these matters. The riches of the house (by condition) indicate the richness of the native's spirit, which will fortify his work in this direction. A heavily configured twelfth house definitely sets one apart from the ordinary flow of life. This seems to have been a favorite subject in the brush drawings of old Chinese painters who pictured a wise man seated alone in a starkly simple landscape, contemplating the secrets of life symbolized by the flow of water that is always nearby. The native is specifically fortified in his quest by the affairs and persons of the houses ruled by the planets in the twelfth house.

♓ PISCES, the symbol of universal understanding, is the natural sign of the twelfth house. Its element is EMOTIONAL, and its position is MUTABLE and forgiving. Its character gathers from the past and blends with the future. The quality is spiritual and immaterial. The form is vague and extended. The strength of Pisces is based on spiritual faith, while the Sagittarian faith is more of an emotional conviction. Pisces resists rational applications as such. Pisceans are often able to carry on in spite of all material obstacles. They always see beyond, behind and underneath what others are pointing at. This gives Pisces an invincible link with another degree of consciousness that tends to defeat the opposition of any obstacle and ultimately prove their point. Pisces people are a little queer by everyday standards. They are a "Sunday" kind of people who seem somehow out of place in the ordinary weekday world. Naturally they are ideal for helping the downtrodden, dejected, outcast and hopeless failures of the world. They see them not as failures in the material sense but as other human spirits seeing themselves for the first time by spiritual standards. Oddly enough, Pisces are not the preachers of the world. They are not given to converting others to their way of life. Preaching is most often a kind of self-selling, which Pisces doesn't need. The Pisces character is more concerned with dissolving fears, dissipating threats, redefining values, and making the spirit whole again. The business of everyday living is very damaging to the spirit and leaves many scars. Pisces know just how to heal these scars. To Pisces these are the real wounds of life—not the physical damage.

THEIR GREATEST STRENGTH IS INNER PEACE.

Ψ   NEPTUNE, the visionary, is the natural ruler of Pisces and the twelfth house. Because Neptune is completely immaterial, its presence or effect can be deceiving. This leaves open the opportunity for people to attribute to Neptune what they want to see. There is no guarantee who is right and who is wrong. The effect of Neptune is to suggest and then fade away. It is up to the one who has received the "revelation" to fit the pieces together and supply his own interpretation. Like the Rorschach inkblot tests, the value is in the response and not in the material fact that stimulated the reaction. In a negative sense Neptune can be blamed for leading people on, to entrap them, deceive them, and defraud them. This is easy because there is no material substance involved—only the spirit or suggestion. But in the positive sense Neptune also inspires, enobles, glorifies, and bathes them in an unearthly beauty. Neptune creates phonies as well as saints, and it very often depends on your frame of reference to tell them apart.

Perhaps the majority of people are most often fooled by the effect of Neptune because they are rather impoverished in the richness of the spirit. Therefore the presence of Neptune in most horoscopes tends toward a negative expression (phoniness). Where you find

Neptune in most horoscopes is where you will find the native most susceptible to deception. Unfortunately, it is failure rather than success that tends to cast aside the deceptive aspects of Neptune and reveal the true insight to which Neptune can inspire us.

IN SUMMARY: The main structural points of the horoscope are the four angles—that is, the cusps or lines showing the beginning of the first, fourth, seventh and tenth houses.
Always remember:
The first house is how the world sees the native.
The fourth house is how the native sees himself—subjectively.
The seventh house is how the native sees other people.
The tenth house is how other people judge the native.

The natural rulers of the angular houses are the four cardinal signs: ARIES, the individuality of the spirit; CANCER, the protectiveness of the emotions; LIBRA, the force of ideals; CAPRICORN, the practicality of matter.

Anyone whose horoscope shows prominence in angular houses in some way occupies a position of leadership and influence over others. Prominence means the presence of at least the Sun or Moon and some other supporting planets in the angular houses. If this condition is not met, the native is DENIED this direct kind of leadership and influence in life.

If the accent is through the first house, the results are due to the force of the native's personality and the development of his individuality. Most people are bound to sit up and take notice of him.

If the accent is through the fourth house, the results are due to the strength of the native's background and the soundness of his methods. His procedures ultimately prove themselves and convince others.

If the accent is through the seventh house, the results are due to the native's talents for handling other people and their guidance and influence in his behalf. He is fortunate in the way he sees and cooperates with others.

If the accent is through the tenth house, the results are due to the native's high position in life or the recognition and esteem that he wins for himself. The public recognizes and treats him as a leader.

The next strongest point structurally in the horoscope concerns the FIXED positions: the second, fifth, eighth and eleventh houses.

Concentration of planets in these areas gives strong determination and unswerving dedication to definite objectives, all of which relate directly back to the native in some personal way.

The second house is the native's source of supply.

The fifth house is the native's outlet for creativity.

The eighth house is the native's capacity for rejuvenation and ability to face change and crisis.

The eleventh house is the native's ideals and those who share them with him.

The natural rulers of the fixed houses are the fixed signs: TAURUS, determination in material matters; LEO, concentration on extensions of the ego-spirit; SCORPIO, plumbing unknown depths of the emotional resources; AQUARIUS, dedication to progressive thinking.

Anyone whose horoscope shows prominence in fixed houses is slated for a more specific role, whose function centers on some type of supply. The second house furnishes supply for the native (money and earnings). The fifth house furnishes supply for the family (children, pleasures and speculation). The eighth house furnishes supply from the partnership alliance of the native with others (co-ownership). The eleventh house furnishes supply or awards for those who have reached a position of command or prominence (friends, honors and group ideals).

The most structurally obscure area of the horoscope is the area of the four MUTABLE houses: third, sixth, ninth and twelfth houses. Concentration of planets in these areas relegates the native to a background position in life where he serves best from behind the scenes providing a service which contributes to something or someone else.

The third house is the instrumentality of the native's own sense of communication.

The sixth house is the servitude which the native undertakes on behalf of others.

The ninth house is the codification of all thinking which culminates in law, religions, philosophy and circulation of formalized learning.

The twelfth house is the service for the salvation of the human spirit after people have faced failure, rejection, injustice and despair.

The houses of the horoscope also group themselves into four sectors or quadrants. Houses one, two, and three are the most personalized sector, where the native is primarily concerned with perfecting himself—through his personality in the first, through his material resources in the second, and through his communication of thoughts in the third. In houses four, five, and six the native identifies with his immediate surroundings and environment—through exploitation of his heritage in the fourth, through extension of his ego by creativity in the fifth, and through acceptance of duty and responsibility in the sixth.

As the native passes over the Nadir (cusp of the seventh house) and rises above the horizon, there is a profound change in orientation. The native now aligns with factors outside his ego sphere and joins with others in a common purpose—through partnerships in the seventh, through possible mutation into a new form in the eighth, and through promotion of principles in the ninth.

At the level of the tenth, eleventh and twelfth sector the native has been judged and labeled in the tenth, honored by followers in the eleventh, and revealed in his true light in the twelfth, which is the court of last resort before beginning all over again.

This sequence of consciousness is important in interpreting the present effect of planets as they pass through our natal horoscope map. These are called TRANSITS and are covered in the chapter on developments and predictive trends in the horoscope.

The horoscope divides itself in half by the horizon (first and seventh houses). The lower half is more subjective in application, dealing with the native (in first, second, third) or his immediate environment (in fourth, fifth, sixth). The upper half has a more objective orientation—or out in the world. In seven, eight, and nine the native concerns himself with others (seven), their crisis (eight), and their principles (nine). In ten, eleven, and twelve native confronts fame (ten), group values (eleven), and spiritual salvation (twelve).

The horoscope also divides itself in half by the center axis (houses four and ten). When the planetary positions give accent to the left-hand sector, the native is primarily responsible to himself and must create his own pattern out of his own resources. The native is self-made. When the position of the planets gives accent to the right-hand sector, the course of the native's life is largely determined by outside factors over which he has little control. The native tends to be a victim of circumstances or of the control of others.

Chapter 4

THE CHARACTER OF YOUR DESTINY

THE HOUSE POSITION OF THE SUN

The character of your destiny—the challenge of your fate—is shown in the horoscope by the condition of the house that holds the Sun. The Sun represents the ego-drive, which accounts for more than half of the characterization of the native. That is why Sun sign readings in astrology are so amazingly accurate. The percentage of accuracy is even higher in those cases where the Moon or the ascendant is also in the same sign as the Sun. This native would then represent a true type for that sign.

Whatever the nature of the ego may be, it can fulfill itself only by meeting the conditions of the house that it occupies at birth. This defines the type of experience and situations through which the native must resolve his purpose or destiny. The degree to which the native meets the requirements of the house of the Sun is the only true measuring rod for judging the native's success or failure.

Since the Sun also represents strong masculine people, the presence of the Sun in a house indicates that men and the driving aggressive qualities that suggest masculinity enter into the affairs of this house.

WHEN THE SUN FALLS IN THE FIRST HOUSE, the native's challenge is to develop a fully individualized identity. Nothing else is more important than that the native realize the full potential of his unique ego as embodied in the personality. This native could never be overly encouraged to follow the "me first" attitude. To the native the conditions of fate always act as a challenge. There is always some reluctance to respond sufficiently to the challenge of one's destiny. The native with the Sun in the first house initially tends to hold back and not push forward, as he must learn to do. He has to be encouraged and/or forced by circumstances to do this.

The Sun in the first house indicates that the native is crowded in his immediate environment by other outstanding ego types who must be pushed aside if the native is to realize his own individuality. The presence of a planet in an area of experience (the houses) always indicates a two-way street; the native gives out in kind and receives back in kind. The presence of the Sun indicates the native's necessity to exert his own ego domination. At the same time the native experiences the effect of other strong egos trying to dominate him. This creates the challenge of his fate. Men or father images in some way play an important part in molding the native's sense of identity.

WHEN THE SUN FALLS IN THE SECOND HOUSE, the native must solve his ego requirements through realization of successful earning powers. The nature of all types of supply that the native may use becomes a field of specialization. The native may become an expert at showing others how they may improve their earning powers or talents for scouting supplies. The second house need not be considered exclusively in terms of money or monetary values. It should include general nourishment, raw materials and supplies of all sorts that may be converted or used by the native in some way. Strong masculine types and their interests contribute to his discovery of how to increase earnings both for himself and for others.

WHEN THE SUN FALLS IN THE THIRD HOUSE, the native must fulfill his ego through communication with others. This usually involves some form of free exchange or interaction of stimuli, where one side stimulates the other. Not only is the third house the exchange of news and views, but also it represents the marketplace or situation under which mental exchange takes place. The marketplace suggests customers, shopkeeping, clients, interviews and merchandising in general. The presence of the Sun in this area suggests a necessity for strong aggressive attitudes in order to hold one's own against similar competition.

WHEN THE SUN FALLS IN THE FOURTH HOUSE, the native's concentration becomes more subjective. There is a looking backward and inward to the native's background or heritage, which in some way must be restored or reactivated for present-day purposes. The native gives much thought and subjective appraisal to methods and techniques as the best possible manner in which to attack significant problems or objectives. In early years the native is likely to be suppressed considerably and disciplined by a parent or parent substitute. In later years he becomes a stern symbol in his own home. Emotional security and how to achieve it is a matter of natural concern for him. The native has talents for viewing this matter and can become a specialist on the subject for others.

WHEN THE SUN FALLS IN THE FIFTH HOUSE, the native must express himself in some creative form, which in effect becomes an extension of his ego. This can involve the arts, all forms of entertainment, games, speculation, gambling, children and the interests and concerns of children such as their early or primary education. The native can become something of an authority on or creator of romance situations. He is also interested in the romantic side of other people's lives. There would be some interest in sexual matters, especially the angle of sex connected with romantic love-making or creating children. The native should assume a positive and authoritative manner in all these matters because this is his field of specialization. The native at the same time may feel some subjective lack on his own part; which gives him cause for concern. This is part of his challenge: to overcome this feeling of inferiority and achieve superiority.

WHEN THE SUN FALLS IN THE SIXTH HOUSE, the native needs to dedicate himself to some kind of duty. This usually involves some activity or function connected with daily living—jobs, vocations, health, waiting on others, looking after requirements for housing, food, beverage, supply. It would also show a natural concern for getting others to assume their rightful responsibility on such matters as public officials connected with community needs and services. Since this is the house of subordination, the native is most likely to be under the dominating authority of a father image whose direction and example the native should be willing to follow.

WHEN THE SUN FALLS IN THE SEVENTH HOUSE, the native must look to other people for his primary source of direction. Since the Sun represents the individuality of the ego, this placement of the Sun is somewhat unfortunate. In the seventh house control passes to others. The native usually enters into open competition with others on most matters. Their resistance forces the native into action; but invariably the native must give in or concede to outside domination. The native is due for considerable frustration until he can accept the wisdom or desirability (in his case) of letting others take over his affairs. While this represents a sacrifice of independence, at the same time this placement of the Sun provides extensive cooperation from others willing and anxious to help the native. The native usually develops an agreeable means of handling and getting along with others. The individuality suffers, but adaptability and congeniality are developed to a point of specialty.

FOR PLACEMENTS OF THE SUN IN THE EIGHTH TO TWELFTH HOUSES, THE EGO HAS LESS NEED FOR PERSONAL SUBSTANTIATION. THERE IS MORE INTEREST TO THE NATIVE IN WHAT HE CAN CONTRIBUTE TO OTHERS.

The above is also true for the Sun in the seventh house, but this position is generally found less effective because only in certain select cases does the ego sufficiently adjust to this outside control in order to get on with the possibility of contributing to others. Most natives with the Sun in the seventh house spend an entire lifetime meeting the challenge of their destiny and learning the desirability of this control.

WHEN THE SUN FALLS IN THE EIGHTH HOUSE, the native is inordinately fascinated with other people's motivations and their probable reactions under test or crisis conditions. These conditions may be from the ancient past, as well as from the present. There is a tendency for these types to drift and satisfy their physical appetites until they are called for some emergency. If they are never called upon, they substitute some sort of imagined situation that suits their curiosity. They have tremendous powers of rejuvenation and they act as "service stations" or "first-aid stops" for others who need rehabilitation or overhaul. The eighth house is an area where people tend to falter. Natives with this Sun placement stand in readiness to help those who do falter or revive those who are overcome. Sexuality is of great interest. They regard sex as a ritual or energizer over and above being a token of romantic affection or for creating children. Since the eighth house is the house of transition or doorway through which one passes from one state or condition to another, it is the house of death and rebirth. Death need not necessarily be considered always a physical death. The native has talents for dealing with all matters relating to death and regeneration. He also has an affinity for the property left behind at death or as dead—discarded as currently of no value. This gives him an interest in restoring life to dead objects or creating an interest in values left for dead (artifacts, antiques, archeology, junk, scrap). The Sun in the eighth house is bound to exert a masculine influence over the sexual attitudes of the native whether male or female.

WHEN THE SUN FALLS IN THE NINTH HOUSE, the native has a desire to contribute in some meaningful way to the warehouse of knowledge, where the thoughts of many are formalized or codified into laws, religions, philosophy, politics and all higher forms of ritualized learning. The native should become affiliated with some cause or principle or outlet which furthers these concepts. The ninth house includes publications and spreading the chosen word over distant areas. This naturally brings the native in contact with persons and conditions that are removed from or foreign to his own background. This native is always advised to remove himself from his original background and take up his work among the "larger assembly" of the world to which he is naturally no stranger. His own thinking is so closely aligned with the larger framework that he should always be "at home abroad."

WHEN THE SUN FALLS IN THE TENTH HOUSE, the native must assume a position of authority, command and executive control. This may not be easy because of the competition and domination of other strong ambitions standing in the way. This must be overcome and the native must eventually be recognized as a figure of importance in his own right. Like the Sun in the first house, this position allows little consideration for taking second place. This position always accounts for considerable worldly ambition whether fully realized or not. The native is bound to incur some enemies on his way up, but this must not stand in his way.

WHEN THE SUN FALLS IN THE ELEVENTH HOUSE, the native strives to express himself through a congenial group that shares his values, aspirations and sympathies. His purpose is their purpose and their purpose is his. These natives are destined for public life and wide associations. The individuality they pursue is not just their own but the embodiment of group values and collective hopes for which the native considers himself spokesman. This position is often self-assumed and self-appointed as the native tends to stand out in groups as their leader who is well suited to further all their common interests. Politics, as well as social or spiritual organizations, can supply the group backing that the native requires. The native in this position does not put himself above the group as a dictator. Rather, he regards himself as their voice and representative. While we have FIRST-AID HELP in the eighth, THE PREACHER in the ninth, and the DICTATOR OR COMMANDER in the tenth, we have the SPOKESMAN in the eleventh and the SAVIOR in the twelfth.

WHEN THE SUN FALLS IN THE TWELFTH HOUSE, the native has two considerations to follow. He must solve or reacquaint himself with the ultimate values on which all things rest. This includes passing judgment on his fellow man, but it need not always be expressed to them. And he must resign himself to a position of isolation behind the scenes, which is the only suitable setting where he can contribute these truths to those who need them.

The twelfth house is the condition of frustration, breakdown, failure, hopelessness, loss of faith or belief, incarceration, and despair. This is an area of darkness to those who have seriously lost their way. It is the area of final judgment and ultimate valuation for the consequences of our acts. Those who find themselves in the twelfth-house condition are at the end of their rope. They are there to find an answer, a solution, a restatement of values, an adjustment of perspective, AND THE BEGINNINGS OF A NEW LIFE. Normally speaking, this area frightens most people. They are not eager to solve its mysteries. But those whose Sun falls in the twelfth house bring purpose, insight, understanding, compassion, and salvation to those who find themselves in any of the twelfth-house conditions.

Their situation is similar to that of a doctor who must perform unpleasant medical duties or a spiritual leader who must listen to the sorrows of his flock. This native must gain insight with which to counsel these unfortunates.

Not everyone needs the services of the twelfth house or falls into this unfortunate condition. But for those who do at one time or another, the secrets of the twelfth house are their only salvation.

That is why the "keepers of these secrets"—those who possess the knowledge which the twelfth house reveals—should be content to REMAIN in the twelfth house and let those who need them COME TO THEM. The twelfth-house native should refrain from promoting his ego in the everyday world, which may not be in need of twelfth-house solutions.

THE TEMPO OF YOUR DESTINY

The tempo of your destiny is the nature of the SIGN which falls on the house containing your Sun. This sign is not necessarily the same sign as the Sun. When it is not, the Sun is always in the following sign, which appears on the next house. For example, if the native has 12° of Libra on the cusp on the third house, 6° of Scorpio on the fourth house, and the Sun at 1° Scorpio, the Sun is in the third house but under the sign of the next house and not the sign on the cusp of the third.

Any planet in the sign of the following house (not in the sign of the house where the planet falls) shows an inherent condition of disappointment or regret of the nature of the planet toward the affairs of the following house.

In the above example the native would always show disappointment toward the home conditions of his fourth house, which would generally stem from insufficient recognition of his ego (Sun) by persons or conditions of his fourth-house family.

The qualifications of the "tempo" of the destiny that follow should be added to the characteristics of the destiny (above).

IF ARIES IS ON THE HOUSE OF THE SUN, the native's primary contribution in meeting the challenge of his destiny is the way in which he brings the individuality and force of his personality to the problem. If the planetary ruler Mars is in the:

First house: all aggressive and competitive forces that will exert the native's ego over others are mandatory in order to secure a footing.

Second house: the native needs to raise money aggressively to finance his original projects.

Third house: the native must be forceful in thought and communication to advertise his ego in the marketplace.

Fourth house: the native must from time to time force himself into new methods of aggressive action. At the same time he is compelled to resist parental domination, which in his case is mostly misguided. The native must also be well prepared to defend whatever he tries against something already established.

Fifth house: the native must be prepared to take chances in order to put his projects across.

Sixth house: the native must serve a period of apprenticeship and service before launching his own conceptions.

Seventh house: the native must actively solicit the cooperation of others, even though they initially put up some resistance.

Eighth house: sexuality is often an opening gambit to gain the native's objectives, or a restoration of programs left for dead by others could be in order.

Ninth house: the native needs to make foreign contacts, travel, and expand his formal education and intellectual capacities.

Tenth house: the native must be aggressively competitive with those in higher authority, even if a fight ensues.

Eleventh house: the native must argue within his group or with his friends before he knows where he really stands. The opposition of friends is more helpful than harmful.

Twelfth house: the native must go behind the scenes and experience the actual suffering of despair and breakdown before he can realize the full import of his mission. The native can learn much from others who have failed.

IF TAURUS IS ON THE HOUSE OF THE SUN, the native must pay attention to the financial structure of all his plans and keep everything orderly in the financial department. If the planetary ruler Venus is in the:

First house: the native can raise or invent ways of bringing in financial backing.

Second house: the money somehow flows in readily and with care should always be available.

Third house: the source of financial backing should come from writings and communication of news and views.

Fourth house: the native must cast about for some talent in his background or heritage that can be exploited for financial gain.

Fifth house: money can be realized through creative efforts, the entertainment world, advertising and speculations.

Sixth house: the native must work or apply himself in subordinate service in order to finance his schemes.

Seventh house: money should be forthcoming from others who believe in the native and want to help.

Eighth house: the native may inherit money or discover some new value in dead objects.

Ninth house: the native may have to go far from home base or deal with products of a foreign nature or publish something to attract money.

Tenth house: people in high position are disposed to assist the native if he can gain their favor.

Eleventh house: financial backing should be available from friends or groups who share the native's aspirations.

Twelfth house: the money should come from research or some behind-the-scenes secret backing or fall into the native's possession through some roundabout way not originally intended.

IF GEMINI IS ON THE HOUSE OF THE SUN, the native's solutions in life are largely of a mental nature requiring expressive attitudes that sell or persuade others through writing, talking or compelling communication. If the ruling planet Mercury is in the:

First house: the native has a decided talent to perform all these functions with individuality original to himself.

Second house: these services can be bought or will themselves produce good financial returns.

Third house: the native must get in touch with others, as in a marketplace, which provides absolute freedom for circulation of all kinds of opinion. The native needs to obtain the seeds of thought through interchange of ideas.

Fourth house: the native must dig up the answers from within his subjective thoughts. His parents and their thoughts are of some help and guidance.

Fifth house: the native has much to gain from observing children and their games. This position is somewhat akin to not knowing what you are going to create in words until you have already done it. Letting the imagination run free and wild is favored.

Sixth house: the native needs order, discipline and a serious intent to his purpose.

Seventh house: the native must look to others for encouragement and inspiration of his ideas. The native does best when developing other people's ideas.

Eighth house: the native must be prepared for many profound changes in his thinking and to expect a certain amount of violent reactions to what he tries to express.

Ninth house: the native needs higher education and a familiarity with the expressed thoughts of many others on the same subject. Getting away from familiar contacts helps.

Tenth house: the native must look to higher authority and be willing to sit at someone else's feet until he has earned the mark of authority for himself.

Eleventh house: one must seek others who share his views and proceed in a joint cooperative effort.

Twelfth house: the native must seek his own inner counsel and carefully do his own research, which may lead to many frustrations and setbacks before he has the matter right.

IF CANCER IS ON THE HOUSE OF THE SUN, the native has a natural talent for knowing how to get what he wants, as well as a good sense of timing for closing in at just the right moment. He must, however, experience a good deal of emotional tension and a certain maturity before he can wisely utilize his sensitivities. Things usually work out right if he is patient enough and bides his time. If the ruling planet Moon is in the:

First house: the native has remarkable talents for attracting public attention and making a big show of everything he does. This attracts support and sympathy for him.

Second house: the native will have many changes of fortune but will somehow manage to recoup and finance things over again. The earnings come from the public, which supports the native when he is constructively turned on.

Third house: the native has talents for expression and communication and for seeming to sense exactly what the general public wants at any moment. This native has a nose for news almost before or while the news is being made. There is an assured market for what the native expresses.

Fourth house: the native is very moody and reflective, which can lead to long periods of relative inactivity. The native will shut himself up in order to concentrate on some subjective source of support. This native is usually provided for, so he does not have to go outside to beat the bushes for what he needs. He should have protection provided by home and background, which disappears if he wanders away.

Fifth house: the native is skeptical and changeable toward the very area that must sustain his sense of security—namely, creative efforts to extend his ego, childish things, certain risks and gambles, entertainment and romanticizing.

Sixth house: the native easily aligns himself to fields of service and maternal sympathy for workers and job conditions.

Seventh house: the native receives much inspiration from others, in either sympathy or competition. Other people dominate the native's emotional reactions, which in turn must be stabilized in order for the native to fulfill his purpose. This suggests a lifelong partnership as a good solution.

Eighth house: the native's interests are aroused by unusual events that may frighten some people but inspire the native. The native may be the spiritual heir from several sources.

Ninth house: the native has talents for publishing and advertising and exploiting the collective thoughts of many people. This is the position of the inspired teacher.

Tenth house: the native has some important connection with the public and draws his inspiration from this interaction of his contribution and their response. This is a position of possible fame.

Eleventh house: the native's source of inspiration is fortunate, being supported on many sides by well-wishers, and there is a comforting sense of being far from alone. The native must find a way of identifying with group values, which is easy for him to do.

Twelfth house: the native is drawn to the background of life to deal with the less fortunate and the downtrodden. Emotionally, he can accept this assignment because he feels drawn more to these people than to those who have no problems. This native has many subjective, sad thoughts, but he can give much counsel to those particularly in need of emotional security.

IF LEO IS ON THE HOUSE OF THE SUN, the native must find a position in life where his authority will not be questioned and he can play the king among his subjects or the father among his children. The ego must have this kind of elevated authority in order to perform its best; otherwise, there is always a deep sense of resentment at having to be second-in-command when he needs to be first. If the ruling planet Sun is in the:

First house: the native must fully develop a dynamic originality and a supreme sense of authority, which immediately is evident in his personality.

Second house: the native must have money and evidence of personal property to support his authority. He should be talented at making money for himself.

Third house: he should concentrate on mental traits and expressive and persuasive speech.

Fourth house: he must develop a deep (but genuine) sense of pride in his background, which carries on a family tradition and absolute integrity of purpose.

Fifth house: the native must utilize all opportunities to extend his ego in creative matters. He should appear romantic, be willing to assume risks, and be understanding of children.

Sixth house: the native should lend dignity to all forms of labor and service and work to make this condition true. Nobility in all walks of life, especially the humblest, is the keynote.

Seventh house: the native must learn to get along with all types of people, even though they tend to get the edge over him with their egos. This is something he must learn to give in to and live with.

Eighth house: the native may have to wait for special occasions or heroic moments to show his worth. In the meantime he should avoid any situation that would besmirch his integrity, for there is a tendency to do just that. This native profits most from concentrating on areas that other people have passed by as exhausted or no longer profitable.

Ninth house: the native must look to the coded thoughts of others as a cause to which he can hitch his own star. He should be prepared to travel some distance to find what is right for him

Tenth house: the native must fight for a position in life which may mean the overthrow of someone there before him.

Eleventh house: the native must align himself with groups and work through them for a common cause.

Twelfth house: the native's ultimate support comes from the background of life—the hidden resources that are often not known or appreciated until some misfortune has brought them to notice—such as inner fortitude. The native has to experience much sadness and resignation before he can accept this "imprisoned" position for his ego, which (under Leo) is normally out in front leading the band.

IF VIRGO IS ON THE HOUSE OF THE SUN, the native is slated for housekeeping chores, which involve endless details and the pursuit of perfection before things can fit just right. The native usually seeks a subordinate place since he feels that is where the most effort for reorganization and proper housekeeping is needed. Order is the essence of Virgo. If the ruling planet Mercury is in the:

First house: the native must originate some angle that will at the same time promote his own individuality and bring attention to himself. There is a necessity to be outstanding (like taking the world's fastest dictation) at whatever service one performs, however servile.

Second house: the native's sense of detailed organization should be applied against the general source of supply (usually money).

Third house: the native should apply his critical sense of perfection toward technical journals and more exacting forms of communication.

Fourth house: the native should apply his knowledge toward

established concepts of behavior, methods and techniques, that tend to carry on traditions and general security concepts.

Fifth house: the native has a freer territory against which to apply his critical faculties, but this is an area not generally given to analysis and scrutiny. Perhaps entertainment criticism, or research on romantic novels or romantic trends in history or the technicalities of rearing children would be in order.

Sixth house: there should be a natural outlet for technical papers on health, education and welfare ideas, vocational problems and job opportunities.

Seventh house: the native should turn his critical observations toward the relationships of others—their reasons for cooperation or dissent. Of interest, too, are all ways in which people can relate to each other and the causes for divorce and separation, as well as all legal contests.

Eighth house: there is much mental curiosity and perfecting criticism directed toward the problems of meeting crisis situations, death and its implications, methods of rejuvenation and adjustment to complete changes of circumstances in mid-life, etc.

Ninth house: application to the law in all its details would be natural. Any field of higher education that involves organization and technical detailing would be indicated.

Tenth house: the native has a natural and scientific interest in analyzing the factors of success, how to get ahead and adapting oneself to the demands of executive administration or exercise of commanding authority.

Eleventh house: there is an interest in all kinds of propaganda, which gather the ideals and inspired aspirations of many kindred spirits. The native is apt to be highly critical of his friends' thinking unless it is precise and detailed. One usually doesn't demand this of one's friends.

Twelfth house: the critical faculties are directed toward alleviating the general conditions of unfortunate members of society in institutional confinement. There would also be a research interest in the subconscious motivations people have and the reasons for their downfall.

IF LIBRA IS ON THE HOUSE OF THE SUN, the native has a faculty for bringing others together for the purpose of resolving difficulties or restoring cooperation and harmony or just getting one side to see fairly the other side's point of view. Libra acts as the go-between, taking first one side and then the other, not being exclusively devoted to either. The aim is to smooth over something that seems out of order or unbalanced. Libra sees the solution as closer socialization and just getting together on the matter. If the ruling planet Venus is in the:

First house: the native must develop his own personality so as to attract both sides to his cause before he can let them go to work on each other. This native would be very attractive physically and in personality, and most people would feel honored just to be around him. This is the pattern of a lovely person or a loving person.

Second house: the native usually has monetary means at hand to supply most of his comfort requirements. There is a possibility to make money from things that beautify or enhance or "pretty up" the picture.

Third house: the native has a persuasive charm in meeting and handling people of different views. There is an ease of expression—probably a talent for music. The native is in contact with many people—as in the marketplace, business firms, or dealing with customers or clients.

Fourth house: the native does best in matters concerning the home, its enhancement, improvement, beautification, or adjustment of problems. The native adjusts well to either the old or the new in conventional standards. He feels a natural sense of emotional security, so he is able to sell this idea to others.

Fifth house: there are talents for entertainment, the performing arts, pleasant dealings with children, primary education, romantic indulgences, and a fair amount of luck at games of chance.

Sixth house: there is an interest and an ability to make working conditions attractive, pleasant and easy. There is a fortunate touch in dealing with the sick (excellent for nursing), healing practices, and an open-mindedness about progressive ideas on health, education and welfare.

Seventh house: the native is able to handle all types of people successfully, for he seems to please everybody and offend no one. This is the pattern of the ideal peacemaker, who is also fair and impartial. The native leans toward others and, if anything, sacrifices himself a little for the sake of cooperation.

Eighth house: the native has a talent for giving others a rejuvenating lift through display of his affectionate nature. Underlying his charm is a certain sexual suggestiveness, which is pleasing to those so inclined. The Libra charm here is more detached and clinically objective in the handling of others. This is a good pattern for difficult fields of service calling for a great deal of moral fortitude and guts in time of crisis.

Ninth house: the dedication is more toward principles than practical issues. There is a love of people, of country, of God, of principle, all of which result in a slight cooling of the more personal Libra feelings.

Tenth house: there is always an eye on the main chance or a preference for concerning oneself only with people in high position whose authority and respect are worth the effort. A material sense of values and status enters the sense of affection.

Eleventh house: the native is very social and well qualified for any type of participation in which everybody feels closely united in friendly sympathy. Certain politicians fit into this category who are perhaps a trifle naive in their conception of the degree to which they truly represent the happy, constructively oriented section of society.

Twelfth house: there can be a real dedication to helping the downtrodden in hospitals, prisons and all institutions that care for the unfortunate. His awareness comes out in acts of kindness and loving care rather than harsh disciplines and callous rejections.

IF SCORPIO IS ON THE HOUSE OF THE SUN, the native has certain peculiarities that set him apart from others. These differences may not be apparent on the surface, but the native tends to wander off by himself and in some way separate from the crowd, although he may not voice any particular reason for doing so. Scorpios do think differently from others on most subjects. One reason for this is that they seem strangely aware of the temporal nature of everything—that nothing is permanent and the moment of change or necessity for complete reversal may happen at any time. This sometimes gives them a peculiar sense of humor, as though they had the laugh on everybody else. Scorpios tend to be unproductive until just the right emergency comes along. Then they can become extremely useful and charitable. They seem to know just what to do in times of emergency, as though they had been through it all before, which they may have been—in their vivid imaginations. Scorpios are especially prepared at all times for the necessity for complete change, even to the point of completely giving up the old situation. They take these emergencies with great calm and a great deal of curiosity and even secret amusement or pleasure. It is as though Scorpios saw or were aware of something that the rest of us did not see. This gives Scorpios an edge on situations, which they enjoy having. It also gives them a certain smugness, as though they could see both sides of the wall at once. Perhaps they can in some way. This is an ideal frame of mind for times of change, stress or crisis. Their attitude is basically forward looking and eager for change and progress, even at the expense of old associations. Scorpios have a talent for certain destructive acts that can be regarded in certain perspectives as constructive. To them a good end justifies a form of evil means. Whatever they may be doing Scorpios are well advised to keep things to themselves because general awareness of their actions may bring violent opposition from the parties who are most apt to be replaced. One must remember that the planet Pluto, which rules Scorpio, always has two phases of action—one tearing down and one building up. In the Scorpio scheme of things there is always one side that has to be torn down to make way for a new one to go up. Pluto is the force of the natural revolutionary, so all these elements are present when the native's destiny is under Scorpio energized by Pluto. If the ruling planet Pluto is in the:

First house: the native invents his own forms of revolution and is very apt to be regarded with suspicious eye by the public. He obviously seems and acts like a troublemaker or bomb thrower, provocateur, rabble-rouser or professional malcontent. This position for Scorpio despels the secrecy that is usually preferred for most Scorpio projects.

Second house: the native may have to appropriate his financial backing from others with or without their consent or knowledge. There could be something illegal about the native's earning power, which may be taking advantage of a situation created by some fluke or error. Pluto in the second house usually shows two sources of income, one or both of which may be questionable or not entirely ethical or orthodox.

Third house: this position creates an unsecret source of attention for the Scorpio native, since his expression, outbursts or propaganda efforts all lead directly back to himself as the source. The native's tone of expression is chilling, threatening and controversial.

Fourth house: the native is better able to keep his true intentions under cover. He is usually deeply engaged in upsetting or planning the overthrow of established traditions, which he feels stand in the way of progress. The native feels the need to strike at the basic roots of institutions and to attack their background, their foundations and the sense of false security that they might hold for others. The native was probably introduced to this kind of lawless thinking early in life through a parental influence.

Fifth house: the native must take great risks or gamble compulsively in trying to put his undermining projects across. There may be great extravagance in claims in order to attract attention. This would also create an unsatisfactory situation in sexual relations, particularly as far as romantic notions are concerned. Sex would be something to be exploited for "the cause" along with most everything else. Reactions to and from children would not be satisfactory or conventional.

Sixth house: the native's revolutionary tendencies would be directed toward conditions of employment, service, servitude and all types of obligations and duties. Participation in labor movements is favored, as well as reviewing all forms of duty obligations.

Seventh house: the native is likely to be in the front line of attack against obvious enemies who might oppose the changes he feels are so essential. This is a position of open conflict in which the differences have gone beyond theory and the target has been singled out for open attack—an indication of disruptive and violent reactions to and from other people.

Eighth house: this would be the most secretive application of the revolutionary Scorpio tactics and therefore desirable for Scorpio. Sexuality is definitely something to be exploited or used here as an instrument for whatever else Scorpio may have in mind. This would surely be indicative of a very sensuous nature but also one capable of giving a great sense of uplift to others who come in intimate contact with the native. There is also a possibility that the native would keep his natural proclivities to himself—unused against the public except in the common good when called on at times of great crisis or emergency. Then the native would be tireless at helping others through the difficulty.

Ninth house: the native's sense of attack would be directed against the bastions of traditional laws, codes of ethics, outmoded philosophies, out-of-touch religions, and such. The native would essentially direct his efforts at the principles behind institutions rather than the advocates of these principles. This is an intellectual revolutionary rather than a mob-scene bomb thrower.

Tenth house: the native must direct his upsetting efforts against those in high position who seem to direct the show, which the native feels is out-of-tune with what could or should be. There is a marked dissatisfaction with all the symbols of authority and a resistance to all orders from the top. The native is very apt to earn a bad reputation—certainly in some quarters, although he may be a hero to those on his side.

Eleventh house: there is a tendency to be less active physically against the outmoded forces of opinion and to lend lip service and moral support to groups dedicated to similar disruptive interests. One's friends are of course very nonconformist and given on occasion to violent tactics.

Twelfth house: the native definitely prefers to work under cover, perhaps as an espionage agent. There is much probing into subconscious motivations or the secret negotiations of one's enemies. Scorpios are always more inclined to sense an enemy before they distinguish a friend. The main effect of the Scorpio type operating through the twelfth house would be to undermine, expose, and jerk the rug out from under the opposition rather than to fight it in the open. From the twelfth house, action has to be directed this way.

IF SAGITTARIUS IS ON THE HOUSE OF THE SUN, the outlook is sunny, optimistic, expansive and righteous. They are as though they had the approval of unseen multitudes—an invincible army all in the right. This position of rightness must always be assumed by Sagittarians. It gives them the faith they need and the unshakable conviction that makes them fearless. Sometimes it is naïve and unrealistic in terms of the immediate situation or outmoded in terms of the needs of the present majority. The rightness of a Sagittarian is based on moral principles that the Sagittarian believes to transcend any condition currently to the contrary. The essence of the Sagittarian belief is a code that is built up from the contributions of many individuals—not just one person's insight. So when changes must be made to adjust to new circumstances, ONE SAGITTARIAN ALONE WILL NOT ASSUME TO MODIFY WHAT MANY OTHERS HAVE BUILT TOGETHER. The Sagittarian is definitely pushing or selling a principle which he feels is greater than either you or I. He won't back down. He may go down with the ship, but he is not going to give up this allegiance once he has identified with its principles. The Sagittarian temperament can be ideal in certain circumstances but totally useless in others. There is a comfort and a solace in the Sagittarian attitude, but one can't always afford that indulgence. Their natural way is to sweep all opposition before them in one noble gesture. This sometimes works and sometimes doesn't. If the expansive Jupiter, ruler of Sagittarius, is in the:

First house: the native may be quite a spellbinder. His personality and his identification with his cause are so closely interwoven that it is hard to see one without the other. This could produce a brilliantly successful leader or promoter who is bound to have some measure of success.

Second house: the native should be successful at making money and initiating or creating natural sources of supply.

Third house: the native is fortunately gifted in speech and expression.

Fourth house: the native is slower to get started but easily dedicates himself to the traditional virtues, and he seems so "right" and successful. His home and family life are bound to be satisfactory, no matter what else happens to him

Fifth house: this is fortunate for gambling and speculation and begetting many offspring and being obviously successful in affairs of the heart.

Sixth house: the native enjoys a fortunate vocational setup. He likes his work, and it gives him satisfaction and rewards.

Seventh house: the native has great influence with others. Many people are willing to cooperate with the native, but his welfare is generally in other people's hands.

Eighth house: the native is lucky at handling other people's money and acting as a trust agent for the dead. There is a great faith and optimism in a time of crisis if it should arise.

Ninth house: the native should be successful in publishing, promoting some form of higher education, and all ninth-house activities, including of course law and religion.

Tenth house: the native tends to be well honored and enjoys above-average recognition and a place of high esteem. Depending on the time and place, the native tends to be on the right side at the right time, thus saving himself from the greatest pitfall, being out of touch, which Sagittarians are prone to be.

Eleventh house: the native may appear to receive more honors than his position would warrant. His popularity with groups may be difficult to analyze, but nevertheless he will be popular and appear to be genuinely successful in most of the things he is interested in. Whether he really is, is another matter; it will appear to his friends that he is.

Twelfth house: the native finds his rewards in secret, behind closed doors and with inward satisfactions. His direct contributions will be less noticeable to the general eye, but his influence behind the scenes may be enormous. His best work will obviously be with the less fortunate in life and for this he may have to take his remuneration in well-meant gratitude, not in coin. His riches will be more spiritual than material.

IF CAPRICORN IS ON THE HOUSE OF THE SUN, the native will be doggedly persistent in striving for what he thinks he needs. Capricorn usually wins out by persistence rather than superior talents. After all the flashier entries have dropped out of the race, Capricorn will still be plodding toward the finish line. What Capricorn usually strives for is a fair measure of worldly values, which are obviously desirable and materially comforting. Capricorn loves possessions and hangs onto them forever. If the ruling planet Saturn is in the:

First house: the native is generally deliberate and slow to act or respond. But by the same token he is always surer and more secure in his appreciation of his self-worth. His personality well qualifies him for the tasks he seeks in life.

Second house: the native's best projects are much in need of proper financing and a certain abundance of supply, which is very slow to materialize. The native's early life may be spent in financial want, but his financial resources are bound to improve in mature years.

Third house: the native needs serious and convincing ideas and a formal style of communication to solve the challenge of his fate. Early years are marked with depressing setbacks in his ability to communicate—particularly with those closest to him in his environment. His ability to formulate individual thinking is painfully slow to materialize.

Fourth house: the native has serious flaws in his family background, which in early life act as a disadvantage to giving him the recognition he so desperately needs. He gradually makes up for this lack by a kind of general overhaul or self-improvement program from the ground up, and eventually he stands out by the sheer magnitude of his efforts.

Fifth house: the native is naturally reluctant to take chances or assume risks or EXERT THE FORCE OF HIS EGO OVER SITUATIONS, yet these are ultimately the only ways in which he can accomplish his purpose. His chances in any of these directions are always much better than he assumes. He learns this eventually—the hard way—after having missed out by inches on many good situations.

Sixth house: the native is reluctant to get down to brass tacks or learn his trade from the ground up, yet this is the only way that he can perfect the technical skill that he will later need. The native is held back in early life by extremely difficult conditions surrounding his vocation, health or duties to others.

Seventh house: the native is reluctant to compromise himself with others, especially older people, who are at the same time the only ones who will eventually help him achieve what he wants in life. The native suffers in early life through unfortunately harsh experiences with others, which leave deep scars and sour his attitudes toward the world.

Eighth house: the native is reluctant to accept changes and any drastic overhaul in programs after he has invested a certain amount of time and effort. Yet life will tend to force such sweeping changes on him and he will several times be required to start over again from scratch. A death or extraordinary event late in life will somehow make up for much of the sour situation that the native has had to endure.

Ninth house: the native is reluctant to accept the mental conclusions or convictions on principle of others who have gone before him. Yet eventually he will come to see that theirs are basically more in common with his own views ONCE HE HAS INTELLECTUALLY GONE A LITTLE FURTHER INTO THE MATTER. There is a necessity in this position of Saturn to acquire a very solid education, which may take many years and persistent effort. The native is particularly resistant to the views of older and wiser people, but he will get over this.

Tenth house: the native is convinced that all the established forces of tradition are initially against him in his determination to rise in the world. Some unfortunate relationship in early life with a domineering parent, usually the father, is apt to retard seriously the native's natural determination to get ahead. It may take the native almost a lifetime to get over this domination and to feel confident that he is actually plugging away in the right direction. As long as this parent (or another person) lives, the native will always be under his thumb and perhaps even long after he is gone. Eventually the native will come to feel that their ambitions are not really so divergent as they once seemed; in fact, the native may ultimately regard them as indentical goals sought by two different people.

Eleventh house: the native is initially reluctant to identify with groups on a common basis since no group seems particularly anxious to adopt or acknowledge the native as truly one of them. It will take many years of effort for the native to prove to himself and to others that indeed their hopes are a common sympathy and indeed he is qualified in maturity to be their spokesman. Friendships are more often doomed to frustration and denial than to an opening up of inspired channels in the native's life. Older people will usually prove more charitable toward the native, although it may take him some time to appreciate this.

Twelfth house: the native is reluctant to acknowledge personally the value of subconscious motivations, especially in his own life. He is apt to suffer many serious setbacks and moments of deep despair until he finally releases some favorite superstitions he has acquired and gets down to the nitty gritty of permanent value structures. His innermost concerns must stand up to the supreme test of workability and living proof. This may not come about until very late in life when he will discover that much of his time has been wasted either avoiding real values or championing false ones.

IF AQUARIUS IS ON THE HOUSE OF THE SUN, the native is immediately set apart from the mainstream by the extreme independence and original attitudes that his individuality both assumes and demands. This person will always to some extent feel out of step with the crowd—usually ahead of them. At the same time the native feels unusually sensitive to the hopes he shares with others on an idealistic basis. There is a unique sense of brotherhood or comradely spirit. People in general do not like to be reminded of their innate difference. They usually prefer to believe that these differences do not show or stand out and that they can get by on the qualities that make it seem as though they belonged or should be accepted as one of the group. Aquarians unconsciously seem to point up in some way the possibility of such differences between individuals and at the same time to make them stand out as impossible to overlook. Actually Aquarians are trying to sift out the unique from the mediocre and help it along or draw it into prominence. They do this, however, by creating an awkward attention to the matter, which seems out of place, eccentric and nonconforming—more of a shame than a blessing. In the structure of society it definitely takes more courage to be an individualist than to snap into line and play along with the crowd. Not only do Aquarians get out of line, but they draw others of similar bent along with them. Aquarians can adjust to the

consequences of this, but other sensitive souls who are not so fortified by the Aquarian sense of independence suddenly feel isolated
and insecure. Unfortunately they frequently blame their Aquarian
friends for getting them into this embarrassing situation. While
Aquarians are basically gregarious, they inevitably are disruptive of
the bonds that presumably hold sympathetic groups together.

As suggested elsewhere (Chapter 3, "The Houses of the Horoscope") perhaps the real function of Aquarius is to prepare others for
the possible conflict between the recognition that life presents in the
tenth house and the ultimate judgment of that recognition in the
twelfth house. The suggestibility of such contrast by Aquarians creates in others a feeling of being not too sure or secure or trusting
about Aquarians. While Aquarians may ultimately do good, their
more immediate effect is apt to be unsettling, disconcerting and
generally disruptive—having created more problems and questions
than they care to answer. Aquarians, if they will constructively
realize their greatest strength—THEIR CONVICTION TO ACT IN-
DEPENDENTLY—are surely the most self-sufficient sign in the
zodiac. They are often the most misunderstood and somewhat the
least appreciated. Once the Aquarian/Uranian "blowup" has occurred, most people look the other way. Far too few acknowledge
the ultimate good that comes from this blowup. It cleans the air,
extends our vision, and brings new relationships and meaning into
our lives. As befitting their nature, but which is often overlooked
until matters blow up in their face, Aquarius is ruled by the explosive
planet Uranus, which might also be called the mischief-maker
because it operates so suddenly, without provocation, and invariably
throws everything off base or changes its direction. Some people love
this; others dislike it intensely. Uranus, the ruler of Aquarius, is
basically an unstable quality, which is both its virtue and its vice. If
constructively held in check (as shown in the horoscope by its
general condition), it leads to ingenious, outstanding achievements. If
not favorably conditioned in the horoscope, it leads to wild, uncontrollable excesses, imbalance, and eccentricity. If Uranus is in the:

First house: the native's eccentricity—such as it may be—is obviously
apparent in the native's everyday personality. This may make the
native difficult to adjust to, or it may make him harmless but
obviously different, if not to say queer. The native usually doesn't
care what anybody thinks and goes right on his merry way doing
just what comes naturally to him, which may be quite out of step
with conventional modes of behavior. The native may possess a

one-sided talent that borders on some kind of genius. This may also at the same time make him relatively unfit for normal behavior or adjustment.

Second house: Uranus in the second house of supply is anything but regular or conventional in the manner or type of nourishment that the native draws to himself. It should generally be considered favorable for supplying him with the most unusual kind of supply for whatever HE NEEDS.

Third house: the native's thought patterns and style of communication are most unusual, if not to say unique. The native is bound to be brilliant on some subjects on which he is uniquely gifted, but his everyday responses may leave much to be desired.

Fourth house: this is not so favorable a position for Uranus because it introduces the most unstable qualities into the native's subjective nature, which should be developed as the foundation from which the native can project his programs. The native's sense of emotional security is very much in constant jeopardy, but at the same time he tends to become responsive to the most volatile and uniquely progressive ideas. Since the fourth house is HOW THE NATIVE SEES HIMSELF, the presence of Uranus encourages the native to even more outlandish behavior than generally apparent, and this can create a very unstable and somewhat unreliable person. At the very least, in his approach to certain problems the native on occasion is capable of the most ingenious methods, which if developed enough can lead to genius. Their brilliance, however, will have to be pursued by others, for the native will have long since switched his attention to other matters.

Fifth house: this position of Uranus generally encourages wild fancies of the ego and extremely unconventional, romantic activities and attachments. Since the fifth house itself encourages far-out activities and all sorts of ego extensions, almost anything can be expected from this position of Uranus. If Uranus is well fortified, it can lead to brilliance in creativity; if not, then to the wildest sort of ego indulgences.

Sixth house: since this is a tied-down area of life, the Uranus principle is working to help or resist the more tedious and offensive forms of obligation and human slavery. On the whole the final results should be more constructive than not, even though it may prove so at the expense of those who would hold others down.

Seventh house: this position for Uranus should be more constructive than not because it passes the unpredictable quality from the native's nature to the effect of others on him. It is not the native who blows things up as much as unexpected reactions to and from others prompting the native to think differently and introduce new concepts which he would not have conceived on his own.

Eighth house: this naturally introduces into the native's life unusual events, which are unexpectedly and explosively produced by Uranus. The effect should be good because the aftermath and possibilities resulting from drastic changes are almost limitless and therefore favored for growth and introduction of new thinking.

Ninth house: the ninth house suggests rigid formation or codes of formalized thinking that invariably outgrow their original purpose and intent. Uranus here is most responsive to the change in conditions that these principles SHOULD reflect. This is generally an excellent focus for the Uranian flash of insight and extended vision. Ninth-house rituals won't like it, but how else will institutions adjust to the purpose that gives them birth?

Tenth house: Uranus here suggests conditions over which the native generally has little or no control. His breaks or opportunity for recognition seem to rest on the most improbable chain of events, which most often seem to work against the native rather than for him. The generalized judgment of others is a rather resolved thing—not casually bestowed. Therefore, to be upset or realigned (especially in the native's favor) must take a most unexpected series of events more like an intervention of fate or destiny itself. This can come when the native least expects it and for the wrong reasons. The solution here is to GO ON ACTING INDEPENDENTLY and when the break comes, DON'T LOOK A GIFT HORSE IN THE MOUTH. An illustration of this would be a writer who has written many a brilliant work but receives the Nobel Prize for something he considers his worst effort.

Eleventh house: Uranus here can generally do little harm. The situation that is constructively blown apart tends to be the native's allegiance to groups with which he is apparently not truly identified. This may be generally disruptive of friendships but is consistently beneficial to the native's own sense of growth and unique destiny.

Twelfth house: apparently the native should have some conscious concern with the condition of those less fortunate in life who have suddenly and catastrophically been cast into a position that demands all their resources. The native apparently has some unique approach to such problems, particularly in getting to the bottom of such inner resources as others may require at a moment's notice in times of misfortune, failures or rejection by society.

IF PISCES IS ON THE HOUSE OF THE SUN, the native has tremendous resources for finding a sense of peace both within himself and in helping others discover this for themselves. Pisces sees life not as just a cold, material fact, but as a reflection of an ideal of which the physical manifestation is but a poor imitation. To Pisces the hidden eternal principles are the reality and the outer form is only a shell. On the whole this is a contrary conception of life to most people, who see the outer form as reality and the inner light as unreal and sometimes a deceptive illusion. This difference in perspective and alignment of values puts the Pisces type on a very different wavelength from that of the average person, which in no way bothers Pisces. Pisces are generally secure and self-assured in their beliefs and seldom have cause to question them. Pisces' concern in life is to find a quiet, safe, protected and relatively obscure position where they can pursue their habits and expand their inner awareness. On the whole LIFE COMES TO THEM WHEN IT NEEDS THEM. It is basically unsatisfactory for Pisces to go out in the world and actively seek any kind of a position that would place them in a front-line attack. Sometimes because of other factors in their makeup which urge them against their better nature, this obscurity is hard for Pisces to accept. Pisces is ideally intended to remain in the background, guarding the answers that are needed at a time when all material considerations seem to fail and a spiritual salvation is the only solution possible. Not all Pisces types are so spiritual about what is held up. Some (as in advertising and sales promotion) are pleased just to hold up a shining dream and let others make of it as they will. . . . Pisces never try to force their views on others, but they are always ready to share their insight with those who seek them. To most people the Pisces approach would seem strange, unnatural, isolated and lonely, but Pisces are always comforted by their inner knowledge, which provides an "expansion into the infinite" far beyond the restrictions of individual egos. Perhaps the chief function of a Pisces is to salvage the essence from the past and in some way reflect this into the future. Since Pisces deals best with ABSTRACTIONS, others may not readily follow or appreciate their real contribution. VALUES and VALUE STRUCTURES are the key factors around which Pisces thread their life. Their discovery, their enhancement, their purpose and their salvation value are what Pisces tries to project. Their natural medium is with some kind of IMAGERY, which creates an illusion of life and yet eventually becomes the true reality. The force of their belief is a subtle kind of transportation where first the spirit and then the whole person is carried along in a mesmerized way. In the end the spirit or guiding light is all that matters. Most people do not get this message immediately. Their consciousness must absorb this "enrapture" very slowly. It plays on the higher emotions and more refined feelings. The artistry of those who weave dreams, cast spells, and lift up the spirit, releasing it from all earthly considerations is the dedicated work of Pisces. Usually Pisces' work is cut out for them. Fate leads them gently to it. Their problem in life is to open their eyes and accept what fate has provided. The key that unlocks the Pisces understanding lies with the illusive and mysterious Neptune, ancient god of the sea, whose presence is only felt or suggested—never seen or proved. To those who would believe, Neptune's power to lead can be more persuasive than all the other planetary forces in the universe. If Neptune is in the:

First house: the native has strange powers apparent in his personality that suggest a divine kind of inspiration. These powers should be conscientiously purified lest they be used to lead others astray or defraud them in some way. Usually these powers have been given the native to use on HIMSELF in order to see and sense realities more clearly. They are not intended to cast spells over others or misguide them in any way.

Second house: the native has creative powers in securing his own sources of supply. He has some unusual talent that can prove to be an Aladdin's lamp in providing resources for worthy purposes.

Third house: the native is able through speech and communication to create a condition in other people's minds that encourages them to see life the way Pisces feels it to be. The native inspires others with his expression.

Fourth house: the native is very subjective in his use of ideals as a way of life. His tendency is to dig deeper and deeper into his own makeup rather than to try and project outward or influence others in any way. The native has much to give of an inspirational nature, but he must be sought out and is available only to those chosen few who for some reason are led to his private doorstep.

Fifth house: the native is more mundane and employs a lighter touch in suggesting values beyond appearances. There is even laughter, entertainment and gaiety involved in how the native uses his inspirational powers.

Sixth house: the native is naturally drawn to fields of service and helping the oppressive conditions of labor, health, and other routine affairs of daily living.

Seventh house: the native does not draw his inspirational power from himself but gathers it from others and this helps to bring it to light.

Eighth house: the native possesses unusual luck in getting in and out of extraordinary situations that could peril most people. The native seems divinely protected in some way and has no fear of death or what lies beyond. In fact the native is fascinated by such matters. This pattern would suggest certain occult powers that, among other things, might enable the native to sense that during certain states of consciousness some part of him leaves the body and travels around. This is called astral projection and is studied by parapsychologists.

Ninth house: the native has unusual beliefs, practices and rituals, which he regards as a kind of religion. He may feel this is a projection of something out of the past that today has value for him. The higher mind is in touch with beliefs not shared by others in the contemporary scene, and there is some tendency to self-delusion. Neptune is not well placed in the ninth house because this is the area of the higher or collective mind, and since Neptune is more of an emotional conviction on the personal level (even though of so-called spiritual focus), it tends to distort the rationality of formalized thinking in favor of fanciful projections or deceptive illusions.

Tenth house: the native is acknowledged for his spiritual powers and ability to inspire others in an idealistic way. This may lead to trouble or protected fame depending on the condition of Neptune and of the tenth house and its related planets.

Eleventh house: the native has unusual friends who inspire him in idealistic ways. The native draws much spiritual support from being in touch with others of sympathetic views and hopes. There is some tendency to be deceived by one's friends, as well as to deceive them in some way. Friendships have a tendency to dissolve and lose their concreteness especially in times of need, when practical matters are pressing.

Twelfth house: the native is irrevocably drawn to places of seclusion and solitude where he can be alone with his thoughts and his philosophy. Isolated research is especially favored or some lonely post where the native is free to expand his awareness of the infinite.

IN GENERAL THE FOLLOWING QUALIFICATIONS ARE NECESSARY WHEN THE RULER OF THE HOUSE IS FOUND IN THE:

First house: the native must utilize some aspect of his own personality to draw attention to that quality most needed to boost him over the top. The native has the talent in his personality and only needs to develop it further.

Second house: the native needs money to finance the kind of program he has in mind, and in this case he must earn it himself. The native has the necessary qualification to turn some asset he already has (indicated by the planet in question) into a profitable income.

Third house: the native must turn to some mental asset he has and effectively use this in speech and style of expression.

Fourth house: the native must look to his background and heritage to provide him with the needed technique and method to attack the problem. Since the fourth is in direct opposition to the tenth, he must be prepared to defend whatever he tries against something already established.

Fifth house: the native must be prepared to assume risks and take chances in some effort to extend his ego in a creative manner.

Sixth house: the native must subject himself to conditions of labor and service and subordinate his pleasures for more serious responsibilities.

Seventh house: the native must subordinate himself to the control and influence of others who are the only ones who can lead the way for him.

Eighth house: the native must usually wait for some extraordinary event to occur, which will make possible something that otherwise could never have come about.

Ninth house: the native must thoroughly educate himself so that he is conversant with the codes, principles and rituals of those who have gone before him on the same matter.

Tenth house: the native must assume a position of authority on the matter whether or not he has really earned the right in the usual manner. Even though this authority may be disputed or contested (as it will be), the native must stick to his guns and act with the absolute conviction that he has the executive prerogative to do so.

Eleventh house: the native must seek the association of others with sympathetic ideals or purpose. In this matter it is better to work through groups than on one's own.

Twelfth house: the native must explore his subconscious and develop a perspective of ultimate values with which to pass final judgment on the matter.

As is always true, any planet, wherever it may be located, is forced into action by those planetary forces that aspect it by hard angles (conjunction, square or opposition). It is encouraged to act by those planetary forces that aspect it by soft angles (sextile or trine). For further details on aspects see Chapter 9.

Chapter 5

THE FOCUS OF YOUR EMOTIONS

THE HOUSE POSITION OF THE MOON

The Moon in your horoscope shows the range and focus of your emotions. Ideally the Moon, which symbolizes feelings, sensitivities, awareness and understanding, should be the magnetic balance of the Sun, which symbolizes the willpower and ego-force. Polarity between these two primary forces of life ensures balance and perspective. There is some polarity if the Sun and Moon are 45° or more apart. There is little or no polarity when the Sun and Moon are less than 45° apart, down to the exact conjunction of being together (which is generally unfortunate). If the Sun and Moon are less than 45° apart, it is better if they are at least in different signs, as this alone gives some distinguishing characteristics.

The degree of emotional tension that the native may experience from time to time is directly related to the polarity of the Sun and Moon. Hard-angle aspects (see Chapter 9 on aspects) create tension. Soft-angle aspects alleviate tension.

THE FOCUS OF THE EMOTIONS IS SHOWN BY THE HOUSE POSITION OF THE MOON. If the Moon is in the:

First house: the personality is nervous, changeable, impressionable, and flighty BUT SUPERSENSITIVE TO PUBLIC REACTIONS. The native should be before the public in some way that caters to their whims (even though this makes the native nervous).

Second house: the sources of income and problem of possessions is constantly brought to the native's attention. There should be profitable activities coming from something that deals with the public or women's affairs.

Third house: the mind is impressionable, sensitive, intuitive and talented for voicing what the public wants to hear. This is favorable for dealing with clients, customers or the flow of the public in and out of a marketplace.

Fourth house: the subjective nature is overly sensitive about background, heritage, and the most effective procedures or methods with which to start any programs. There are many changes in and around the home. There may be some notoriety connected with the parents or something in the background of the family.

Fifth house: the sense of creativity is pronounced, although there is much uncertainty as to exactly how to utilize this. This is unfavorable for gambling or speculations, for there are too many uncertainties and an inability to move when the "iron is hot." This pattern is favorable for entertaining and the primary educational training of children. Romantic sentiments cause tension and moodiness.

Sixth house: duties, daily routines and health matters are all subject to nervous reactions and/or psychosomatic disorders in the native. Sentiments lean toward helping others.

Seventh house: native is supersensitive in reactions to others. There is a talent for tuning in on other people's thoughts and motivations almost before they are aware of them themselves. This is a position which certainly places the native in active cooperation with the public in some way.

Eighth house: most of the time the native is moody and introspective and vaguely detached. In times of crisis or emergency he can be amazingly calm, cool and collected. He keeps his emotional control while others get hysterical. This position is best for the unusual situation in life—not so favorable for ordinary everyday living. There are many sensuous preoccupations.

Ninth house: the native longs for distant places and the generally unobtainable. Wherever they are or whatever they have, they emotionally long for something else. There are vague intellectual leanings but seldom carried through to completion. Many changes in ideas, principles and affiliations.

Tenth house: this is the most favored position for success before the public as some kind of celebrity. But this position may have its ups and downs—in vogue and out of vogue. The public eye makes the native nervous and tense, but he seeks it anyway.

Eleventh house: this is a very favorable position for the Moon making the native responsive and sympathetic to all interests of community or group value. There is much public spirit and eagerness to join with others of like sentiments to put ideas across. This is favorable for politics and for becoming a representative of the people.

Twelfth house: the native is emotionally saddened by the harshness of life and the injustices often imposed on the less fortunate. There is much philosophic concern over values and purpose and answers that can solve or assist those in trouble. The emotions are deeply fortified with a sense of the subconscious and the inner purpose behind things. On the surface this native is usually hard to reach emotionally. He is too conscious of the deeper aspect of life to waste time on superficialities.

THE MOON IN ARIES: the emotions are masculinized and made forceful and aggressive. The feelings compete with the ego and want to dominate the motivations. The native feels with his ego.

THE MOON IN TAURUS: the emotions are attracted to material possessions and the comforts and satisfaction that comes from material wealth. The emotions are earthy and practical.

THE MOON IN GEMINI: the emotions are light, adaptable and attracted to mental stimulation. There is a superficiality that requires variety and effectiveness at the moment rather than duration and depth of feeling. The native feels with his mind.

THE MOON IN CANCER: the emotions become protective, moody and possessive. They are overly sensitive to anything that would threaten the home, family or personal security. They usually do not see clearly on any of these matters because their feelings take over. However when concentrating on matters that do not involve their personal security, they have great sensibility about matters which affect people as a whole. This is the pattern of the "universal mother" who at the same time is overly protective with her own.

THE MOON IN LEO: the emotions are carefree, gay, extensive, and daringly pleasure-seeking. Leo lends a nobility to the emotions but also makes it difficult to back down or compromise, which should be a natural quality for the Moon. The native is strongly attached emotionally to anything that belongs to him or reflects personally on his ego, which causes a lack of objectivity and a blind spot in the emotional perspective. At the same time the native is unlikely to be very responsive emotionally to anything or anybody who does not directly contribute to his own ego enhancement. The emotions are self-centered and somewhat pompous.

THE MOON IN VIRGO: the emotions are cool, deliberate, detailed, objective and analytical. In most respects they are the very opposite of the Moon in Leo. In spite of all the above qualifications, the native cannot be considered as enjoying his emotional life any less, but others may find him emotionally "a strange fish." There is some tendency for the native to become so involved in analyzing his own emotional reactions as to lose track of the emotional object itself. Analyzing the reactions becomes more important than the reaction.

THE MOON IN LIBRA: the emotions are outgoing, appraising, argumentive and self-balancing. With Libra the emotions turn off whenever they feel there is no fair exchange. Libra emotions never waste an ounce of feeling that is not returned by others. On the other hand, they are more likely to be the first to respond to others on the emotional level but quickly turn to someone else when this is not returned in spirit. While not as shallow as emotions in Gemini, Libra emotions are not much deeper and a good deal less penetrating than under other signs. The charm, sociality and talent to attract are more important than other considerations. Libra emotions tend to like what compliments them or reflects their own allure.

THE MOON IN SCORPIO: the emotions are secretive, intense, penetrating, objectively detached and deeply sensuous. The emotions under Scorpio are almost the opposite of those under Libra. Scorpio is less concerned with surface attractions and highly keyed to the potentialities beneath the surface. Very often the deeper they are and the more digging necessary, the more attractive they are for Scorpio. They love to put matters to the test. The Scorpio nature is very jealous and will not tolerate any sort of competition. They can, like the scorpion itself, destroy what they cannot have for themselves. Emotional involvement with this type tends to stir up all sorts of hidden and unsuspected qualities in both parties, which adds to the fun but can also get out of hand. Any quality of our nature (that is, any planetary force) is subject to exploitation in the sign of Scorpio, for Scorpio finds other uses for even the simplest things. Fortunately, the objects of affection that Scorpio selects for itself generally tend to have qualities that can stand up to the Scorpio testing treatment. If not, then Scorpio discovers this very early in the game and drops the object for something more interesting.

THE MOON IN SAGITTARIUS: the emotions are jubilant, enthusiastic, optimistic and strongly based on faith and uplift. The emotions tend to get carried away on the moral plane which often leaves the physical and material plane unattended and lost. More realistic, earthy types tend to avoid the Sagittarian spirit as just not "with it" for them. Sagittarian emotions are loyal but inflexible and coded or ritualized. The native goes through emotional stages as if scanning a driving manual without seeming to become very much involved in any one step. It is the whole pattern that is important to Sagittarius, not just the beginning, the middle or the summation.

THE MOON IN CAPRICORN: the emotions are stubbornly persistent, serious in tone, reserved in expression, and keyed to what is expected or desirable UNDER THE CIRCUMSTANCES. Other types may be less aware of the circumstances involved, being more intent on an effective presentation of themselves unaccompanied by balance sheets, material background or future profits. Capricorn tends to see the whole picture with a certain appraising eye, which is considerably aware of material advantages over and above any emotional gratifications. The native is always conscious of the price involved, even with emotions. He likes to budget his emotions because he is well aware of just how much he can afford in this department. He seldom overextends his emotional budget.

THE MOON IN AQUARIUS: the emotions are unconventional, visionary, erratic and independent. The native tends to feel qualities in situations or people that he himself introduces or empathizes into the situation. The introduction of these added elements is not wholly unjustified because he is responding to something which he is aware of, but the other party involved may not be aware of these qualities in himself. This introduces a surprise element in all contact with Aquarians. The Aquarian emotions are seeking something unique, which generally rules out the ordinary and the mediocre but not the strange. Aquarian emotions tend to be warm and friendly but not especially intimate, suggestive or penetrating. Their brilliance (such as it is) lights up momentarily and passes away just as quickly. It particularly avoids the implication of responsibilities, which tend to defeat the best of what Aquarians have to offer.

THE MOON IN PISCES: the emotions are subconscious, deeply convicted, tolerant, inspirational, idealized and mature. There is always attached to any planetary quality falling under Pisces a spiritual implication, which is suggested but never forced or demanded. The ideality of the matters is always stressed over either the practicality or even workability. Pisces emotions tend to become fixed on the most improbable objects, as though they sought the least likely candidate imaginable. Protective relatives and friends of natives with the Moon in Pisces often have cause to feel that the native is being purposely arbitrary in some of his emotional attachments. This is not true. The native may see something in the object of his affections which no one else can see (influence of Neptune), but he does not do this to be arbitrary. He is actually guided and drawn to things on a spiritual wavelength that transcends other considerations, particularly material ones. He is particularly drawn to sad or dejected cases because he can understand them so well. Sharing this understanding gives the native with the Moon in Pisces a confirmation of an added dimension in his life. Without this his life would feel one-sided or flat and hollow.

Wherever the Moon falls in the horoscope (by house) is where you will find unstable conditions and mixed emotions that the native feels for the matters and persons of that house. It is in this department of life that the native will experience the most frequent changes of attitude and mood. The native may return again and again to a position on the matter which he formerly held, but there is always some uncertainty that causes tension, nervous strain and emotional maladjustments. It is this very movement however that gives a sense of life to the matter, and the native generally has a great deal more depth of understanding than he usually gives himself credit for.

What you long for with the Moon takes the actuality of the Sun to make possible. A difference between the two creates the hum of life, the buzz of action and reaction, the throb of reality. This is why it is necessary to have some polarity between the Sun and the Moon. This is what often makes life a headache but prevents it from being a bore.

Chapter 6

THE IMAGE OF YOUR PERSONALITY

THE ASCENDANT & ITS RULING PLANET
(THE 1ST HOUSE)

The house divisions of the horoscope map set the scene of the action. They identify the focus through which the native's interests must operate.

The signs of the zodiac that fall on these areas of action describe the weather conditions under which the action will take place; they establish the tempo and character of the action; and they provide the costume and the mask the native wears to carry out his project.

Since the signs are stationary divisions of space and the houses are sections of the earth circle (which is rotating on its axis), it is more correct to phrase this as which house is falling UNDER which sign influence.

In erecting the horoscope map the starting point that determines ALL THE OTHER FACTORS IN THE HOROSCOPE is the point of the left-hand horizon at the moment of birth. We call this point the ascendant (AC) or cusp line, which marks the beginning of the first house of the horoscope.

Next to the sign position of the Sun, which identifies the ego-drive (and its house position, which shows the character of the destiny), the ascendant of the horoscope is the next most important consideration. As already covered in Chapter 3, "The Houses of the Horoscope," this is the quality of THE PERSONALITY IMAGE WHICH ATTRACTS ALL INITIAL CONTACT WITH THE NATIVE. This is HOW THE WORLD SEES THE NATIVE.

The tempo or character of the personality is shown by the sign on the ascendant.

THE ARIES PERSONALITY IMAGE ON THE ASCENDANT: This attracts all the qualities of the Aries individuality together with the Mars aggressive impulses. The native displays a unique and un-compromising personality, which is courageous, enterprising, ego-centered, rash, impulsive, hot-tempered, ardent, loyal and frank. The native also attracts and brings out these qualities in other people, since this is the type of sign on his "front door." Others who are looking for just this fresh new approach seek him out to give him this kind of assignment. Everything important in the daily contacts initially starts for him an Aries/Mars way. That is to say, with a bang and generally accompanied with much initial enthusiasm, optimism, purity of intention and a certain naive trust in others with regard to their following along and being as trustful as he is. If strong enough, the Aries/Mars attitude can sweep the day and carry the victory, but often enough the whole show collapses along the way through some disastrous flaw or unsuspected oversight. Aries can only pick up the pieces, patch up the mistakes, and start over again or take off with some new adventure. This is Aries, the herald of spring, the call of the open road, the glory of battle. If you want the most enterprising front man you can find, seek an Aries ascendant.

The planet Mars controls and triggers Aries, so we look in the horoscope for the house location and condition of Mars. With Mars in the:

First house: the native initiates himself. He has the capacity to turn himself on and to fuel his own enthusiasms. In fact these are the ONLY ones he is able to respond to. There is some tendency to be overly competitive with other egos, and the initial reaction is to fight first and ask questions later. The native is extremely ener-getic and sexually conscious, which generally works to his advan-tage. This Aries personality is better able to sweep people off their feet by the force of his personality. His concentration is ex-clusively "me first, last and always."

Second house: the personality works best when directed toward efforts to make money and increase earnings. This is naturally favorable for financial success. The native never stops experiment-ing with ways to make money for himself.

Third house: the native turns the force of his personality into some kind of effective writing, communication or descriptive thinking. The native will be mentally restless and constantly moving around the neighborhood. This leads to adventures, fights and exercise of competition against his neighbors, brothers and sisters.

Fourth house: the native rebels in some way against his background and parental authority and general conditions in the home. He will radically change his methods many times. There is a tendency to throw over a good plan in favor of a new approach before the old one has time to prove itself. The native needs a good home situation but will be constantly changing it. There is apt to be considerable uncertainty and self-doubt as to the soundness of his own approach, and at the same time the native is against allowing anyone else to decide such matters for him. The situation here tends to put the native constantly at war with himself over his fundamental programs. This is a "foot on the banana peel" type of security.

Fifth house: the native is naturally creative and productive and very romantic in his love-making. There is a fondness and talent for gamble and speculation, but the risks are usually high and dangerous. All romances are fated for stormy sessions, and with the native's children there are fights that arise through a sense of competition. Sexual promiscuity would be frequent and intense, as the dynamics of the native's individuality are considerably enhanced by any sexual aggressiveness.

Sixth house: the native is far more subdued, and spontaneous action is considered a close second to duty and obligation, although the native may get very aggressive on matters relating to certain responsibilities. The native has a talent for being useful, if not to say essential, in serving others. There is considerable opportunity for sexual adventures in and around the job and while being of service to others or while others are being of service to the native. This placement of Mars would provide some degree of balance or restraint for an otherwise "too much" of the Aries temperament.

Seventh house: the native's personality has to be turned on by others. He does not take the initiative. He is considerably subject to outside domination in most of his affairs. This is generally unfavorable for smooth or peaceful relations with partners or in other alliances. The native lends himself to control by others yet resists at the same time, leading to fights and aggressive acts. In the end the native gives in. With Mars as the sexual force there is some suggestion of sadistic or masochistic abuses. The native wants to be taken advantage of, although he may initially put up a fight.

Eighth house: the native's sex life (with consequent effects on his personality development) tends to be unsatisfactory. The secrecy of the eighth house encourages hidden excesses of a sexual nature. The native is capable of rising to tremendous deeds of courage in times of crisis and catastrophe, but most of the time he over-indulges in sexual fantasies of a questionable nature. The eighth house is an "undercover" area, and with the natural sexual impulses handicapped in this way and controlling the dynamics of the personality, it is difficult to move in a constructive and healthy direction. At times of crisis (either in his own life or in general) the demands of the situation take the native's attention off his personal problems and channel them into constructive acts of heroism.

Ninth house: the native must travel far from his initial beginnings in order to find himself. There is a tendency to devote oneself to causes and principles that at the same time lend themselves to violence and revolt. The native would be naturally drawn to violent movements or strongly controversial positions—in fact, this is the only kind of principle that turns his personality on. This position indicates much foreign travel and restless adventures, which should be encouraged to bring out the best in the native's personality.

Tenth house: the native is geared to fight for his ambitions and a position in the world. He will also suffer much severe competition from those above him until he can force them out of the situation, which he needs for himself. This is inevitable. This sense of aggressive competition is music to his personality. The native is likely to acquire a reputation for dirty fighting.

Eleventh house: the native strives aggressively to defend and protect those who share his interests and sympathies. The native will expect and demand that he be acknowledged as leader, and then he will lend his courageous spirit for a common purpose. But until he has won his point, there will be fights and violent disagreements among the friends he has chosen. His friendships are probably more important to him than his family or the direct objects of his romancing. Spirited physical competition with close friends leads to sexual emotions.

Twelfth house: the natural instrument of forceful action is considerably hampered by being secluded in the house of disappointment, failure and subjective values. The native is drawn to people who are at least temporarily out of commission, behind the eight ball, or in some state of rejection by society. This condition of others (which might be considered some kind of sickness of the moment) is the very thing that turns this native on. If the other person were well, the native wouldn't be attracted. The sex life is very secretive and should be kept so, lest it offend others who wouldn't appreciate the circumstances. This native is unfortunately somehow unable to do much for himself, but he can heroically help those who are down and out.

The aggressive nature of Mars is always coupled, forced, or blocked by the action of other planetary forces with whom it aspects by conjunction, square, or opposition, respectively. The Mars nature is encouraged by any planetary force in soft-angle aspect (the sextile or the slightly more effective trine).

With Aries on the first house of the personality (or how others see the native), Libra is always on the seventh house of others who touch the native's life (how the native sees others). This makes the Aries personality extremely susceptible to anyone else who is willing to trade affections. Libras have a talent for beautifying their environment, and the Aries personality is sensitive to this. This is a stabilizing factor for the Mars urge and opens the Aries heart to ANY display of affection and/or comforting efforts on the part of others. The Aries personality generally assumes that others WILL LOVE HIS EFFORTS. Since the Libra type is always bringing up the other side of the picture—turning the coin around for fair play—this keeps the Aries defense system up and active, always ready for an argument, contest or chance to win his point. Aries expects this and generally meets it. The Libra type may actually agree completely, but he invariably takes an opposite position to put others on their mettle, and this particularly keeps the Aries pot boiling.

With Aries on the first house of the personality, Cancer is always on the fourth house of how the native sees himself, and Capricorn is always on the tenth house of how others judge the native. With Cancer on the fourth the native is cautious in method (once he becomes organized) and proud and protective of his family and background. Capricorn on the tenth assures a practical goal and one which is in keeping with obviously desirable values, which all those with common sense will appreciate in the maturity of their experience.

After considering this somewhat unique coincidence, which occurs only for the Aries personality (that is, having the other cardinal signs always on the four angular houses of their horoscope, and this coincides with the natural order of signs to houses), one notes that the exuberance of Aries follows to a considerable extent the age cycles of growth. That is, the impetuosity of youth is soon tempered with the responsibilities of family considerations (Cancer on the fourth), the attractiveness of partnerships (Libra on the seventh), and the practicality of ambition (Capricorn on the tenth). So the Aries personality is most pronounced or typical in youth but is quickly tempered and modified with age and responsibility. The Aries quality of the personality does not survive youth too well. The aging factors soon take a strong hold on this personality type to the point of possibly suffocating its true nature.

THE TAURUS PERSONALITY IMAGE ON THE ASCENDANT: This gives the native a personality that is careful, deliberate, practical, stubbornly consistent and very conscious of all material values. They have a talent for keeping records and make excellent clerks or accountants and excel at any kind of housekeeping routine. They always appear dependable and attract the kind of assignments in life that call for these qualities whether or not they are thrilled with the assignments. Their personalities suggest natives whose feet are firmly planted on the ground at all times, and they naturally gravitate to conditions of comfort, ease and abundance that at the same time are pleasant and attractive. They demand a situation that is orderly, comfortable and colorful. They do not as a rule appreciate too many changes in their immediate environment. Once something is set, they prefer to leave it alone as long as it serves some practical purpose. They are very habit-prone in their daily living—so much so that they work themselves into a rut but endure it rather than instigate disruptions. They may be very upset inwardly, but they tend to leave their outer conditions alone.

The planet Venus controls Taurus, so we look in the horoscope for the house location and condition of Venus. It is naturally important where Venus falls because Venus is a gentle planet and the Taurus personality responds best to gentle methods. It does not like force or harsh treatment. It is particularly responsive to comforts, pleasures, color and decoration. With Venus in the:

First house: the native himself has a talent for creating Venus-like atmosphere. While he has a talent for this, he is less likely to create these comforts for others, as Libra would. Taurus usually stops when the situation is comfortable enough for himself. Venus in the first house always lends a certain physical beauty to the native.

In Taurus this tends to be of a practical earthy quality—the clean-cut conservative type.

Second house: the native is especially good at adapting his personality to moneymaking pursuits, which are generally profitable. This is a very strong moneymaking pattern. The pursuit of profit is uppermost in the orientation of the native's personality.

Third house: the native has a grace and charm of expression that is very persuasive in any kind of communication with others. There is much fondness for gossip and neighborhood news and views and social relationships. The brothers and sisters are likely to have much influence on the native and his well-being.

Fourth house: there is much love for home, family background and a tender relationship with parents. The home life is usually happy, and the native is most expressive around the home or projecting from the home as a base of operations.

Fifth house: the native has romantic talents and is very attractive as a lover or sex object. There is a certain amount of luck in gambling, speculation and around places of entertainment and in all pleasure-loving pursuits. Relationships with children are very gratifying.

Sixth house: the native is fortunate in and around his place of work. The vocation is attractive or stems from an activity that creates attractive conditions professionally. The native has congenial relationships with those above him and below him in station. Working conditions are always pleasant.

Seventh house: the native lends himself to agreeable domination by others to whom he is attracted and for attractive reasons. The native has an agreeable talent for getting along with others and creating affectionate reactions himself. This is a happy and fortunate pattern for all kinds of social relationships. The native is primarily controlled or influenced by the other party.

Eighth house: the native operates best in dealing with others at a time of crisis or emergency. The native would be especially sensitive to deaths, the problems connected with deaths, or in handling property which is connected with the affairs of the dead. This could also include dealing with antiques, since they are the artifacts of a dead society. The affectionate nature suffers some distortion due to the *sub rosa* nature of the eighth house.

Ninth house: the native is affectionately disposed toward travel, foreigners, foreign countries and products of foreign countries.

Anything in sharp contrast to the native's own birth origins or background or original mode of thinking is foreign to him. The native is happiest (and TAURUS PERSONALITIES NEED TO FEEL HAPPY) when associated with some cause, law, religion, educational pursuit or publishing enterprise. The native is well advised to remove himself at some distance from his original beginnings. He will always receive more appreciation in this way.

Tenth house: the native should capitalize on his personality. He should find some way to sell attractiveness (beauty aids), happiness and the comforts that help in this direction. The native should eventually be celebrated as a beauty or beautifier. The native can also make himself valuable as a decorative accessory or supplier of comforts to someone in a high position who is perhaps too busy or untalented to do this for himself. This position assures the native of a good reputation and affectionate regard from others.

Eleventh house: the native is ideal as a group organizer or one who is able to gather the dreams of others and give them a practical application. This position makes for social talent on a large scale and a place of affection in the hearts of many friends.

Twelfth house: the affectional nature is turned toward those less fortunate in our society who may be singularly lacking in the very social assets that the native seems to have. The native is pushed into the background of life's affairs, but this unfortunate position will provide the more secure happiness. It may take him some time to appreciate this, however. One's true vocation is apt to be revealed only after many setbacks and deep disappointments, which it is hoped will sweeten and deepen the native's love nature rather than harden and frustrate it.

Venus is always joined, forced or blocked by any planetary force in hard angle to it (conjuction, square or opposition). Venus is encouraged by any planetary force in soft-angle aspect to it (sextile or trine).

The Taurus personality always has Scorpio on the seventh house. Thus the Taurus personality is always somewhat suspicious and skeptical of others, but the very secrecy and suggestiveness of their nature leads Taurus on. Taurus, an earthy sign, is very susceptible to the sexual undertones of Scorpio, which of course brings out the sexuality of Taurus. Since Scorpios keep other people guessing about themselves this also intrigues the Taurus personality. Taurus personalities tend to size others up by the hidden potentials of their sexual nature.

They are attracted to partners largely for sexual reasons, and it is generally impossible to become involved on a partnership basis with anyone that is not sexually attractive to the Taurus personality.

Due to the tilt of the earth in certain latitudes, sometimes Taurus has Cancer/Capricorn on the fourth/tenth axis, which is soundly constructive, or Leo/Aquarius, which is considerably less desirable. Cancer on the method gives a talent for doing the right thing at the right time. And Capricorn on the reputation and final judgment keeps one consistently on target and mindful of practical goals. The pattern with Leo on the method is good for originality and the individuality of creative efforts but is considerably less adaptable and a good deal more opinionated as to the sureness of his own method. The Aquarius label on the reputation is most uncertain. The native seems to strive for the unattainable or the unpopular and at best ends up a genius to a few but a nut to most people.

THE GEMINI PERSONALITY IMAGE ON THE ASCENDANT: This gives the native an ease and facility with words, ideas and a general ability to express himself eloquently on a variety of subjects. The native will attract attention by his quick perceptions and his talent for comment, gossip, communication and verbal gymnastics. He will seldom be at a loss for opinion, comment or criticism, whether asked for or not. His most noticeable virtue will be the way he can talk himself into (or out of) situations that would stump most people.

The mental planet Mercury rules Gemini, so the native has the kind of mind that forms a perfect mirror, or reflection, of news and views of the moment. With Mercury on the:

First house : the native shows considerable ingenuity and originality in expression of his views. He would be more noticeably brilliant than other Gemini types, who all seem however to share some degree of this brilliance (if only a surface smattering of many subjects). Gemini has often been accused of superficiality (and not without reason), but with this position of Mercury there is more individuality, inventive thinking and independence in all the native's expression.

Second house: the native applies his clever and critical mind to moneymaking schemes that can result in some fast-talking slick programs, not all of which may be too sound. In any event the native can turn his talkative personality into some kind of financial return.

Third house: the native's thoughts become slightly more critical, and the native strives to create a style or quality of communication that is entirely his own. He would aim to write for writing's sake.

Fourth house: the native's talents for writing become subjective, and there. is much examination of one's background and heritage. This is not a position favorable to individual freedoms, since the native's personality is subjected to parental authority and there is a reluctance and an inability to break free from one's background. The background is favored in this struggle.

Fifth house: the native's efforts are highly creative, romantic and courageously daring. His efforts have merit in the field of entertainment and other pleasure-seeking activities. The native is apt to sacrifice his individuality on some highly risky undertaking that, although intended to be entertaining or creative, could be of questionable merit.

Sixth house: the native's efforts at writing and self-expression take on a more serious tone and lay great stress on duty, technical matters and elaboration of instructions on organization and "how to" publications, health matters, job instruction manuals, and the techniques of writing.

Seventh house: the native's talkative personality is directed at getting along with people and devising schemes to hold people together and minimize any differences that would keep them apart. This is a position favorable for debate and contests between speakers and for settling legal differences or controversial views otherwise unreconcilable. The native is predisposed to lean more to the other person's view than his own.

Eighth house: the native's views are confined to a very specialized area not usually understood by the public. In many respects the subjects of most interest are those that are considered dead issues or too frightening for ordinary discussion. Science fiction, death, or even pornography as the exploitation of sex are subjects of the eighth house.

Ninth house: the thoughts are channeled in far more serious areas such as law, higher education, religion, philosophy, publishing, travel, history, promotion for its own sake, advertising and more serious literary pursuits.

Tenth house: there is a possibility of fame through writing. The native must certainly devote a great deal of conscious effort to creative expression that has career recognition possibilities. The Mercury in the tenth house could be in Capricorn, Aquarius or

Pisces, any of which is possible as a significant breakthrough that could capture a wide audience. The Capricorn Mercury would be more solid and respectable. The Aquarius Mercury would be more free-swinging and offbeat. The Pisces Mercury would have the more mysterious suggestiveness and be well suited for films or television.

Eleventh house: the native is apt to waste his best efforts on friends without fully capitalizing on the career possibilities. It would be favorable for house organs and publications that further the aims of special groups, a field of special values or hopes.

Twelfth house: there is a turning inward to the subjective and sub-conscious reasons behind what happens to people. This position is favored for research and technical experiments that probe into unusual conditions and seldom-acknowledged areas of experience. It could also include fiction built around tragedy or the misunderstood people of the world. Film making and writing and performing for the films is felt to be a twelfth-house subject because there is an image, mask or film between the performer and the audience. This is typically Neptunian—the image vs. the real.

The Gemini personality always has Sagittarius coloring the world as Gemini sees other people. This gives a natural hopefulness, optimism and trust in others, which in turn tends to keep the Gemini viewpoint healthy, objective and full of positive application.

The Gemini personality has three possibilities for the fourth/tenth house axis. One has Cancer (public sensitivity for timing) on method, with Capricorn (the practical and persistently determined) on judgment—always a talented and sound combination. Another has Leo (the self-assured) on method and Aquarius (the progressive) as the goal. The third gives Virgo (the critically careful with much detail of organization) on technique with Pisces (the idealist) on goal.

The mental versatility of Mercury is coupled, forced or blocked by the three hard-angle aspects to any planet (conjunction, square or opposition). The thinking is flattered or complimented by either of the two soft-angle aspects to other planetary forces (the milder sextile or the stronger trine).

THE CANCER PERSONALITY IMAGE ON THE ASCENDANT:

Cancer on the ascendant always gives the native talents for attracting and influencing the public, particularly women and matters of feminine interest. The native seems to sense what the public wants at any one moment and is prepared to cater or serve these needs. Anywhere that Cancer falls is in fact where the native is supersensitive to public needs and has powers for attracting people. There is also much moodiness and the quality of turning on or off, which is self-protective for Cancer. Timing, which is so vital in everything, is a natural talent in the personality, and the native knows how to make the most of it. The native may be too gentle at times to deal with the harsher realities of life.

The sensitive and fickle Moon rules Cancer, and like the tides of the ocean she has many moods and highs and lows. Control of the Moon is a gentle art and shows a feminine influence both given and received.

When the Moon is in the:

First house: the native is acutely sensitive but somewhat unbalanced and overly temperamental. He may be possessed with one special talent to an extraordinary degree, but this may prove more of a debilitating liability than an overall blessing. The native tends to go to extremes in behavior and to be very high-strung and generally unmanageable. When the native is "in tune" he should be capable of influencing large audiences.

Second house: the native is extremely sensitive to any situation that has profit-making possibilities. He should also be able to sense how others could improve their earnings. One might consider professional counseling on such matters.

Third house: the native is particularly sensitive to all sorts of communication work and news gathering and even mental telepathy or the possibilities for it. What is being accented is communication coupled with extreme sensitivity to emotions and thought transfers. ESP is a possibility.

Fourth house: the native's personality is somewhat dampened by being submitted to parental domination or excessive subjective appraisal. Anything that filters or comes between the native and a direct reception of outside stimuli would be generally undesirable. In this case the interference is initially from conditions in and around the home. Later it comes from the native's own sense of protective criticism.

Fifth house: the native is very outgoing in his emotions and eager to register an impression on others through some emotional creativity. This is a position of an inner seed coming into flower and receiving public reaction rather than the native receiving his inspiration or go-ahead from the public.

Sixth house: the native is very responsive to duties and obligations and a sense of service toward responsibilities of public interest. The public, through the obligations which it imposes on the native, generally shapes his emotional responses.

Seventh house: the native is again subject to a filter or intermediary between outside stimulation (or inspiration) and his own reception or awareness. The native in this case must get his sources from others. And others in the process are largely responsible for the shape and/or direction of the native's emotional responses.

Eighth house: the native is considerably freer, in the course of his emotional direction. The interests are less personal, being almost wholly consumed with a curiosity about other people's reactions, particularly under stress or in times of extraordinary conditions. The native's emotions have a tendency to wander far afield and to explore hidden depths of feeling and possibilities for change. There is an acute sensitivity to matters that others neglect as dead issues.

Ninth house: the native considers himself a spearhead or advance publicity agent for some particular code or form of thinking that has much tradition or sense of historical buildup behind it. The native in this sense is not alone in his beliefs since he emotionally ties himself to a tradition or principles that have the force of law or religion. This is the pattern of an inspired and gifted teacher, who is particularly responsive to what the student really needs at the moment.

Tenth house: the native is again subject to the filter treatment, which is also evident in the fourth and seventh house positions of the moon. This time the controlling agent is those in command who stand above the native in authority, and this influences the recognition or acknowledgment he will receive. This involves the goals and ambitions, which make him sensitive to following the dictates of those whom he senses will in some way affect his outcome. This requires the native to submit to a control in his emotions that he would normally not permit.

Eleventh house: the eleventh house placement of any key or controlling factor is generally a happy and fortunate pattern. It does require, however, that the native seek his focus or outlet in group associations or by joining with others of sympathetic intent as the most advisable way for him to content himself. This ensures the native of sympathetic and understanding associates. However, it reduces or waters down the personal emotions to group values or group levels where individual attitudes would allow for more independence and range of freedom.

Twelfth house: the native is deeply aware of the background nature and collective unconscious which creates and controls that which is publicly "in the air" at the moment. This may give him an air of detachment, reserve and a degree of sadness and mystic quality. The native would naturally gravitate to the background to be available when called as a specialist or consultant. The native would not or should not push himself into front-line prominence or in any way attempt to take over or directly lead the situation.

The sensitive Moon is coupled, forced or blocked in its emotional pattern by any hard-angle aspect it makes to other planets. It is sympathetically encouraged and spontaneously stimulated by any soft-angle aspects.

The Cancer personality image always has Capricorn on the opposite side of the fence dominating the way the native habitually sees the world. Since the Capricorn outlook would be repressive and limiting, it would seem to align all the established forces against the native. He would be considerably held in check and restricted or limited in any feeling of release or freedom TO BE EXPECTED FROM OTHERS.

The Cancer personality image can have (according to the tilt of the earth at various latitudes) four different combinations of signs on the method/ambition or security/judgment axis. It can have Leo/Aquarius (a variable pattern not generally favorable), Virgo/Pisces (favorable for service but taking a back seat), Libra/Aries (a decidedly more influential configuration), or Scorpio/Taurus (suggesting hidden and disruptive emotions).

THE LEO PERSONALITY IMAGE ON THE ASCENDANT: This is immediately indicative of a strong personality that demands constant and responsive attention at all times. The individuality is so pronounced as not to tolerate any competition in the field which will in any way diminish or detract from the native as the center of attention. The native is ideally suited to situations or programs which call for individuality of effort, inventiveness of mind, resourcefulness of nature and aggressiveness of spirit. The combination of all these qualities acting together is needed to clear the field, carry the day, and gain the beachhead. Will power and supreme belief in the self at all times and under all conditions is mandatory. It would be impossible, if not to say tragic, to pretend bashfulness or reticence or feel indecisive in any way. This native feels he was born to lead, rule and exercise prerogatives of position. Anything that stands in the light of the native's sun casts a deep shadow or scar on his effectiveness to fulfill himself with the honor and distinction that he requires.

A detailed presentation of the force and spirit of the all-powerful Sun by house appears in Chapter 4 "The Character of Your Destiny." This can be followed through by taking first the houses of the Sun followed by (in each case) Leo on the ascendant.

The nature of the Sun, even though it springs from the ego, will or spirit of the native, is further enhanced by those forces with which the Sun allies itself by aspect. It is coupled, forced or blocked by the hard angles and sympathetically indulged by the soft angles. The hard-angles aspects are far more indicative of character and development of inner fortitude than the soft angles, which only encourage but do not support or sustain the ego in times of necessity or crisis.

The Leo personality image always has Aquarius coloring the outside world as the native sees it. In this case this is a questional value which works splendidly on otherwise strong and sound foundations but disastrously with weak or vacillating supports. The Aquarian outlook lends itself all too readily to an unreal, fabricated sense of the outside world which at the same time feeds the individual ego (in the personality) to unjustifiable extremes. The Leo personality image leads to a glorious all-or-nothing flourish—impressive but sometimes empty.

The Leo personality image sometimes has Virgo/Pisces (critical and penetrating) or Sagittarius/Gemini (generally fortunate and impressive) on the method/ambition axis. But in temperate latitudes it mostly has Libra/Aries (good) or Scorpio/Taurus (not so good) on this axis.

THE VIRGO PERSONALITY IMAGE ON THE ASCENDANT: This native is a born perfectionist in all that he assumes or undertakes. He appears detailed, organized, disciplined, objectively critical and sincerely desirous to fill a need or augment a service to which he feels obligated. The Virgo contribution, such as it is, may not be exactly what others feel they want or need. Virgo considers his opinion on this to be superior generally because Virgo is objective and knows what he is doing and the best way to go about it. The uncontrollable point is in getting others to appreciate the real value of the Virgo contribution with its sense of "perfected details." Too often Virgo merely gets stuck with the short end of the stick—which is to say, with all the petty, nuisance jobs that no one else wants to bother with. And unfortunately many Virgos accept this assignment with too much philosophical rationalization.... "Well, as long as it has to be done, I might as well do it myself and see that it gets done right." It takes a superior or strongly oriented Virgo to resist being stuffed into pigeonholes and save his sense of perfection for where it has real value.

Virgo (at the moment) is keyed to the vacillating, reflective, and to some extent shallow Mercury. It is naturally important how Mercury is fortified under stress by strong hard-angle aspects to other planetary forces besides being pleasantly favored by whatever soft-angle aspect it makes. If Mercury is in the:

First house: the native shows originality of thought, individuality in thinking and self-dedication of spirit in choosing and accepting the duties that life forces on him. This is an above-average, strong Virgo/Mercury position.

Second house: the native tends to accept those assignments which seem profitable and likely to produce a certain aboundance of "supply." The interests are personal and material.

Third house: the interests are personal and mental as the native concerns himself with perfecting some special techniques connected with communication, styles of expression and the collection and dispersal of news and opinions.

Fourth house: the native is more independent and constructive as to the duty assignments he will accept, since any and all obligations which he assumes must meet rigid standards of subjective perfection. Initially, his thinking is strongly influenced by home conditions and parental examples, which eventually give way to subjective inventory and better exploitation of his natural background and heritage. Home conditions are always important to the native, and standards of perfection are demanded of the family and of anyone who touches in some way on the native's emotional security.

Fifth house: the native is more vulnerable to being "taken" or "put upon," so to speak, because he responds automatically to almost anything mentally that will offer an extension of his critical and appraising personality. Very often this can lead to risks and speculations that may not be sound. Remembering that Virgo personalities tend to concentrate on the details, they are very apt to get carried beyond their depth because they DO NOT have their attention on the larger frame of reference.

Sixth house: this is a sound, suitable pattern for work-hungry Virgo, but his duties are apt to be more routine, subservient and limited. The native, while generally well qualified for critical tasks, is more content to waste his best efforts with background details and let others direct the course of action. In this position of Mercury, Virgo almost prefers it that way.

Seventh house: this is a somewhat stronger and more constructive pattern for the Virgo personality because, while others control the native, they are interested in him and he is liable to get better assignments than he would generally choose or accept for himself. Two heads or two egos are better in this pattern because the Virgo personality subjects himself to any tasks, which may not really be worth his best efforts. Perfecting criticism when highly developed in the Virgo type is too rare and valuable a talent to waste on humdrum back-office slavelike jobs. The control passing to others who are interested helps avoid this pitfall.

Eighth house: this position of Mercury is also favorable because the native is swept into new opportunities or out of worn-out situations by the tide of circumstances, which is generally an intervention of fate. Since the Virgo personality generally does not sufficiently exercise what control he has over duty assignment, here at least fate takes over and sets the course in a progressive and expedient direction. The Virgo personality will be just as happy in his new assignment, and, ten to one, it will be far more needed than what he would have chosen for himself.

Ninth house: the native is rather fixed in his direction, which adjusts itself to a course already set up and determined by others who have gone before him on the same principles. The native takes up where others have left off. The principles being followed have the force of law or religion for the native. This is a favorable pattern for scientific pursuits and most forms of higher education, which require a familiarity with vast numbers of facts, figures, measurements and HAIR-SPLITTING REFINEMENTS.

Tenth house: the native's critical faculties are made the object of conscious ambitions. The native is far more selective and self-determined as to exactly what goals he will follow and the detailed assignment he will accept. The course is for ABSOLUTE PERFECTION in all matters.

Eleventh house: the native is somewhat suspended between the devil and the deep blue sea with too great a possibility of ending up on the losing side. Group objectives are substituted for individual values, and the native joins with others in the service he seeks to provide. This is usually a dirty-end-of-the-stick deal, but the native's hopes remain high, even if out of perspective.

Twelfth house: the native is guided and influenced by his inner conviction, which in this case can lend constructive support to an otherwise overly obedient servant. The pattern here may be likened to the native's capacity for being of help and his service being coupled with the forces of fate or destiny, which push or pull him into an assignment. This can be extremely important in many ways that may not be immediately apparent to other people. As long as the native is deeply convinced, the tasks that he assumes are right for him and ultimately for many others who will be helped. This is true only because this pattern gives him spiritual insight on the matter.

The Virgo personality always has Pisces coloring and diffusing the perspective from which the native sees others. This lends an eternal hope and Christian-like faith to the ultimate goodness in man, perhaps to the exclusion of the most glaring of humanity's mistakes and shortcomings. This spiritual (but sometimes unreal) attitude in life has both its virtues and its vices in shaping the Virgo personality. Its virtue lies in enabling Virgo to accept his lot in life and dedicate himself to service and general helpfulness, especially with tasks and duties that no one else wants or appreciates. Its vice lies in overencouraging Virgo to accept routine tasks that are unworthy of the precious Virgo talent for hair-splitting refinements. Also, because Virgo on its own makes so much of the trees that it misses the point of the forest, it doesn't help avoid the routine pitfalls of life by looking at the world in general through the glasses of delusion. Not that all of Pisces is delusion by any means, but one has to have a natural talent for getting the best that is involved with inspirational Neptune and the "spiritual way." One just can't look at the whole world by spiritual standards. But that is exactly what the Virgo personality does. Pisces, on the other end of the Virgo personality axis, is just not a quality that materially strengthens the picture. It is, in fact, more often an invitation to fantasy and retreat.

The Virgo personality sometimes has Sagittarius/Gemini on the method/recognition axis, which (under the circumstances) is another foot on the banana peel, or it has Scorpio/Taurus which is a good deal stronger, down-to-earth and practical. There is more determination here to break tradition with the past and head for material goals that are sound and productive.

THE LIBRA PERSONALITY IMAGE ON THE ASCENDANT: The native has definite social talents and a pleasing and gracious manner, which is apparent to everyone. This factor alone assures one of a happy and comfortable life—which is promising a great deal. The native makes an initial impression of being more interested in others than himself. This pleases and flatters people, and the native is assured of willing cooperation and sincere interest in his welfare. Libra personalities are attractive, even though they may not all be physically beautiful. There is always something about their personality that more than makes up for any physical shortcomings they may have. Almost everyone is willing to overlook their faults and concentrate on the charm and appeal of their friendly outgoing nature. They are the most automatically forgiven people in the world.

Venus, the soft spot of sentiment, holds the key that brings out the charm in the Libra personality. If Venus is in the:

First house: the native is physically attractive, as well as having a charming and persuasive personality. There may be a considerable amount of conceit and some degree of a Narcissus complex (being in love with the image of oneself), but there are generally plenty of people willing to pay the price just to be in his good favor, for they see Libra as an attractive ornament or enviable possession. This person is favored in life with luck, beauty and protection.

Second house: the native is generally fortunate in all money matters, and financial comfort is generally indicated which flows to the native without too much fuss or effort.

Third house: the native is favored with charm and grace of speech, delivery or style of communication. He attracts many people by his persuasive salesmanship. He may be a little insincere, but it sounds good coming from him and he gets away with it.

Fourth house: the native usually comes from a happy and secure family background, which enables him to flower early in life. This is the pattern of the fortunate one who is born into life of beauty, security, happiness and comfort. Who could ask for more? The native has a protected life and a fortunate way of regarding or adjusting to most of life's problems.

Fifth house: the native is very successful in all affairs of the heart, romance, love-making, enjoying children and being charmingly entertaining. This position is favored for popular entertaining and doing those things which give others pleasure. There could be a certain sadness underneath, which, however, is seldom allowed to show or mar the native's outgoing performance.

Sixth house: the native happily applies himself to the more irksome responsibilities that always prove useful and constructive. The native may be taken advantage of, but he seldom seems to mind and it does not sour his happy nature.

Seventh house: the native is especially gifted in dealing with all kinds of people. The native always seems ready to compromise at just the right moment in order to strengthen the other person's hand. Consequently, others feel indebted and are grateful. The native has many happy and gratifying relationships.

Eighth house: the native has hidden resources that are very potent and dramatic when suddenly brought into play during times of emergency or in handling sudden events which tend to sweep ordinary people aside. There is a strong sexual undercurrent which others sense, and the native is able to capitalize on this. This is sometimes crafty but always exhilarating. The native's reputation (or morality) is not above reproach by more conventional standards, but this is unlikely to interfere with the native's pursuit of pleasure.

Ninth house: the native is interested in teaching and converting others to the principles and laws that he believes in and that more or less follow established traditions. The native feels caught up in a sense of history, which adds to his own stature and impresses others.

Tenth house: the native is favored for some degree of success and recognition that relates directly back to the native's charm and personality. This distinction which the native earns may not last forever, but it assures him of above-average conditions surrounding his ambitions. The native's sphere of influence is greatly extended; his reputation can be far-flung and universal.

Eleventh house: the native happily identifies with others of similar purpose, and together they program themselves for something they enjoy in common. Not only is the native's life fortunate and happy, but he surrounds himself with those similarly blessed and together they multiply their luck.

Twelfth house: the native's favorable situation in life is not nearly so apparent in this position of Venus. In fact by many standards the native may be more often found in generally unfavorable conditions—like working around unfortunate people. But the native is content to enrich his spiritual values and know that he is part of the program that represents the ultimate values rather than just the material advantages that good fortune brings to some people. This native is truly at peace with his inner self, and this realization cannot be taken from him—no matter what happens.

Venus, the symbol of sentiment, is not a strong planetary force; therefore it is fortunate when fortified by hard-angle aspects, which give character, depth and purpose to an otherwise pleasure- and comfort-seeking quality. Venus is encouraged in its indulgent nature when in soft-angle aspect to other planets.

The Libra personality image always has the individualistic and aggressive Aries on the opposite seventh house of the horoscope. Aries always strives to bring out and encourage the best that is in us, and Libra finds it natural to respond to this constructive force from others. The Libra personality opposite to Aries is, on the whole, more fortunate and a good deal more rewarding than the Aries personality opposite to Libra.

The Libra personality has either Capricorn/Cancer on the security/recognition axis, which is very favorable, or Aquarius/Leo, which is considerably more free-swinging and harder to make gel.

THE SCORPIO PERSONALITY IMAGE ON THE ASCENDANT: The Scorpio type is a very complex individual with many varieties of subtypes. Basically he has a split personality. He seems to be drawn in two directions at the same time. The extreme of one direction may at times seem destructive to some people, while the other extreme has all the potential of a great liberator or freedom fighter. The Scorpio natives have very mixed emotions about these two directions in their lives and which road they should pursue. Frequently they find themselves heading in one direction only to switch around suddenly and head in the other. They are often unaware of what their real or ultimate intentions will be until they have pursued the matter at some length or gone too far to back down. At heart they are born reactionaries. Deep in their hidden thoughts (which they like to keep to themselves) they feel vaguely dissatisfied with some condition or situation in which they find themselves. Initially they are not sure what to do about it, except to build up a conviction that it must be changed or altered in some way. Scorpios come to regard themselves as self-appointed instruments of necessary and desirable change. They feel instinctively drawn to their destination by intuition, which they seldom rationalize or even express in conscious communication. They regard themselves as fated to act in some way as agents on an assignment given them by some mysterious force. The degree to which they accept this challenge and effectively bring about change differs widely from type to type. Some are merely vaguely detached, lost, secretive souls who wander in and out of situations and never start any decisive action. They merely become preoccupied with imagined solutions or give sympathetic support to others who are stirring up resentments or throwing rocks at the present establishment. Others take a stronger stand and register their reactions in some form of rebellion. Some even become violently anti status quo, which leads to some form of anarchy, rebellion or revolutionary tactics. And still others devote themselves to a new idealized state or concept, which they somehow bring to life in spite of the existing state of affairs that opposes and challenges it. In any event they come to stand out because of their peculiarities or the degree to which they do not fit into the prescribed mold.

Sexuality as a regenerative force, as opposed to procreation, is of great interest to Scorpios. Here, again, we encounter very mixed emotions. Some Scorpios use sex freely as a vehicle for exploitation, while others regard it as a sacred trust only to be used in extreme emergency. Either way there is an explosive violence somehow connected with the Scorpio sexuality. Some indulge in this, while others merely dwell on it in secret.

The Scorpio personality images vary widely, but all reflect to some degree these basic orientations and other people sense these with decidedly mixed reactions. Some people are intrigued by them, others avoid them, and some are openly suspicious of or actively hostile toward these people. Scorpios come to be regarded as either troublemakers or persons who seem to get into trouble or attract trouble. All of which is true, but it should be remembered that in the whole of life and the natural state of things THERE IS A VERY DEFINITE AND POSITIVE VALUE TO THE SCORPIO FUNCTION. Change is inevitable. Death is necessary, and if the old material is not removed, there would never be room or possibility for new life. The Scorpio type intuitively knows all these things, and he lends himself to nature's laws, whether or not these laws are understood by others. At the very least they all have hidden resources that are essential in times of crisis, and they help others face these emergencies and pull them through.

PLUTO, the two-faced sword, is the key to the mysterious

operations of Scorpio. Wherever you find Pluto in the horoscope, there you will find a split condition or a situation that has two sides or angles. One side is favorable, the other generally less favorable. One direction may be disintegrating while the other direction is taking on new form. There is always potential disaster afoot and the possibility of new construction from the ground up. Neither state is set or definitely finished. One condition is merging or being transformed into another totally different one. There is death on one hand and the wonder of rebirth on the other.

If Pluto is in the:

First house: the native is a more active revolutionary, and he doesn't particularly care who knows it. He is born with a greater sense of conviction as to exactly where his mission lies, and he is more prepared to do something about it—now. His violent reactions are apparent, and his proclivities for moving into something even more dangerous are always regarded with certainty. This native may be labeled by some people as dangerous from the beginning, but this may make him an instant leader of the rebellion rather than an outcast from the establishment. A great deal depends on other factors such as the condition of Pluto, other planetary forces which it aspects, the character of the native's destiny, and other planets in the first house.

Second house: the native's concentration is on money and resources and how to take them. Under the pattern of the Scorpio/Pluto configuration some means of force may be necessary in order for the native to get what he considers should be his.

Third house: the emphasis is on communication and learning to express or articulate the particular dissatisfactions that the native feels should be changed.

Fourth house: the native initially rebels against his background, which he feels does not truly represent him. Later he formulates programs designed to overthrow existing conditions which he is against. He is more interested in jerking the rug out from under the opposition than in confronting it face-to-face or taking over in its place.

Fifth house: the native is more daringly creative in his attitudes about change. In fact he may be in love with the romance or adventure of it or for the sheer pleasure it gives him.

Sixth house: the native devotes himself to secondary roles that lend support to his general sympathies while he brings up the rear or supplies the logistics.

Seventh house: the native enters into direct confrontation with the enemy in the guise of "others." Others in turn single out the native as "one to be watched," so they keep a sharp eye on him. The native tends to be thrown off guard by those who offer more practical solutions than he has, or he casts in his lot with those who are better organized and more carefully programmed. He takes his ultimate lead from others.

Eighth house: the native enters into secret negotiations or waits until fortuitous events cast him into the role meant for him. The native is a bit more aware of the spiritual consequences of his commitments and seeks intuitive guidance in these matters.

Ninth house: the native aligns himself with a movement or principle that has already been established and has some precedence or code of behavior which the native accepts as law or religion. At the same time his intellectual code may be at complete variance with other codes, which it tries to undermine or change. The native's approach is an intellectual one working through the formal system of a movement rather than using a more physical street-riot attitude.

Tenth house: the native places himself at the disposal of someone in command or control of a situation who is also committed to instrumenting significant changes. He does his bidding as his agent or employee. He acknowledges others as his masters until he is able to step forth in some degree of leadership. This is a position of personal ambition with an eye to what the native can gain from his affiliations.

Eleventh house: the native makes a social, friendly, comradely show of his interests and commitments. He seeks the sympathetic support of others who share his views on a friendly basis. He will accomplish more, in the disruptive changes to which he is drawn, by joining groups.

Twelfth house: the native needs no outside confirmations that the course he sets for himself is correct. He has deep inner convictions that ultimately his position will win out no matter what it may cost individuals like himself in the process. The native early resigns himself to the more obvious limitations of his project, so he is better prepared than most for setbacks, denials and frustrations. He relies on his own spiritual forces to see him through and has almost a complete lack of trust that others will be by his side when he might need them most.

The Pluto quality being essentially the reflection of a social force rather than a personal characteristic is considerably affected by the planetary forces that it aspects. Naturally it is more strongly affected by hard-angle aspects than soft angles.

The Sun would give it integrity.

The Moon would give it sensitivity and emotional support.

Mercury would give it articulation.

Saturn would give it structure and purpose.

Mars would give it initiative and courage.

Venus would give it softness and adaptability.

Neptune would give it inspiration.

Jupiter would give it faith and uplift.

Uranus would give it independence and sudden advantages.

Somewhat the same modifications or characteristics would be suggested as above when Pluto is the sign that the above planets rule.

The Scorpio personality always has Taurus on the opposite seventh house of others. This makes the native aware of practical solutions and the power that money will buy. In fact Scorpio personalities invariably come to think that money either solves everything or is the root of all evil. This is not, of course, universally true, but it is generally at the root of most of the inequities which Scorpio/Pluto sets about to change or correct. Since Taurus (those that Scorpio habitually has his eye on) is ruled by the love nature of Venus, Scorpio is doubly convinced of the effectiveness of sexuality when dealing with others—either opposing them on some matter or getting them to go along with his ideas in partnership. This tends to keep the Scorpio type from being completely bad in everybody's eyes because some people like him and have in fact offered him some degree of love and affection along the way. Scorpio is never completely down on everyone. He exempts those who have come in direct contact with him and concentrates his disruptive policies against strangers. The Venus love shield stops him from hurting those he has made contact with.

The Scorpio personality sometimes has Capricorn/Cancer on the method/ambition axis (which is sound, constructive and publicly effective) or Aries/Libra (which is more personal and dynamic). In temperate latitudes, however, he mostly has Aquarius/Leo (which can be offbeat, screwball and self-centered) or Pisces/Virgo (which is equally odd but slightly less volatile).

THE SAGITTARIUS PERSONALITY IMAGE ON THE ASCEND-ANT: the native exhibits a certain fire of enthusiasm which stems from his conviction concerning certain principles or patterns of thought. Like the other enthusiastic types (called FIRE signs), where the Aries exuberance is based on the spirit of his individuality and the Leo spirit is based on the power of his will and the extent of his ego, the Sagittarian faith is based on the strength of his principles and the rightness of his efforts.

The Sagittarian's spirit is keyed only to success and moving forward. Failure is not in their vocabulary. In fact it is very difficult for them to accept or admit anything less than success and upward, onward progress. When the tide is against them—not necessarily because they are inherently wrong but because more powerful planetary forces are in control—Sagittarians are somewhat at a loss as to just what to do or how to act. They can't stop being themselves, which is a positive declaration, but this may at times be tragically out of step with conditions around them as they really are. Sagittarians have a developed sense of history in which they see themselves as an important link in some invincible chain of significance which has to be right because it has been proven time and time again. They are ill prepared for changes in circumstances which would temporarily or permanently outdate the principles or concepts on which they stand. This blind spot in their makeup is apt to be a critical pitfall in times of crisis or change. When the going is good, they flourish magnificently. Then God is in his heaven and all's right with the world. But when all hell breaks loose Sagittarius is most apt to be left standing at the gate, a hollow voice in an empty land.

Jupiter, the symbol of abundance, keys the direction of the Sagittarian philosophy. If Jupiter is in the:

First house: the native has within himself the power to perform miracles in making everything seem right in the world about him whether it is or not. He has an air of distinction and the mark of success, which is very convincing even when without foundation. This native is hard to put down because he believes in the power of positive thinking so strongly and his integrity is generally above reproach.

Second house: this is a fortunate placement of Jupiter and indicates a certain abundance of resources and the talent for creating materially successful situations. The native should eventually be handsomely paid for his efforts. With Capricorn on the second house, the native works hard for his money. With Aquarius there are many ups and downs in fortune, but the native is essentially lucky and inventive with money.

Third house: the native is fortunate in his type of expression and in getting his ideas across to customers and clients in the marketplace. His whole personality has favorable "exchange value."

Fourth house: the native is fortunate in his family connections and the obvious richness of his background or heritage. The native has many fixed and solid assets to draw upon. He is generally fortunate in his choice of programs, and most situations at least start out well for him, even if they all don't end up exactly as hoped.

Fifth house: the native is fortunate in love, gamble, speculation, and affairs connected with children, their interests or primary education. He has a lucky touch in all of these areas.

Sixth house: the native is fortunate in his field of work. The conditions and relations with fellow workers are generally favorable and constructive. There is luck on the job.

Seventh house: the native receives fortunate cooperation from others, who favor him with material benefits.

Eighth house: the native is lucky in stumbling upon "dead situations" that bring good fortune to him.

Ninth house: the native makes fortunate contacts with institutions of higher learning or organizations that publish the same principles in which he believes.

Tenth house: the native is fortunate in life and receives a degree of distinction and fame, which brings profit and honors.

Eleventh house: the native is favored with influential friends who supply what he may lack.

Twelfth house: the native receives secret support from those who stand behind him but do not wish to be known publicly or advertised in the usual way. The native's inner convictions are well supported, and he frequently has proof of the rightness of his position, even though everyone doesn't truly understand what he is trying to accomplish.

The nature of Jupiter as a planetary quality is such that it needs support and structural foundation from other planetary forces in order to be really effective in life. Hard-angle aspects are particularly important because they strengthen the native's character, while soft-angle aspects tend to weaken or spoil the character since they give benefits without effort or struggle. Human nature tends to value most what it pays for in one way or another. And it tends not to value that which it gets for nothing.

The Sagittarius personality always has Gemini on the opposite seventh house. This draws the native toward mental contact with stimulating people who give him ideas and valuable suggestions, of which optimistic Sagittarius invariably makes good use. The native, however, tends to see others only in their surface images, since he feels it is not necessary to look deeper. This is not altogether a sound, realistic way of seeing the world and tends to keep the Sagittarian's head up in the clouds and out of touch with the totality of life. This may be OK if one just happens to be on the right track but can be fatal if one just happens to be off the beam.

In temperate latitudes the Sagittarius personality usually has Pisces/Virgo on the security/ambition axis (which under the circumstances is weak) or Aries/Libra (which is resourceful and much more mutually receptive for getting a better picture). Sometimes it may have Aquarius/Leo (unfavorable) or Taurus/Scorpio (much better).

THE CAPRICORN PERSONALITY IMAGE ON THE ASCENDANT: Capricorn is a hard-nosed sign which limits the native to established, material objectives and doing things the sure way. On the personality (ascendant) position it labels the native as old, rigid, fixed and determined, even as a child. It is not a colorful image and certainly not a spontaneous, joyful one. It lays a heavy hand on all those with whom it comes in contact. Capricorns are above all super-realists—at times far too much so. As a personality type they can be depressing but admirable in their way. They act like the voice of doom, which may be inevitable but not always welcome at the beginning. This is the way in which Capricorns affect others. The pure Capricorn picture (unless considerably relieved by other factors) is oppressive. They often achieve their goal eventually, but in the process they considerably limit everyone else around them. They are solid, down-to-earth, disciplined, hardworking people, who never tire or give up what they once set their mind on doing. They are seldom satisfied with any back seat in life since they also have their heart and purpose set on a fair share of all the material advantages. But they have to break a number of backs getting there. Capricorns have a way of grinding others down to dust. This seems to give them a source of satisfaction by minimizing or eliminating or exhausting their competition. It takes very extenuating circumstances for other signs to stand up to Capricorn. There has to be a reward in it somewhere, and for this we would have to look in our own horoscopes. The quality which Capricorn stresses most is security in the material sense. If you feel it is right, you will have to prove it in cold hard facts to satisfy Capricorn. Nothing else will impress them. If you are good at handling such figures, then Capricorn will stop and listen to you. They may not do things any differently, but they will pay attention to what you say. They are invariably fair and just and they expect others to be the same. Like Virgo they do not generally ask for more than they are prepared to give. In fact Capricorn is prepared to give more than he receives. This is very unlike Libra who is more concerned with an even exchange and generally prefers to see the cash in hand. Capricorn firmly believes that if you sow good deeds, you will harvest accordingly. The question in dealing with the Capricorn type is really the extent to which you can afford this grinding down to dust that Capricorn effects. For some this is constructive and helpful but for others it kills off their only assets and destroys them in some way.

Father Time as symbolized by the relentless Saturn is the force that guides and preserves the persistent Capricorn. If Saturn is in the:

First house: the native is capable of intense disciplines and a dogged persistency which hardens his shell and better insulates him from life's ruder shocks. He is slow to respond or react but when once aroused, is also slow to cool down. He is a steady pusher and inherently strong and durable. Perhaps "tough" is a better word for Capricorn than "strong." He is thick-skinned and seemingly insensitive.

Second house: the native is interested in money and intends to get a fair share of it or know the reason why. He invariably does acquire money, although he may find it hard to enjoy it. The native's early life is generally marked by a scarcity of resources, while his later years may be distinguished by a certain abundance because he is loath to part with it or spend it.

Third house: the native is faced with an early struggle to express himself adequately or communicate effectively with others, especially customers and clients in the marketplace. Eventually he develops a certain "exchange jargon," which, while overly serious and at times intimidating, is nevertheless effective for what he is trying to sell.

Fourth house: the native's early life and background are limited in financial advantages. He works hard to correct this and to discipline himself to expect less, therefore not to be in want. Parental restrictions are severe in youth and continue in effect into the native's mature years, where he finds it hard to break old habits of frugality and doing without. The native is careful and deliberate before he undertakes a set program to obtain a fixed goal. There is always a problem of getting going, but eventually the native accomplishes something, although it usually turns out to have been done the hard way.

Fifth house: this position is unfavorable for gamble and speculation and getting along too well with children. It kills romance. The native waits too long to make up his mind about such matters, and by then it is generally too late. The native will gravitate to certain older people who are harsh and firm but are somehow attractive to the native. Sexual gratifications are unsatisfactory.

Sixth house: the native is ambitious to find ways in which he can serve others and help alleviate the harshness of their daily burdens. He insists on doing this through very realistic and practical channels, which may prove even harder on those he is trying to help. The native learns something from this, but others tend to feel only the heavy yoke of his discipline.

Seventh house: the native is drawn to others who are older to discipline him and provide the golden key that will make it possible for him to earn some degree of recognition in life. Other firm, severe types have a strong influence on the native and retain a close grip on all his affairs. The native does not mind this; in fact he may rather enjoy it, like sharing his burdens with others. There is some hint of masochistic/sadistic tendencies, which may become involved in close relations with partners.

Eighth house: the native is naturally reluctant to accept the pressure of the times or the effect of sweeping changes in his life. Yet inevitably he is swept into and out of situations, and sometimes he is required to start again almost from scratch. The native has strong sexual powers (although somewhat hidden and secretive) coupled with some sort of guilt complex which encourages him to submit to situations generally intolerable for others. The sadistic/masochistic problems are even stronger here than with Saturn in the fifth or seventh houses.

Ninth house: this is a favorable pattern in that the native's disciplines are keyed to established beliefs or principles. The native submits himself to doing work in connection with building up and filling in the needed support for the points in the system that have fallen by the way or been lost sight of in the shuffle. The native's concerns are mostly mental and intellectual, releasing his emotions from the more arduous limitations of the Capricorn/Saturn configuration.

Tenth house: this is a favorable position for Saturn and ensures that eventually the native will receive some degree of success and recognition for his long and heavy labors. The native is deeply ambitious, although he is painfully slow about putting these goals into effective operation. One would wonder at times if he would ever really make it. The native wants to be almost overly sure of himself before the public eye. Many obstacles stand in his way such as tough resistance and required proof from people in authority. He may have to wait until all those senior to him have passed on before he gets his best chances.

Eleventh house: the native sees early in life that he must hitch his wagon to a group that shares his convictions and ideals and will lend him a helping sympathetic hand. At first this is difficult because those in control do not exactly see the native as one of them. It takes many false starts and much hard work to convince others that he indeed belongs in the group. He does not make friends easily, although he values friendship highly. The fact is, he expects too much from friendships.

Twelfth house: the native is deeply troubled most of his life as to the real nature and influence of his inner motivations. He is deeply aware of these subconscious elements, but he doesn't know what to do about them. Generally they just depress him and frustrate his best efforts to move forward. The Capricorn/Saturn pattern being keyed to material goals is thrown off base when complicated by spiritual considerations. Usually his problems stem from some spiritual principle that he is well aware of but has somehow overlooked. After many harsh setbacks and crushing defeats (all of which have an inward effect) he manages to get his wagon back on the track and be off again. There is little outward indication of joy or values or appreciation or even proof of what supports his endless efforts. Only late in life does he come to understand himself and what it is that he might be seeking. He generally finds that material goals are not what he wants but that the trouble with spiritual goals is that they are so immaterial—especially at the bank when making a deposit.

Saturn is naturally so strong and compulsive by itself, that it hardly needs to be fortified by additional planetary forces. But Saturn nevertheless still needs to be prodded in a constructive manner or it ends up beating itself to death against impossible odds. The hard-angle aspects that force Saturn are always beneficial. The soft-angle encouragements lessen the harshness of Saturn and make a few tough jobs easier.

The Capricorn personality always has sensitive Cancer on the opposite seventh house. This makes him very vulnerable to the gentle people in life, those who seem to have only their feelings to protect them. Actually Cancer people have much more—they have, for instance, a switchboard which tunes in and out and ideally protects them from the messages they do not want to hear. But Capricorn doesn't always understand this. It is impossible for him to comprehend how anyone can ignore or play blind to a material fact. Cancers can be blind to this. Capricorns never. The interesting question is: Who is really blind? Capricorn, who over-responds to isolated material facts, or Cancer, who conveniently threads his way between that which he wants to see and that which doesn't concern him? Both are a little blind in different ways. Cancer and Capricorn types tend to block each other's effectiveness in such a way that leaves little hope for compromise. All opposite signs of course block each other by introducing a slightly opposite point of view. But with Capricorn and Cancer the opposition is perhaps stronger and less reconcilable than with most other pairs of signs. Some oppositions are mild with each other. The Cardinal oppositions are more apparent with Capricorn/Cancer having the edge over everyone. The Aries/Libra axis contrasts the individual viewpoint with that of many others. The Capricorn/Cancer viewpoint contrasts material pigheadedness with emotional sensitivity.

In most temperate latitudes the Capricorn personality has Taurus/Scorpio on the method/ambition axis, which is strong. Sometimes it has Aries/Libra, which is also good, or Gemini/Sagittarius, which is slightly less favorable.

THE AQUARIUS IMAGE ON THE ASCENDANT: Aquarius on the ascendant is generally less favorable than other signs. First, because most people don't understand or appreciate the nature of Aquarius. Second, there is generally less use or need for Aquarians in the everyday world. Aquarians are a special kind of people given to independent viewpoints on life that invariably do not fit in with accepted modes of thinking. The mass of humanity looks with disfavor on those who deviate from what everyone else is doing or thinking. This quality may indicate a degree of brilliance, if not to say genius, on the Aquarians' part, but it stirs up such a frightful resentment that it is difficult for the native both to do his thing and hold his own at the same time. Fortunately this doesn't seem to bother Aquarians, but it does put rocks in their path.

One must remember that we are talking about the ascendant and one's public image—this is the native as the world sees him on the surface. The personality is what shows. As might be imagined, there is less good in having something showing on the surface that causes misunderstandings from the start and turns other people against the native before he even has a chance to prove his value. The Aquarian conception is an indispensable part of the universal picture. But it never works as effectively when it shows to its worst advantage as when it cuts loose on an end play and makes an uninterrupted run for it before those who would suppress it are aware of what has happened. Aquarians, to do their best, have to catch others off guard, as befitting their ruler, Uranus. This is why Aquarius is somewhat unfortunate on the ascendant and not because of the nature of what Aquarius can contribute.

The Aquarian type has to be very strong inwardly and well fortified with other planetary patterns in order to rise effectively above the crowd. Most of the time this "extended vision" they have leads nowhere. But occasionally a flash of brilliant insight lights up the sky and a whole new world opens up. Unfortunately this is the exception rather than the rule. Aquarius represents a quality which is really reserved as a condition for those who have arrived at a station or time in the cycle of life which is one step removed from the label that life puts on most of our efforts. It is a privilege and (if you will) an honor that one receives for past credits.

Aquarius is keyed to the erratic Uranus, which is a planetary force of social involvement rather than individual development, as the other planets are (except Pluto, which is also a social force). Uranus as a force gathers steam and then blows up. This breaks patterns and disrupts groupings, so everything must rearrange itself in a new way, supposedly as an improvement. At least Aquarians like to think so. After the blowup Uranus settles down to generate more steam until it blows up again. Such natural behavior to Aquarians is looked upon with dismay and shock and resentment by others. This isn't easy even for Aquarians because they regard themselves as a friendly force, liking group associations and seeking sympathetic friendships. The blowup which they cause is often as much of a surprise to them as it is to others. It is suggested elsewhere in this book as to the possible real intent of the Aquarius/Uranus contribution. In connection with the effect on the personality it is enough to point out the erratic, unpredictable and apparently uncontrollable potential that is always present.

If Uranus, the unpredictable, is in the:

First house: the native is obviously an eccentric of some kind. The extremes of his attitudes and the independence of his position invariably stand out and mark him at once as different. This native has more control over the "genius" quality that makes him distinctively what he is.

Second house: the native's finances are chaotic but run in lucky streaks for him.

Third house: the native's thoughts and ideas are obviously unique and perhaps in time can be reduced to some sense or order. The native indulges in wild flights of imaginative thinking. This would be good for science-fiction writing.

Fourth house: the native has some quality that marks him as distinctively different from others, although this may not be immediately apparent. This is far less obvious than when Uranus is in the first house but is perhaps even more explosive and far-reaching in the fourth. The native conceives ingenious methods and techniques with which to tackle his objectives. The native learns early in life to adjust to erratic behavior, since his parents and home life are so different to begin with. Eccentricity comes naturally to him.

Fifth house: the native's independence is carried into relationships with others through romance, love-making, relations with children, and a rare kind of luck that is undependable but occasionally impressive in gamble or speculation.

Sixth house: the native has strange health conditions, habits and daily routines, which suit him perfectly but are hard for others to follow or diagnose. There is something unique about his vocation or how he goes about it or the eccentricity may be evident among his fellow workers.

Seventh house: the native is oddly affected by others with whom he suddenly comes into contact. Others act as a catalyst for the native in bringing him into unusual contact with certain factors that he understands and can make use of. His relations with others are erratic and as suddenly terminated as they begin.

Eighth house: the native is suddenly swept into situations that initiate fundamental changes in his views (which aren't too stable or consistent anyway). On the whole these new circumstances are unique and surprise even the native, who is usually prepared for almost anything in life. The native has strange secret habits that are for him a source of inspiration and revitalization.

Ninth house: the native is attracted to strange cults and long-forgotten beliefs. His beliefs, which are anything but standard, may seem crazy to some people. The native is well advised to remove himself far from his native background in order to be among friends who will appreciate him.

Tenth house: the native is assured of a unique place in life which is in some sense tailor-made for his personality. He seems obviously destined for the final outcome, which comes suddenly. The native comes under the influence of unusual people who exercise great authority over his affairs. He becomes their follower until he eventually invents something on his own.

Eleventh house: the native's interests are socialized and he expands best when in the congenial company of others who share his unusual views. He does not wish to be alone, nor does he care to personalize his ambitions. He would rather find "his group" and string along with them.

Twelfth house: the native is far more isolated here than other Aquarian types. Basically he is thrown back exclusively on his inner resources, which are the only things that will sustain him when he needs support. This he has learned time and time again. His inner life is subject to rude shocks and devastating flashes of insight, which all further convince him that he has within himself all that he needs to face the strange life he has.

As already stated, it is very important which planetary qualities Uranus is tied to by aspect, since on its own it is only a solitary, erratic force working in the dark. To be effective in the personal life, it must have hard-angle aspects to other key planets (particularly the Sun, Mars or Saturn, which are the planets that get things done). Hard angles concentrate the inventive qualities of Uranus, while soft angles disperse them.

The Aquarius personality always has Leo on its opposite seventh-house position. Since Leo is keyed to the ego-drive of the Sun, the Aquarius type always notices other outstanding personalities and is guided by these uniquely individualized people who travel with him on life's highway. He tends to ignore the mediocre and the ordinary, since he is a special person who feels bound to a unique destiny. The Leo types, being strong personalities, readily accept the eccentricity and independence of Aquarians, and they generally make a good team rather than waste time blocking each other.

The Aquarian personality sometimes has Taurus/Scorpio on the fourth/tenth axis, which is favorable because it is down-to-earth, but mostly in temperate latitudes it has Gemini/Sagittarius, which is less favorable because it contributes to the "head in the clouds," which Aquarius has too much of already.

THE PISCES PERSONALITY IMAGE ON THE ASCENDANT: The Pisces type, like the Aquarian, is not an everyday kind of person. In his case the native is in touch, or gives the appearance of being in touch, with a realm of consciousness that is not given to everybody else. This is the realm of the subconscious and constitutes the inner values we have and the ultimate value structures we may need in life. Eveyone has inner values, but not everyone is as closely in touch with them as the Pisces type. In Pisces there is a deeper conviction and a reference to the role that our inner motivations play every day. This awareness also sets them apart from other people but not nearly as obviously as it does for Aquarians. Aquarians are noted for their eccentricity, while Pisces are noted for their inner peace. As mentioned before, Pisces are not the preachers of the world like the Sagittarians. They go about their business and accept what must be with philosophic calm and emotional resignation. In many ways this gives them an edge on their fellow men, for they do not waste time or effort chasing rainbows or fighting windmills. The reality they feel is just as real to them as the reality of the material world which the rest of us deal with every day. The focus in their case is on a spiritual level, and this answers all their questions. The true Pisces type should be naturally calm, collected, peaceful and poised. They are not easily upset or hardly ever thrown out of perspective even when blocked, frustrated or challenged. They are inwardly accustomed to these interrogations, and they handle them with finesse and inspiration. Pisces natives naturally concern themselves with situations that the rush of life tends to leave behind as "no longer in the race." To Pisces nothing is ever wholly lost or totally without redemption. It is more of a challenge and infinitely more gratifying for them to restore the unfortunate to health than to chase after the material advantages. Although some Pisces types do work with material resources, their path is generally spiritual.

Pisces personalities are guided on their way by the inspirational light of Neptune. To those who are not exactly keyed to Neptune (because everyone isn't), this planet tends to fool and deceive rather than inspire and purify. But to Pisces in particular it is their inspirational guide. If Neptune is in the:
First house: the native has unusual psychic resources on which to

draw whenever needed. There could be a saintly or mystical quality about the native which others are drawn to as they would be to a religious person whose very presence benefits a kind of healing. The native can mesmerize others in such a way that they will not harm him if that was their intention. This is a position of divine protection.

Second house: the native is able to tap unusual resources for his source of supply whenever he has need of such to help him in his dedication. Generally the native should be reluctant to use this power for personal gain. It is a gift for social purposes.

Third house: the native has rare gifts for soothing and inspirational speech that fascinates his audience. The general effect is unreal but significant. Others are inspired by his communication.

Fourth house: the native is well qualified for the role that life provides for him. Pisces people are generally led to their work rather than forced to seek it on their own. The native looks within his subjective self for the practical applications that will enable him to find his goals. His early upbringing encourages this, and a spirit takes over in later years as a guiding light. There is some unusual condition in and around the home which the native accepts as quite natural but which others might find odd or strange.

Fifth house: the native is talented in fields of entertainment, creating romantic fiction, dealing with children and in some cases is lucky in games of chance or speculation. Usually, however, the native does not wish to gamble in the ordinary manner, but he will in some degree commit himself to some sort of risk in spiritual ways.

Sixth house: the native is closely drawn to the conditions of labor connected with our daily routine. Health and the care of the body are of special concern. The native prefers a more humble station in life so he can be closer to those who interest him.

Seventh house: the native takes his cue from others who drift in and out of his life mainly for the expressed purpose of delivering an inspirational message. The native sees life as a pageant performed in a mist, where no one is clearly defined and no standards are absolute. He feels that all we need to know will be revealed to us at the right time and what we do not need to know is blessedly lost in the mist. The native has no fear of others or what will be revealed to him by others. Everything fits nicely in place, and in the end the picture is made whole and complete.

Eighth house: the native is drawn to unusual states of consciousness where the spirit is felt on occasion to leave the body and contact other levels of consciousness. This is hard for others who are not keyed to the realities that Pisces knows to understand or accept. The native has hidden talents that even he is not aware of, except in times of emergency when he is able to perform functions or rise to states of consciousness which he never anticipated. The native has an other-worldly attitude, which is perhaps more irregular and unusual than other Neptune positions. The power of sexuality is a potent force for the native.

Ninth house: the native is drawn to codified thinking that has been formulated by others who share his views. The reaction is more mental and the native sees life as more of an intellectual challenge than a physical struggle. The native can acutely sense history as though he were living it.

Tenth house: the native is ambitious but not for himself alone. He hopes for power and influence so that he might reveal to others the framework which he so devoutly accepts for himself. Somehow he feels the necessity for some position of power and influence in order to reach effectively those he wants most. In the beginning he is drawn to some spiritual leader who opens doors for him within himself. Eventually he aspires to do this on his own for others.

Eleventh house: the native seeks others with whom to share his hopes, and together they will spread the truth as they see it. The native has transferred his inner awareness to a collective unconscious that he feels resembles and amplifies his own image.

Twelfth house: the native is more withdrawn and secretive about himself and what he wishes to do in life. His personality shuns the light, and he prefers to work in the background. Recognition is of less importance for what he does. In many ways he is trying to prove to himself something that he feels from time to time needs nourishment. This placement is apt to produce a solitary, lonely figure who feels little need for communication with others or the usual interests of daily life. The salvation motivation is more personal and less social or collective. The native feels that first he must resolve some inner problems from his past.

Neptune is a spiritual force that in most people is decentralized or over and above the demands of everyday living. Very few of us are personally keyed to this other-worldly quality. When considering Neptune, it is most important to see if it is strongly aspected to other key planets (like the Sun, Mars or Saturn, which do things). Hard-angle aspects are always more effective and significant than soft angles.

The Pisces personality image always has the critical Virgo outlook on its opposite seventh house. Both of these natives are used to selective standards of behavior. The Virgo native (to whom Pisces pays close attention) consciously selects and organizes the minute details of situations by which he distinguishes basic differences between otherwise unclassified material. Pisces in turn consciously dwells on the inner spiritual aspects, (which he can sense just as clearly as Virgo is able to pick out significant distinguishing details) which he uses as a framework to fit material back again into the whole of life. Both natives live in a more refined and rarefied environment by their own choosing. Both are specialists who read into life more than meets casual observation, since most people overlook or purposely ignore details or spiritual aspects. Both tend to feel that everyone has a specialty because they both have.

The Pisces personality only has Gemini/Sagittarius on the fourth/tenth house axis. This gives him a mental approach to problems, together with a boundless faith in the correctness of the outcome.

SPECIAL NOTE

A word of comment is in order to avoid possible confusion on the reader's part in case he feels as though he were going around and around and needs some landing space to get his bearings.

The techniques of analysis, whatever tools are used—scientific, medical, psychological, occult—should be used to divide the whole into significant parts, analyze each part and understand its function, and then reassemble the parts into the whole. Psychiatrists and particularly psychoanalysts have often been accused, and justifiably so, of taking their patients apart and leaving them in that condition. When challenged as to the value of this, they have been known to shrug their shoulders and reply, "What did you expect?"

Astrology starts with a whole and ends with a whole. It merely breaks down the parts for closer observation. This is what we have been doing here, but the reader may be confused as to where this is leading him. At this point let us review the following:

We as individuals are more obviously the type of the sign that falls on our PERSONALITY than we are of the type that falls on our EGO (or Sun, as so familiarly known as Sun-sign astrology).

It would be far more significant and useful if the public could read in the daily papers about their personality sign than to read about their Sun sign. The personality factor is far more indicative of what WE RECEIVE IN LIFE and the way we are generally TREATED BY OTHERS.

The reason why so-called popular astrology (such as newspaper columns) cannot do this is nobody knows what his personality sign is unless his horoscope is calculated. But as a matter of fact, the people writing the columns arrive at their comments for the astrological types as though the Sun signs were on the ascendant position—namely the personality. The readers, if they know their ascendant, might get a little more out of the columns if they followed the sign on their ascendant instead of their Sun sign.

It also might be well to remind the reader that astrology reveals the meaning of life and not necessarily the literal facts of the situation. Therefore, particularly in thinking about the personality image, it is in no way intended that all Aries personality types or all Virgo types look alike physically. There is a feeling however that comes through the personality which captures the spirit of the Aries type or the Virgo type and this is what is important.

The Sun is out in space. We are down here on earth. To know where the Sun is (say, on the day you were born), a measurement is taken from a point in space to a point on earth. Since all factors are in motion, this must be taken as of a given moment in time. The astronomers, who were originally astrologers, have mapped all this information out in advance, and any planet's position can be known at any point in time—in the past or in the future.

To identify the IMAGE OF YOUR PERSONALITY, which is only one part of the total you in your horoscope, you must make the reverse calculation. The measurement is taken from a point on the earth (say, your place of birth) to a point in space—the point of the eastern horizon at the moment of your birth. Setting up this map and writing out these measurements is the method of casting a horoscope.

What the horoscope shows is the following:

THE IMAGE OF YOUR PERSONALITY. Your personality is a quality that you obviously have. In fact you are stuck with it whether you like it or not. This is the part about you that is on the surface, and the public sees and reacts to it as you go about your business. You use your personality consciously and automatically every moment in every way. See Chapter 6.

THE QUALITY OF YOUR EGO. This is shown by the sign and condition of the Sun. This is something that is trying to emerge and direct the course or purpose of your life. This identifies the quality or characteristics of your WILL as it follows the urges of the EGO. This is buried WITHIN the personality. It is not immediately apparent to those who merely deal with us on the surface (as in dealing with our personality image). This is something that enters the picture AFTER people know us better and discern a pattern of behavior which follows the form or pattern-type of the ego.

THE CHARACTER OF YOUR DESTINY. This is a refinement of the picture which shows the PATH the ego must take to fulfill itself. This is identified in the horoscope by the house placement of the Sun in relation to the whole of life (which is the complete circle of the horoscope). See Chapter 4.

THE FOCUS OF YOUR EMOTIONS. The emotions are symbolized by the Moon, which is the polar or magnetic opposite of the ego-drive symbolized by the Sun. The FOCUS of your emotions is shown by the relationship of the Moon (its house position) to the rest of life. See Chapter 5.

Other things shown and described in your horoscope are:

HOW THE NATIVE SEES HIMSELF (in the fourth house). Chapter 12

HOW THE NATIVE SEES THE WORLD AROUND HIM (in the seventh house). Chapter 15

HOW THE WORLD COMES TO JUDGE THE NATIVE (in the tenth house). Chapter 18

YOUR RESOURCES, EARNINGS AND MONEY (in the second house). Chapter 10

YOUR THINKING AND DIRECT COMMUNICATION (in the third house). Chapter 11

YOUR BACKGROUND, HERITAGE AND SENSE OF EMOTIONAL SECURITY (also in the fourth house). Chapter 12

YOUR CREATIVITY, AMUSEMENT, PLEASURES AND LOVE-MAKING (in the fifth house). Chapter 13

YOUR DUTIES, OBLIGATIONS AND RESPONSIBILITIES, INCLUDING THE RESPONSIBILITY TO YOUR BODY (in the sixth house). Chapter 14

YOUR PARTNERS, COMPETITION AND EFFECT OF OTHERS ON YOUR LIFE (in the seventh house). Chapter 15

HOW YOU FACE CHANGE AND VIEW THE SPIRITUAL CON-SEQUENCES OF YOUR ACTIONS (in the eighth house). Chapter 16

YOUR PRINCIPLES AND YOUR CODES OF BELIEF AS EX-PRESSED IN LAWS YOU LIVE BY, YOUR RELIGION AND PHI-LOSOPHY (in the ninth house). Chapter 17

YOUR AMBITION AND MATERIAL GOALS (in the tenth house). Chapter 18

YOUR DREAMS AND HOPES AS SHARED IN FRIENDSHIP (in the eleventh house). Chapter 19

YOUR INNER VALUES, SUBCONSCIOUS MOTIVATION AND FINAL REACTION TO YOUR LIFE (in the twelfth house). Chapter 20

YOUR WAY OF THINKING (the condition of your Mercury). Chapter 8

YOUR INSTINCT FOR SELF-PRESERVATION (the condition of your Saturn). Chapter 7

YOUR ENERGIZER FOR ACTION (the condition of your Mars). Chapter 8

YOUR CAPACITY FOR LOVE AND AFFECTION (the condition of your Venus). Chapter 8

YOUR SENSITIVITY TO INSPIRATION (the condition of your Neptune). Chapter 8

YOUR FAITH IN JUSTICE (the condition of your Jupiter). Chapter 8

YOUR SPIRIT OF INDEPENDENCE (the condition of your Uranus). Chapter 8

YOUR POWER TO REVITALIZE AND REACT TO CHANGED CONDITIONS (the condition of your Pluto). Chapter 8

In making an exhaustive study of any of these special departments or tools in the native's life, the reader is again cautioned that there is a primary structure of reference in which ALL these subjects have THEIR OWN PLACE. Any isolation of a subject for the purpose of analysis must always be treated with reference to the overall pattern out of which you have extracted the subject.

Astrology considers life in a spiritual context. The purpose of the individual life pattern (which takes precedence over all other consid-erations) is contained in THE CHARACTER OF THE DESTINY. This is the PRIMARY STRUCTURE OF REFERENCE.

It seems advisable to remind the readers of this because from here on in we will pursue the refinements of analysis on individual subjects.

PERSONALITY IN OLD AGE

As stated before, in the practice of everyday living the packaging is often more important than the contents because that is what the public primarily reacts to. Most people have little time or interest to look further. You attract what the sign of your front door says, whether you like it or not and regardless of what lies beyond. The assignments one receives in life are handed out according to the way others see you. This is why Taurus personalities tend to get Taurus-type jobs (money management and record keeping) and Libra personalities tend to get Libra-type jobs (socializing and beautifying their environment).

The problems of old age between personality types vary considerably according to the sign on the ascendant. *In mature years it seems more important to satisfy the needs of the personality image* (sign on the AC) than to satisfy the ego-drive (sign of the Sun). This is probably because our ego weakens with age but our bodily requirements go on until death.

On the whole the signs of OBJECTIVE ORIENTATION (Scorpio through Pisces) fare much better in coping with the problems of old age than the signs of SUBJECTIVE ORIENTATION (Aries through Libra). The subjectively oriented signs need some sort of substantiation of their personal identity in order to be fulfilled and this is undoubtedly more difficult to obtain in very mature years when one's scope is obviously limited in all directions.

For example, when considering the sign on the ascendant:

ARIES NEEDS ACTION. It is most essential for the Aries personality to keep as physically active as possible. They must keep their five senses alive and working or they will lose their sense of purpose. It would be extremely difficult for them to suffer a physical impairment which would diminish their native energies. When they have lost their sense of push, they are ready to give up.

TAURUS NEEDS HAPPINESS. The comforts of life go a long way in making Taurus feel happy. They can in fact make up for a great many other shortcomings in their past. Money usually has a great deal to do with comforts, so this is important too. Since the Taurus type continually accumulates all the Venus products, what is needed is usually for Taurus to count his blessings, which may be considerably more than he realizes.

GEMINI NEEDS TO COMMUNICATE. Ordinarily communication involves sending and receiving. But in Geminis' case (particularly in old age) they really don't need much understanding from an audience. They just need someone to talk to. The kindest thing for Geminis is to place them around others where they can jabber away, whether or not others pay much attention. This mental exercise is as necessary to Geminis as food and water.

CANCER NEEDS TO BE WANTED. This may be impossible to satisfy in later life because Cancers attach themselves to certain people with lifelong devotion, and when these affectionate objects are gone, Cancers are inclined to give up and fade away. If at all possible the older Cancer personality types should be kept at home around those they love and cherish, even though they are no longer an active part of the family circle. Nursing homes are strange and frightening to Cancer.

LEO NEEDS RESPECT. Since there usually has to be a reason to merit respect, Leos must often resort to fabrication to gain the respect their ego demands. This is sometimes easier to gain from strangers than from friends of long standing if Leo is not exactly all he claims to be. Leo easily warms up to strangers, especially when the home ties are not all that he might wish, and they usually aren't for Leo.

VIRGO NEEDS TO SERVE. Although it is nice to be appreciated for what one does for others, Virgo is so certain that his contribution is the right thing that often it is enough just to be given a task that is useful and constructive. The more detailed it is, the better. Virgo is another type that should be kept around the family circle rather than being shunted off to a rest home, where there is little possibility of being trusted with odd jobs.

LIBRA NEEDS BEAUTY. The breath of life to Libra is to be surrounded with beautiful things (including himself). They simply cannot endure surroundings that are dull, drab and depressing. They would rather die. Sometimes when there is nothing else for Libras to work on, they can be kept quite happy just trying to beautify and ornament themselves. Since beauty costs money, Libra is usually more expensive to maintain than other signs. They can be equally satisfied in their old home or a new one as long as they feel attractive.

The objectively oriented signs are, from the beginning, more self-contained, which allows them to project themselves outward toward the world. What they need from the outside world as they grow older hasn't changed as much as they have. They have grown weary, but the world lives on and they can accept this ongoingness of life without personal frustration. They need less from the outside for themselves.

SCORPIO CONTINUES TO SATISFY HIS CURIOSITY. The Scorpio personality is naturally secretive and mysterious, so they can be left alone and still find plenty to absorb their thoughts and interests. The Scorpio type (like the Pisces) adapts to old age better than any other sign. They make excellent listeners (always in short supply). Since they have faced death many times in their imaginations, it holds no fear for them.

SAGITTARIUS CONTINUES TO SENSE PROGRESS. The Sagittarian type usually finds it easy to adjust to old age. Their natural enthusiasm and optimistic attitudes close their eyes to material deficiencies, and they respond positively to any ray of sunshine. They simply ignore what does not fit in with their scheme of things.

CAPRICORN CONTINUES TO EXTEND HIS POSITION. Capricorns adjust to old age very nicely, since in spirit they were born old. Even if they have not managed to achieve as much as they hoped for, they like to keep right on trying to the end. They usually keep active, so it is best to let them decide matters for themselves—they will anyway.

AQUARIUS CONTINUES TO PURSUE HIS FREEDOM OF VISION. Aquarians in old age can cause considerable distress to their families because they tend to fall apart mentally or emotionally but not physically. In fact, their bodies, when released from the tensions previously imposed by their minds and emotions, seem to grow stronger than ever. They are very apt to become eccentric, which is really an exaggerated state of their real self (which comformity kept hidden). Old age seems to release this. Sometimes they have to be locked up and looked after, but they are happier than we assume.

PISCES CONTINUES TO SEEK INWARD ANSWERS. Pisces, like Scorpio, is more prepared for death than other signs. They dwell so naturally in the subconscious that they do not feel at all unnatural to be left alone or isolated. In fact they may prefer it that way. They are independent and self-sufficient when it comes to leaning on others. They want to follow the dictates of their "inner voice" without interruption.

In trying to help others through their problems in old age, the key that unlocks or releases the satisfaction of the personality for each one is to be found where the ruler of the sign on the ascendant is found.

IF THE RULER OF THE ASCENDANT IS FOUND IN THE FIRST HOUSE, the native holds the key to what turns his personality on and off. This is an ingredient that he manufactures for himself. It is largely up to him. During active life this greatly contributes to the dynamics and individuality of the native's personality, but it makes it somewhat more difficult for others to deal with him in old age if he does not want to help himself. The native will always have the potential to do for himself if life demands it.

IF THE RULER OF THE ASCENDANT IS FOUND IN THE SECOND HOUSE, money and being able to pay for what the native feels he requires has a great deal to do with the conditions under which the native's personality will flourish. It is better if this comes from the native's own resources rather than from others, for the second house represents that which is earned.

IF THE RULER OF THE ASCENDANT IS FOUND IN THE THIRD HOUSE, the native needs mental communication with others to bring out the best in his personality. He will respond to ideas only after outside stimulation.

IF THE RULER OF THE ASCENDANT IS FOUND IN THE FOURTH HOUSE, the native generally has to fall back on his inner resources—to re-create some aspect of his background or family connections. He must especially feel emotionally secure. Without this feeling (of which the native has to be convinced) there is little that others can do. But his resources for falling back on himself are strong. He has been doing it all his life.

IF THE RULER OF THE ASCENDANT IS FOUND IN THE FIFTH HOUSE, the native enjoys simple pleasures—even childlike games are helpful. Sometimes if the native has developed a skill or craft, any opportunity to be creative is good. The native should be allowed to be around children, where he can watch them at their games. It brings back his own youth and the vitality of competition.

IF THE RULER OF THE ASCENDANT IS FOUND IN THE SIXTH HOUSE, the native should be given tasks and duties to perform. Anything that will keep him busy and occupied gives him a sense of contribution.

IF THE RULER OF THE ASCENDANT IS FOUND IN THE SEVENTH HOUSE, the native needs companionship of some kind. He is used to being directed and dominated by others and may be unable to make decisions for himself. Even a stern hand is helpful. The native is accustomed to being told what to do.

IF THE RULER OF THE ASCENDANT IS FOUND IN THE EIGHTH HOUSE, the native is much more difficult to arouse or help. He wants to be left alone, which in this case is usually best. His consciousness finds its necessary level, and he can be content, even though by our standards it may not seem satisfactory. The important thing is to allow him to go his own way without imposing what we might prefer for ourselves.

IF THE RULER OF THE ASCENDANT IS FOUND IN THE NINTH HOUSE, the native is invariably stimulated by strangers, new faces and a change of scenery. Books, news and information on his favorite subject are almost as good as friends and company. The native has a capacity for mentally projecting himself out of his immediate situation, which is a blessing. This is one of the more pleasantly self-sufficient types who respond constructively to their confinements. We can't all read a book and get our mind off our troubles, but this native can.

IF THE RULER OF THE ASCENDANT IS FOUND IN THE TENTH HOUSE, the native has a continuing interest in world affairs, news and views of the day and is helped by keeping in contact with those who are making their mark in the world (even if he only keeps in touch by radio or television). This native was always ambitious in a worldly way, so anything that recalls this struggle or present-day achievements is welcome.

IF THE RULER OF THE ASCENDANT IS FOUND IN THE ELEVENTH HOUSE, the native needs companionship and a feeling of friendly sympathy, even though it may be from a comparative stranger. He has to be coddled and reassured and made to feel that he is not alone and that in fact many share his sympathies and aspirations. This is one of the more difficult cases to help because it is often difficult to find those who will take the time to comfort him. Fortunately, this native warms up to strangers as long as he feels a sympathetic bond of compatible dreams. This native has spent a lifetime making and holding friendships, so there should be plenty to draw from.

IF THE RULER OF THE ASCENDANT IS FOUND IN THE TWELFTH HOUSE, the native is accustomed to solitude. In fact he may prefer it. This native is more resourceful than one might imagine, especially when it comes to inner fortitude and dealing with disappointments and frustrations. All his life he has been used to limitations and denials. Actually this native usually meets old age with much serenity because all his life he has known the final answers and death holds no mystery or fear for him. He thinks of death as another beginning.

Chapter 7

SATURN IN YOUR HOROSCOPE

SATURN'S HOUSE POSITION BLENDED WITH CAPRICORN ON THE HOUSE CUSPS

Saturn, the taskmaster, is the principle of self-preservation and basic security. The location and condition of Saturn is an extremely sensitive and important consideration. In many cases Saturn can be the single most determining factor in the entire horoscope. Self-preservation often takes precedence over ego fulfillment (the Sun), emotional gratifications (the Moon), pursuit of ambitions (the tenth house), development of the personality (the first house), or indulgence in pleasures, love or sex (the fifth house). If the native does not solve this requirement of basic security, none of the other matters can have any permanent satisfaction.

Where Saturn is by house indicates the area of experience where the native's basic security is most vulnerable. The requirements of this house must be given top priority before the native can turn his attention to higher matters. Sometimes only a quasi compromise is achieved, which, if shaky enough, can undermine the native's best efforts all his life.

IF SATURN IS IN THE FIRST HOUSE, the native suffers from a certain inferiority complex, which must be overcome. The sense of personal identity and self-worth is slow to develop, but in this position a solid and reliable personality is eventually bound to emerge. This is one of the more favorable positions for Saturn because the native is able to control the necessary disciplines of life. He learns to do this from the very beginning. Overcoming restrictions and limitations becomes second nature to these natives. Because they naturally move slowly and appraise situations more carefully before they jump, these natives tend to know what they need and are able to concentrate more effectively on its attainment. The personality is marked by a slow, deliberate obstinacy, which keeps plugging away at generally constructive objectives. The affairs of the house under the sign of Capricorn can greatly contribute to the upward progress of Saturn on the personality.

If the sign of Capricorn is on the:

First house: the native has abundant determination.

Second house: the native is fairly assured of adequate resources.

Third house: the native has sound thinking.

Fourth house: the native's background and family lend assistance in his struggle. A secure home life (which comes late in life) is mandatory.

Fifth house: the native has creative talents that can be capitalized on.

Sixth house: the native's vocation is productive.

Seventh house: others always stand ready to assist the native in his struggles.

Eighth house: the native gains through the labors of others.

Ninth house: the native enjoys favorable connections with promotional organizations.

Tenth house: the native is assured of adequate recognition and an esteemed position.

Eleventh house: the native is befriended and protected by sympathetic friends.

Twelfth house: the native receives secret support from behind the scenes.

IF SATURN IS IN THE SECOND HOUSE, the native continually suffers from an inadequate source of supply or financial resources for his best ideas. The native's financial position improves in later life but only after many frustrating setbacks and delays. The native invariably feels that lack of funds is the chief obstacle in life holding him back. Saturn in this position always limits the monetary return for his labors. In terms of earning capacity from his own efforts he will always have to put out more than he is paid for. But he should always have an earning capacity, even into old age. In fact it should get better in old age. This position generally indicates a frugal and hoarding attitude toward possessions but may not always appear so with money itself. Even if money is quickly spent, the native invariably holds onto the purchases. The affairs of the house under

Capricorn should be of primary interest to the native as a natural and eventually assured source of earning power.

If the sign of Capricorn is on the:

First house: the native is able to capitalize on his personality image in some way.

Second house: the native must select one vocation and stick with it to the bitter end. Avoid changing vocations at all costs.

Third house: the native should have business in the marketplace with clients and customers. But the profit margin per unit is small.

Fourth house: the native has something in his background or heritage that can be made to pay off. Favored are real estate, fixed assets, mineral deposits, and products that can be produced at home.

Fifth house: the native gains from the fields of entertainment, children's primary education, sound speculations and serious creative lines of work.

Sixth house: the native gains from work connected with labor conditions or services catering to housekeeping or health matters. Under housekeeping matters we would find hotels, innkeeping, food and beverage services, and anything that catered to providing a home away from home for others.

Seventh house: the native gains from some sort of service that stems from interpersonal relationships—their regulation or promotion. This would involve people in a state of cooperation or in competition or contesting each other in dispute.

Eighth house: the native profits from situations or objects that others have passed over as currently "dead." In bringing them back to life the native creates new value.

Ninth house: the native profits from publishing and the promotion of creeds, laws, programs or principles collaborated by many minds. The native would also be well advised to look far distant from his established base or natural background as a market for his labors (that is, some place originally foreign to him). Dealing with foreigners or foreign products is also favored. The native profits from some form of application of the law. The law could be just application of the truth or reality as a principle.

Tenth house: the native profits from some activity that concerns people in high places. This could involve acting as an agent to secure recognition for others. Promotion of career possibilities such as employment or executive placement is indicated.

Eleventh house: the native profits from organizational work connected with mass movements of public sympathies or social causes. The native must identify his sympathies with those of others of like mind and labor to supply some kind of function that serves this cause.

Twelfth house: the native profits from institutional work, caring for inmates, patients, clients, etc. Research or a service that supports behind-the-scenes activity or probes subconscious motivations is indicated.

IF SATURN IS IN THE THIRD HOUSE, the native must spend concentrated effort in developing a technique of communication with a client or customer. The thought patterns are profoundly serious and well organized. The native invariably gains recognition for the power and influence of his writings. The affairs of the house under Capricorn would provide the subject matter most favored for the native's realistic approach in this direction.

If Capricorn is on the:

First house: the native must concentrate on selling himself. He has some talent that others see or give him credit for which should be developed and spread around as an example.

Second house: the native should concentrate on ideas for making money or counseling others on how they could improve their resources of supply.

Third house: the native must more or less start from scratch in developing his own style of expression, which may take some time. It will also take a long time to build up a following or clientele for one's views and opinions.

Fourth house: the native has something solid to contribute to the development in others of method or technique or general approach to their objectives. This naturally grows out of extensive introspection by the native into his own problems in this area.

Fifth house: the market value of the native's thoughts derives from some connection with entertainment, pleasurable pursuits, primary education or affairs of children. Romantic situations and sex connected with romance are a thought.

Sixth house: the market value of the native's thoughts derives from problems or conditions of labor, vocation, health and housekeeping interests.

Seventh house: the market value of the native's thoughts derives from an understanding of the interpersonal relationships of others (either in harmony or discord).

Eighth house: the market value of the native's thoughts derives from pursuing subjects or conditions not generally understood by most people under everyday circumstances. The ideas are based on extraordinary situations that may arise only occasionally in a lifetime. Sex as a source of revitalization is of interest.

Ninth house: the market value of the native's thoughts derives from publication or promotion of established principles which may need a substantial overhaul or more realistic and truthful treatment.

Tenth house: the market value of the native's thoughts derives from ways of gaining and holding public recognition or career esteem.

Eleventh house: the market value of the native's thoughts derives from organizing the common interests or collective sympathies of wide groups.

Twelfth house: the market value of the native's thoughts derives from presentation of subconscious motivations or probing into sociological factors among the distressed members of society. With Saturn in the third house these facts are brought out into the open and freely discussed.

IF SATURN IS IN THE FOURTH HOUSE, the native must develop a feeling of close kinship with his historical background and heritage. There is a strong parent fixation anyway, which encourages a natural attitude of looking subjectively backward rather than objectively forward. This native would be considerably held back in early life (initially by the family) and would be very late in showing positive development on his own. Once the native is satisfied of the soundness and impregnability of his position or foundation, then he is likely to make a strong mark on those around him because of a persistent stand on some matter of subjective importance.

The scope of his influence, while ultimately sound, is apt to be fairly restricted. The native's primary reference is subjective, and he is unusually late in finding the necessity to accomplish something on his own. The affairs of the house under Capricorn have much to contribute to the native's stability and purpose.

If the sign of Capricorn is on the:

First house: the native must discover the underlying connection between himself and his heritage, which makes it important that he carry on or contribute some sort of basic technique or method analysis. The native has something to give or add in addition to what he obtains from his family connections.

Second house: the native must resolve his subjective approach through a penetrating analysis of methods for obtaining money, increasing one's natural sources of supply or husbanding one's required nourishment.

Third house: the native must resolve his subjective approach through a careful examination of methods of expression or styles of communication and their effect on others. Serious writing is favored, with factual emphasis on news and views and handling customers and clients.

Fourth house: the native must resolve his subjective approach through a consistent effort at rearranging his techniques in such a way that they bring out the very best he has to offer. This will involve much soul-searching and digging within the subjective self. This would be a favored position for medical analytical work like psychiatry or psychoanalysis.

Fifth house: the native must resolve his subjective approach through an objective effort in creativity. The whole area of creativity, as extension of the ego, is of interest to the native. A subjective analysis of gambling and forms of speculation or love-making also is of interest.

Sixth house: the native must resolve his subjective approach through a thorough analysis of vocational problems, health matters and people's concept of duty and service.

Seventh house: the native must resolve his subjective approach through a study of all interpersonal relationships (harmony or discord).

Eighth house: the native must resolve his subjective approach through a study of people's reactions to extraordinary situations under stress or crisis. The eighth house is the area of significant change of direction in people's lives. The approach is how other people face this and preserve their sense of basic security.

Ninth house: the native must resolve his subjective approach through a study of the history of development and trends of thoughts which subsequently become codified into whole systems, as in religion, philosophies, law and all subjects of higher education.

Tenth house: the native must resolve his subjective approach through a detailed study of the relationship between methods and success, effort and recognition, ambition and attainments. This is a very high-powered leverage position of the Saturn/Capricorn axis. The native is well endowed in some way for his task, and from the start he enjoys some degree of recognition for having already attained a position of some merit and esteem. Yet something subjective holds him back, and it resolves upon himself to bring the picture into complete focus.

Eleventh house: the native must resolve his subjective approach through an identification with group aims, group ideals and the factors that tie men together, as opposed to the qualities that distinguish them from each other as individuals.

Twelfth house: the native must resolve his subjective approach through the focus of two very complex areas of subjectivity—the subjectivity of the self and the subjectivity of the collective sub-conscious. Most people would not understand what this means or involves, but the native with this pattern in his horoscope will know what it suggests.

IF SATURN IS IN THE FIFTH HOUSE, the native feels a limitation and a depression about all the affairs concerned with creativity, romantic love-making, children and their education. Yet dealing with any or all of these subjects holds the key to the native's sense of security. The problem is that the fifth-house area is normally one of the outgoing, objective extensions of the ego, which usually performs best when not held in check by the more basic and down-to-earth reality that Saturn demands. The result has to be a tempering of the product in the restrictive Saturn sense. It is somewhat difficult to consider the self-preservation principle and the supposedly joyous expressions of the ego in the same context. In this case they must be considered together. One's children may become a source of security, but at the same time they are bound to involve disappointments and obligations. The same thing might be said for all creative efforts the native might initiate. Sexual love-making (connected with romance) is generally considered a pleasurable undertaking, but the Saturn presence in the fifth house considerably dampens the ardor. One is bound to be attracted to more mature types in this matter, and the more practical aspects of security will be more important than the ecstatic emotions of romance. Saturn in the fifth house should certainly discourage gambling, speculation and taking quick advantage of in-and-out situations. There is some favor for very long-term and thoroughly sound risks however. One is almost forced to seek the material of the house where Capricorn is located as a SUBSTITUTE for all the pleasurable things the fifth house normally provides but Saturn denies.

If the sign of Capricorn is on the:

First house: the native must usually seek delight in impressing his personality on others. This is almost a pattern of being in love with oneself or the image of oneself.

Second house: the native should perhaps fall in love with making money and exploring all possible sources of supply. One could also be in love with one's possessions.

Third house: the native tends to be in love with his thinking, expression and style of communication. There is also a fondness attached to one's clients and customers, brothers and sisters.

Fourth house: the pressures or lessons from the native's past or heritage are projected onto one's children. Probably too much is expected of one's offspring or other creative efforts.

Fifth house: this is perhaps a surprisingly more positive pattern than most of the others for a fifth-house Saturn. The native's creativity is closely associated with that which catches the public eye of approval. The big-business side of entertainment is suggested, as well as the business side of gambling and speculative investments.

Sixth house: the native somehow must approach the obligations, duties and service commitments of sixth-house matters with an eye for creativity and a flair for some kind of advertising or propaganda.

Seventh house: the native may act as an agent for speculating or gambling with other people. Others stand ready to cooperate in obtaining the native's security, which should eventually encourage his sense of creativity, but this may be a number of years in coming about.

Eighth house: the native is exposed to a special kind of luck factor with this pattern since the eighth-house involves other people's money, inheritances and money not earned by the native. The fifth house involves gamble and speculation and all games or investments of chance. The two must somehow be made to meld constructively (the Saturn/Capricorn axis demands this), and yet there are many loose, uncontrollable factors. One is hard put to sense a constructive solution.

Ninth house: the native's creativity, which must somehow be developed to a point of security, is keyed to factors at a distance and a possible audience that is far removed from the native's accustomed home base or background (that is, something foreign to him). Publishing is favored, as well as institutions of higher learning and formalized rhetoric.

Tenth house: this is a fairly strong pattern in which people in high position place some weighty responsibility on the native, compelling him to be entertaining, romantically convincing and daringly adventuresome (whether he feels like it or not). Success, position and the native's creativity are somehow interwoven with strong threads. The Saturn/Capricorn axis is always a strong bond involving obedience, duty and compelling necessity.

Eleventh house: the native is considerably freer in this position. Group values and group sympathies play a romantic role in the native's duty to create something.

Twelfth house: the native is drawn to subconscious motivations and sociological causes for the condition of under-par citizens for his creative material. Any projection of the native's ego in creative bent (which is ultimately mandatory) will be profoundly influenced by a suggestion of subconscious or ultimate value structures.

IF SATURN IS IN THE SIXTH HOUSE, at least this is an area more understandable for the depressing nature of Saturn. Work, duty, obligation, toil and responsibility all are conditions that Saturn suggests. On the whole the Saturn presence lends strength and determination to see the tough jobs through. Early limitations in any sixth-house matters will ultimately be improved in later years as Saturn proves his point: SUCCESS THROUGH STICKING IT OUT TO THE BITTER END. With Saturn's affairs one is almost assured of lasting long enough to see this end (bitter or otherwise). There are apt to be chronic conditions involving service, obligations and health, which are hard to shake. Wherever Saturn is found, there one must persevere, and here we find it in the line of duty. We can look for some easing of the load from the house where the ruler of the sixth is found. On the other hand, the affairs of the Capricorn house tend almost to add to the burdens of the sixth-house duties rather than lighten them.

If the sign of Capricorn is on the:

First house: the native is fully supported in his struggle with duty and obligation by the force of his personality and strong constitution.

Second house: the native is aided by a sound source of supply and earning power.

Third house: the native's capacity for thought and a talent for sensing the appropriate sentiment of the moment help ease the burden of his tasks.

Fourth house: the native's background and heritage and family tradition all blend nicely with the present task to be done. The native has the good fortune, in what he tries to do, to get started off on the right foot.

Fifth house: one's love life and creative efforts must step aside for one's sense of duty and obligation. The native must probably sacrifice even his children to sixth-house obligations. One's children also become an added obligation over and above the normal routine of their childhood.

Sixth house: one's vocation is bound to be rigid, fixed, routine and demanding. Yet it may also lead to important results and involve people in high position and public esteem.

Seventh house: the native is considerably under the heel and boot of others when it comes to carrying out their demands and requirements. The native has little freedom in choice of vocation. There are plenty of others always ready to tell him what to do. Sometimes this can get to be a grind when the native seems subject to almost everyone's whim and caprice. The native must somehow take all this seriously and yet turn out a satisfactory job.

Eighth house: the native is likely to be fully absorbed in looking after the important affairs of people who have passed on. The importance of the affairs they leave behind can be considerable. The native's involvement is heavily obligated and subservient to their laws and wishes.

Ninth house: the native finds comfort in service obligations that cater to some aspect of ninth-house institutions—publishing, law, religion, higher learning.

Tenth house: the native is likely to be servilely obligated with the routine duties attendant to public officials, men of position and authority.

Eleventh house: similar to the tenth, the native is committed to servile duties connected with organizations which cater to group values and sympathies. One's friends impose obligations that become more of a yoke than a pleasure.

Twelfth house: the native may be heavily involved with routine duties and service obligations, but a subconscious set of motivations or a sense of being able to contribute in some way to the underlying causes of important issues is involved. This work could be with institutions such as prisons or hospitals and asylums. The native is somehow able to lighten his burden by identifying with and helping unfortunate people in some way.

IF SATURN IS IN THE SEVENTH HOUSE, the native's sense of security is directly tied to other people. He has no control over this. Others must provide his security for him. There are probably plenty of persons willing to do this, but at the same time they exact a control over the native that is depressing and frustrating. The native must become accustomed to this condition. This would seem to suggest almost a slave or bonded servant illustration, which is pretty much to what the native must adjust. The master is apt to be older and rather severe and certainly demanding. What the native brings with him to help carry the burden is shown by the Capricorn house. The purpose or reward to which this adjustment leads is suggested by the house where the ruler of the seventh is found.

If the sign of Capricorn is on the:

First house: the native brings with him a willing personality and a kind of self-dedication, which is obvious. His whole identity is tied in with discharging his obligations well. In fact he has very little expression of personality outside of this.

Second house: the native tends to place all his possessions and future source of supply in the hands of others who will furnish him security.

Third house: the native's thinking is primarily directed toward pleasing the one who controls his security. His every thinking moment is in that direction.

Fourth house: the native sacrifices control over his own family and/or heritage to the one who controls his security. All his subjective attitudes confirm the wisdom of placing his security in the hands of others.

Fifth house: all the native's ideas of romance, love-making and creative efforts are centered on the one who will ensure the native's sense of security.

Sixth house: the native is attached to those who offer a protection or sense of preservation with complete service and willingness to obey their commands.

Seventh house: this native has even less control over his security than the other Capricorn positions, since all the decision passes into the hands of others. The persons most likely to capture and hold the native in their control generally tend however to be those of honorable intent, firm attitudes and high position or esteem.

Eighth house: the native is cast under the control of others through extraordinary circumstances out of his control and involving the wishes or plans of others who are no longer around or in the picture. The native's condition could be the result of war, crisis or catastrophe.

Ninth house: the native's obligations are centered on or arise from a close affiliation in similar institutions—like both members of the same church, religion, university or legal background. It is the ninth-house matter that ties them together.

Tenth house: the native easily subordinates his own goals or objectives to those of another, who rigidly controls his security. The native at the same time has high purpose but feels he can best reach this goal by submitting himself entirely to the will of a master, whom he hopes eventually will honor him.

Eleventh house: the native would solicit the support of similarly oriented friends and well-wishers and would subject them also to the control of his master.

Twelfth house: the native feels psychologically compelled to follow a master for reasons felt but not articulated in conscious speech or thought. An invisible bond draws the native to his master.

IF SATURN IS IN THE EIGHTH HOUSE, the native feels a deep sense of debt, not to others in particular nor to his own background, but to some sense of a COLLECTIVE PAST of which he feels secretly a part but cannot or does not particularly want to explore further. One might label this some form of superstition, which takes a firm control over the native. A strong sense of personal guilt resulting from the past is suggested for which the native feels spiritually accountable. The native empathizes himself into a position of obligation, which there is no rational way of proving or disproving. Again, this is likely to represent a pattern that most people won't understand, only those who have this pattern in their horoscope. Death is likely to be delayed for these natives until they have somehow resolved this feeling of collective guilt. Since Saturn represents old age, this would indicate a long enduring life in spite of several close calls with death. What other conditions contribute to this sense of collective guilt is suggested by the Capricorn house, while the solution or application of this attitude is suggested by the ruler of the sign on the eighth house.

If the sign of Capricorn is on the:

First house: the native feels even more responsible in some personal way for this sense of collective guilt. The mold or stamp of his personality will in some way suggest this. The native from the start not only will appear serious and old beyond his years but also will suggest a mysterious duty and urgency which will be difficult for others to place. One could say this appears to be a person of destiny and that is the way the native regards himself.

Second house: the native's sense of collective guilt may stem from his possessions or his income, neither of which he regards as spiritually his. The native will wish to use his resources for some secret eighth-house project.

Third house: the native enjoys a reputation that brings him clients and customers, whom he subjects in some way to a disciplined rejuvenation or gradual mutation or helps them over an extraordinary crisis.

Fourth house: the native has acknowledged subjective talents for devising methods and techniques that invariably work. He should use his insights in helping others adjust to important changes in their lives.

Fifth house: the native has an acknowledged creative talent which can be entertaining, educational or just romantically indulgent. He uses this in some way to ease others through the discipline demanded at times of significant change.

Sixth house: the native is acknowledged for well-developed traits or talents for service and duty. He uses this to help out in times of crisis but is always firm, rigid and demanding.

Seventh house: the native has the knack for engaging others to help him with his interests. These are particularly dominant at times of crisis or in poking around in odd situations for which the objective is never too clear or well defined. He is rather more hung up on some mysterious element out of the past.

Eighth house: the native is likely to be engaged permanently in an activity in which he either dwells on the past (as in archaeological excavations) or stands ready for emergency calls at time of need or crisis. On occasion the native would be pushed to heights of heroic effort.

Ninth house: the native has an acknowledged sense of history, particularly concerning the codification of thoughts, which he feels drawn to use in order to recover from the past something that he may feel has been lost or falsely discarded. Combined here are an excellent education, a sense of history and a concern for the past or relics of the past.

Tenth house: the native forgoes a personal goal that is clearly acknowledged as outstanding in favor of recovering something of collective significance from the past. There is a compulsion for some kind of self-sacrifice, which is based on guilt and which is concerned with the transition from one state or condition to another. This is one of those difficult patterns for ordinary people to understand, since most people are unfamiliar with the involvements of eighth-house matters.

Eleventh house: the native sacrifices friendships for his avowed purpose to recover something of value from the past. But he also at times has or can have the friendship and sympathy of important persons behind him. This is a native who uses his acknowledged honors to pay off the collective guilt of the past.

Twelfth house: this is a complex pattern combining two areas of darkness: the eighth house of death or threshold of transition from one state to another (not necessarily death) and the area of subconscious motivations or structure of ultimate values against which all our deeds are judged. The insight of the one supports the guilt complex of the other. This would give the native an unshakable conviction in the rightness of his possible guilt and the need to absolve himself.

IF SATURN IS IN THE NINTH HOUSE, the native feels a repressive obligation or duty to add to or establish the proof of certain beliefs, codes of behavior, religious convictions or system of laws. Not being sure of their present conclusions or positions, he feels more data, more substantiation of cases, or deeper emotional experiences are needed. The position is that of a professional doubter turned against the bastions of ritualized thinking. This represents the type that takes up religion not to spread the word of God but rather to prove to himself that there is a God which he doubts. The more he doubts, the more fanatical and evangelic he tends to become in flaying others for his own lack of faith. This is a somewhat dangerous position, as well as a phony one, for the native is concerned with an area of knowledge for inherently destructive rather than constructive purposes. Societies for psychic research have long been retarded and plagued by a predominance of this kind of attitude. The urge to destroy is obviously just as strong in man as the urge to build. Saturn in the eighth through twelfth houses tends to reflect this as well as any good that it might do. The native most often regards himself as doing good when in fact on the surface he may do more harm than good. It is supposed, however, that ultimately only good comes from the harm that may have been done. This may be the divine way of cleaning house from time to time. The affairs of the Capricorn house contribute significantly to the native's faultfinding. But in the end the native will have to bend to the suggested import of the house that holds the ruler of the ninth house.

If Capricorn is on the:

First house: the native brings the acknowledged force of his whole personality to bear on investigating and rationalizing the claims of his ninth-house subject (religion, law, or whatever). Wherever Capricorn falls in the horoscope always places a stamp for some degree of acknowledgment for the talents of that house.

Second house: the native uses his acknowledged source of supply and earning powers to set the matters straight. The presence of Saturn in the ninth house determines that the native feels there is something to set straight, rebuild, see realistically, or place on firmer foundations.

Third house: the native uses his acknowledged talents for self-expression and communication to adjust the ninth-house problems (see above).

Fourth house: the native uses his subjective powers and sense of divine right by virtue of his background and heritage to set the matters straight.

Fifth house: the native uses his creative talents and forgoes more idle pleasures to further his ninth-house commitments.

Sixth house: the native devotes his job and vocation to his ninth-house tasks.

Seventh house: the native enlists the aid and cooperation (or sometimes enmity) of others in furthering his aims.

Eighth house: the native is assisted in his pursuits by fortuitous events that suddenly sweep away old conditions.

Ninth house: the native must work more independently in whatever he is trying to set right. He must work within the accepted and acknowledged framework already in existence. There is no possibility to attack "the brotherhood" from the outside.

Tenth house: the native has the acknowledged support of recognized authorities and the apparent stamp of approval in his efforts, but his ambitions are not personal objectives. They must be pure of all taint of personal bias or private benefit.

Eleventh house: the native has the enlisted sympathy of others who share his goals and sympathies. His point of suggested effort is not so much personal discovery as it is the collected version of others who happen to share his values.

Twelfth house: the native is deeply convinced of the inner authority for his actions and interests. He might feel to some extent divinely inspired, although at times this inspiration may be based on information from the devil rather than from God.

IF SATURN IS IN THE TENTH HOUSE, it is most often said that this indicates a very probable fall from glory based on some form of personal undoing. This is consistently true for all positions of Saturn because Saturn itself continually calls us to task for an absolutely down-to-earth appraisal of our true foundations for security. Naturally this is always where we feel the most vulnerable and most insecure. Our security has to be carefully and slowly and convincingly built up over many years of effort and experiment. We are probably never entirely satisfied that we have resolved the matter. There will always be some aspect about it to plague and worry us. Saturn in the tenth house shows a firm conviction and absolute necessity to raise one's station in life. This has to be done, no matter what the cost—or so it often seems. This is absolutely mandatory. Ambition becomes almost predatory and ruthless. The affairs of the Capricorn house nourish and feed this determination.

If the sign of Capricorn is on the:

First house: the native's own resources must sustain him on his long journey upward. A proper sense of self-worth would be initially mandatory before anything could be started. This would instill a ruthless "me first" attitude, which would be required in this case to accomplish what has to be done. After all, very few people, particularly self-made types like this, climb to high position without having walked over countless others in the process.

Second house: the native needs money and sound financial backing for what he must do. This should be available, having been somehow won in the past. His sources of supply may be slow to unfreeze however.

Third house: the native needs a remarkable power of delivery to get his message across. This can be done with effort.

Fourth house: the native must purify his background and push his techniques to their utmost. This will require long, hard, subjective probing.

Fifth house: the native must develop his creative powers and ability to extend his ego so as to command the attention of those he would impress. This will take a lot of practice and many false starts.

Sixth house: the native must discipline his health and habits and job organization more carefully to make the grade. Not even minor falls from grace will be allowed.

Seventh house: the native must enlist willing cooperation and minimize any possible disparagement from others. The native will ultimately fail if he loses the effective cooperation of others. He can't make it on his own.

Eighth house: the native may have to bide his time until fortuitous events sweep aside obstacles that otherwise cannot be removed. He must also be prepared at all times to catch the tide of events on its full or he may be left waiting at the dock. Control is out of the native's hands and somewhat tied to probable events, which may take forever in coming about. Then there is no guarantee that they will work out the way the native wants them to. It may take the intervention of destiny itself to secure the beachhead.

Ninth house: the native needs support from groups whose ideas and principles coincide and support his own. His formalized thinking must be fully backed up all the way along. There is no possibility of sketchy thinking or an unprepared sense of history.

Tenth house: control of the eventual outcome is out of the native's hands. It is up to fate what the final judgment will be. If the intentions are pure and the native is persistent and realistic, then the odds are that he will win a fair measure of recognition. He is already assured of striving in the right direction, since the Saturn/Capricorn measuring rod assures this. Any false leads would have long ago been clipped in the bud. But the native can carry the ball only so far. After that public opinion will have to judge the case on its own merits, and there is always the possibility that the native may have to settle for second or third place. If the native is not pure of heart, he may also fall to his ruin when he least suspects it.

Eleventh house: the native needs the sympathy and understanding and encouragement of friendly supporters. He must pick his slogans from their collective dreams. He must identify with some sort of group values to project himself at the winner's table.

Twelfth house: the native needs an absolute inner conviction of the rightness of his ambitions. This may not be so easy to come by, for it is impossible to fool one's subconscious. This is something you have to feel. It is not something you know or can necessarily prove or explain to others. The important thing is to be convinced of it yourself—inwardly. This may come only late in life after many frustrating failures.

IF SATURN IS IN THE ELEVENTH HOUSE, the native feels both obligated and repressed by his association with groups and in trying to spearhead their collective dreams. The native, of course, must have the warmhearted support and encouragement of his friends and a sense of belonging to a special order or group. The native may be continually beset with doubts and reservations as to whether he has sufficiently captured the essence that they have in common. At one time he may be pushing one quality only to find that this is in opposition to another group which desires something else. Somehow the native must mediate these differences and still come out with a positive and truthful position. One naturally looks to older patrician types for guidance and support until one is able to strike out on one's own. The problem is to eventually make it before it is too late for any effective purpose. The character of the eleventh house is apt to disperse one's best efforts in fruitless pursuits rather than concentrate them in one effort in the right direction. Because you are dealing here with group values and group sympathies, it is more difficult to pledge your own sense of security with assurance or conviction. The affairs of the Capricorn house should help resolve this dilemma.

If the sign of Capricorn is on the:

First house: the native must develop a sense of self-identity to the utmost so that his dynamics become an easy rallying point for others of like intent and hopes. One is thus surer that he is in fact their true spokesman.

Second house: the native must to some extent buy his way in and so attract the group that will support him, as well as speak through him.

Third house: the native must authoritatively declare his position so as to leave no doubt where he stands and let others then flock to his side or cause.

Fourth house: the native first has to set his house in order, which may take much soul-searching and subjective appraisal. Then only after he is very sure of himself can he expect to collect or direct a following of similar intent. He may have to go in and out of many groups before he finds the right one that truly fits in with his own background.

Fifth house: the native must go to great lengths to project his ego in all directions so as to attract sufficient attention of the group that will claim him. There may be much trial and error, but with careful accounting on all levels the way should ultimately become clear. Any phase of entertainment or ballyhoo or sideshow attraction (even though childish) is needed.

Sixth house: only serious devotion to routine duties first will bring the native before the group that will eventually consider him their spokesman or champion of their dreams. The way up is long and arduous and once taken should be persistently followed. With Saturn it is persistence—not brilliance—that counts.

Seventh house: the native must first prove his ability to influence others and then to lead them on to bigger and better projects where many can join, as through a collective or a commune. The native should be immediately attractive to most people because he points the way or suggests the power of their acting collectively instead of on their own. The native is an agent or catalyst collecting a few into many.

Eighth house: the native may remain relatively inactive until some extraordinary event pushes or paves the way for him to assume command suddenly or take over. The native must hold himself in readiness until the green light appears.

Ninth house: the native needs first to have a good education and then to align himself with a certain group that is already established through the community of their interests. He must then elevate himself into a position where he can sense their collective hopes and somehow project this into a reality. There is an idealistic theme here, which eventually has to be brought into prominence—but not at the beginning.

Tenth house: this is a somewhat complicated pattern in which the native either has to have already arrived at a position of importance and prestige or at least seem convincingly to have done so. Then he is ready to join the "favored group" that somehow feels it is destined for better things than just worldly values. This may take a bit of doing, and the native must subjugate his personal ambitions or idea of private profit for the advancement of something more altruistic. Personal greed must give way to collective hopes.

Eleventh house: the group spots the native and makes him what he may become. This is sort of a shortcut situation in which one starts at the beginning to dream and yet somehow convinces others of like spirit that these dreams are real and moving. It must be remembered that the eleventh house is not one of worldly ambitions, being somewhat one step beyond that. There is a great deal of idealism, which is nevertheless realistic and desirable in the hearts of many.

Twelfth house: one might say this is more of a religious aura in that the native must be personally assured of his inner purpose, which is not yet proven, and yet be able to capture the enthusiasm and backing of others of similar spirit. This may take a lot of spiritual power and create a situation in which the native cannot afford to show all that he holds in his hand. That which supports him (the twelfth house) must be kept hidden and secret. This is part of the rules of "his" game. Twelfth-house powers are not absolutely convincing when examined in the light of more mundane everyday matters which have never faced a breakdown or been in need of repair. Once you have passed that state, then the rules of the game change. You can't apply the same rules to bright new shiny machines as they come off the assembly line hell-bent for leather. You have to experience life before you can judge it. The answers found in the twelfth house cannot be understood until after the game is over and all the conditions have been met. Until you have been through this, how can you appreciate what it means? That is why the twelfth house is a secret. You will find the answer when you reach the situation that calls for it.

IF SATURN IS IN THE TWELFTH HOUSE, what the native lacks most in his struggle is a firm, inner conviction about his subconscious motivations. He lacks a frame of reference for seeing the structure of ultimate values in their proper perspective. At the same time he is deeply concerned and secretly troubled by this lack in his inner nature, which tends not to support him when he needs it most—that is, when faced with delays, denials, frustrations, failure, loss of hope, or a sense of despair. It is not necessary for everyone to rely on inner values for his everyday actions, but in this case the native is continually made aware that only his inner values will support him. He will become convinced of this as all other contacts tend to fade away in time of "need, leaving him with an acute sense of isolation and a desperate need to develop some degree of inner conviction. This pattern suggests sad and even tragic conditions, which would so desperately force the native back upon his inner resources. There would be some tendency to build on false assumptions, favorite superstitions, even distorted values, but Saturn in its inevitable way would reduce these images to basic realities. Saturn cleans house from time to time by forcing all such values to meet a practical test. It is at such time that the native is painfully made aware of the distortion in his values. The Capricorn house will substantially support the native's struggle for inner security. This is perhaps the most difficult position for Saturn in the entire horoscope—when it falls in the twelfth house. Saturn normally works with everyday realities, factual truths, concrete foundations and material values. The twelfth house dissolves all material considerations in favor of spiritual truths, making the literal functions of Saturn almost impossible.

If the sign of Capricorn is on the:

First house: the native is blessed with an external obstinacy and powers for endurance which will sustain him well in his moments of defeat. A lack of sensitivity, plus a persistent hardness of attitude, will spare him from the more crushing blows that would destroy a more sensitive type.

Second house: the native has a hard-nosed attitude about money, which, while money won't buy everything, will help solve many of his problems simply because he has the financial means to readjust.

Third house: the native develops firm mental patterns that keep him from vacillating in times of personal crisis. The only thoughts he will assume are attitudes for marching forward.

Fourth house: the native has firm unshakable convictions about his fitness for the job and the soundness of his background. This will considerably help shield him in times of need, when reliance on this happenstance is not enough.

Fifth house: the native lays carefully developed plans for extending his ego in creative efforts, which generally prove to be invincible. This reduces the areas of vulnerability from which he can be challenged and/or defeated.

Sixth house: the native has carefully laid down patterns for vocation, health, diet and duty obligations, which are all sound, assuring him that the vulnerability will not come from there.

Seventh house: the native has the avowed support of others who will champion his cause in time of need. He will not be alone during his severest trial. Although their presence, unfortunately, will not be what the native feels he needs.

Eighth house: the native will have the ability to face drastic changes with ease, since he is always somewhat prepared for the worst that any change can bring.

Ninth house: the native will have the support of formalized thought and the institutions that grow out of them. He is not apt to fall down because of his concepts on law, religion, philosophy or any realm of higher principles.

Tenth house: the native will always retain his reputation and public esteem and the support of people in high places no matter what inner suffering he may endure.

Eleventh house: the native will always have some friends and well-wishers who actively extend their sympathy and hopes for his best—if that is any comfort. He will feel it is not.

Twelfth house: the native will have to dig even deeper into his resources, for apparently the answers that he will need are always there if he can sense them. He need not look any further for help.

As stated above, the affairs of the Capricorn house support the native in his need for inner conviction, and his vulnerability to false values will not come from that direction in his life.

The vulnerability for Saturn trouble (no matter what house Saturn is in) comes from the house where the ruler of the sign on the Saturn house is found. This points to the direction and purpose for which this sense of reality is needed. This is where the native is more apt to falter if he does not have what it takes to meet this need.

If the planet which rules the Saturn house sign is found in the:

First house: it is the native who gets short-changed. He cannot effectively present himself to anyone under any circumstance until his values have been realistically placed in order.

Second house: the native's source of income will suffer. His supplies could be jeopardized.

Third house: his sense of communication will suffer. He will not be able to get his ideas across.

Fourth house: his whole emotional security is threatened. He will lose confidence in himself.

Fifth house: his sense of creativity will fail him. His satisfaction from pleasures will dry up.

Sixth house: his health is threatened, his job will suffer, and he will not be able to fulfill his obligations either to others or even to himself in daily matters.

Seventh house: his relations with others are impaired. Cooperation is diminished and discord is increased.

Eighth house: he will find it impossible to face or cope with important changes. He will be unable to accept the psychic implications of his actions.

Ninth house: his sense of principle will be endangered. He will no longer know what he believes in.

Tenth house: his reputation will suffer, his sense of ambition will be gone.

Eleventh house: his friends will seem to desert him. He will seem to have lost touch with his sense of collective hopes that he once shared with others.

Twelfth house: oddly enough, this position is a little less unfortunate than the others because his troubles are buried in the subconscious. This could in extremes lead to some kind of drastic self-undoing or hopeless confusion but in most cases the material limitations are kept in the background as a haunting fear or as something unreal which can be adjusted later.

Naturally, the force of this reality disturbance varies according to which planet is involved—that is, which planet rules the Saturn house.

If the planet is the:

Sun: it affects the native's integrity.

Moon: it affects the native's emotions.

Mercury: it affects the native's thinking.

Saturn: it affects the native's sense of reality.

Mars: it affects the native's sense of action, also his sexual attitudes.

Venus: it affects the native's sense of sentiment, his loving or affectionate nature (which is not his emotions or feelings controlled by the moon).

Neptune: it affects the native's sense of ideals.

Jupiter: it affects the native's sense of justice and what is right and wrong.

Pluto: it affects the native's sense of adjustment to change and his ability to go along with new conditions or progressive movements.

Uranus: it affects the native's sense of independence and possible creative genius.

Saturn is supported or opposed in its normal function by being in aspect (contact) with other planets. This will also involve the affairs of the house where that planet is located (primarily) and the affairs of the house which that planet rules (secondarily).

For the aspect relationships to and from Saturn see Chapter 9, "Aspects Between Planets."

THE CYCLES OF SATURN

Starting at its birth position, Saturn moves by yearly passage counterclockwise through the horoscope seeking solutions for self-preservation and acquisition of basic security. The complete cycle, returning to its original position at birth, takes Saturn approximately twenty-eight years. Dividing the horoscope by the horizontal axis of the ascendant and the vertical axis of the meridian makes four sectors. Each sector represents approximately seven years of Saturn's time.

THE POSITION OF SATURN IN THE BIRTH MAP, BY VIRTUE OF ITS TIMING OVER THE ANGLES OF THE HOROSCOPE, IS THE SINGLE MOST IMPORTANT DETERMINANT OF THE RISE AND FALL OF FORTUNE.

Saturn, "the timer in life," provides the opportunities to move forward, assigns our duties, and at the end acts as chief accountability officer. It thus establishes the ebb and flow of our entire life pattern—whether the native catches opportunity ideally on the crest or flounders hopelessly while the best of life passes him by because his timing is all wrong. We get our breaks in life only when Saturn gives us the green light. Naturally it is important as to our age and preparedness when these breaks open up as Saturn moves from sector to sector.

First, we look to Saturn's position at birth. This identifies our initial consciousness of the importance that self-preservation means to us. Some feel this much more personally than others, as those born with Saturn in the first sector (houses one, two, three). Others are born with a natural preparedness to take on immediate responsibilities as those born with Saturn in the second sector (houses four, five, six). Others seem to begin life with an avowed purpose, sensing immediately the advantages of objective orientation, as those born with Saturn in the third sector (houses seven, eight, nine). And there are those who seem born into positions already established for them from which they immediately reap benefits, as those born with Saturn in the fourth sector (houses ten, eleven, twelve).

The vital moments as Saturn moves around the horoscope are the points when Saturn crosses over the angles from one sector to another and the points of contact that Saturn makes with other planets at their birth position, including contact with its own position at birth.

THE FIRST SECTOR (houses one, two, three) is PREPARED-

NESS. This is where the native develops himself. In the first house the native examines his self-worth, as embodied in the image of his personality. In the second house the native examines or reexamines, as the case may be on the second time around, his resources and source of supply. In the third house the native examines or reexamines his thinking and sense of communication.

THE SECOND SECTOR (houses four, five, six) IS EMERGENCE. This is where the native first objectifies himself outward by accepting certain responsibilities toward his immediate environment. In the fourth house the native accepts the obligations of his family and heritage, which is also his subjective self. He formulates his methods and patterns of technique. On the transit passage of Saturn he reexamines himself on these matters. In the fifth house the native relaxes but seeks serious pleasure in extending his ego to creative fields, taking chances, incurring risks, begetting children, and pursuing the pleasures of love and sex. On the transit passage of Saturn he adjusts his reality on these matters. In the sixth house the native accepts the obligations of service, duties, a job and the responsibility of his health and the routine of daily living. On the transit passage of Saturn he is forced to correct any of these matters that are not fundamentally sound.

THE THIRD SECTOR (houses seven, eight, nine) IS THE CLIMB. There the native finds himself prepared to step out into the world and join or compete with others for considerations outside his subjective self. We call this area the beginning of OBJECTIVE ORIENTATION. It is a real step forward in external affairs. In the seventh house the native joins with others as partners or opposes them in competition. On the passage of Saturn these matters come up for examination and/or correction. In the eighth house the native makes necessary changes due to experience and weighs the spiritual consequences of his actions. On the passage of Saturn the native is forced to reexamine this area of his life and take heed of all that it implies. The transit presence of Saturn in the eighth house tends to purge the air and spirit of certain things that will not be needed in the future. In the ninth house the native formalizes his thoughts into a general system or code of laws. This is a state of advanced learning and involves the symbolism of ritual (or the ritual of symbolism). The transit passage of Saturn in the ninth house causes us to adjust our awareness of principles and possibly discard some angles that are not altogether realistic or truthful.

THE FOURTH SECTOR (houses ten, eleven, twelve) IS THE

CLIMAX. There the native reaches the peak of his material achievement in the eyes of the world and receives the recognition that he has won for himself through effort and application. From here on, the native solidifies his achievements and continues to gain from their application. In the tenth house the native is recognized for himself (good or bad) and receives a label or grading and a distinction. He can appreciate the fact that he has somehow arrived at a maximum peak of production FROM HIS PRESENT PROGRAM. It is the passage of Saturn that brings these honors and/or failures. It is at this time that the native is forced to see what he has done, for better or for worse. In the eleventh house the native gathers honors and benefits from his award. He rejoices with friends of like sympathies and together they form a collective hope or ideal. Since the passage of Saturn in the tenth house brought to light both the nature of the native's ambitions (whatever they happen to be) and the degree to which he had made any headway or achievement in the matter, it may well be that a certain adjustment in friends might be necessary with regard to how these particular friends continue to fit in with his programs. The passage of Saturn through the eleventh house is a time for seeing one's friends in a more realistic light with the possible elimination in the future of some. In the twelfth house the native must make a final review and receive an ultimate judgment of the real worth or import or value implication of what he has been doing. The passage of Saturn through the twelfth house brings all these subconscious factors to a head.

ANTICLIMAX, END AND NEW BEGINNING: There tends to be another climax—perhaps a final valuation—as Saturn crosses over the ascendant bringing an end to the previous twenty-eight year cycle.

For those natives whose natal sun is in the tenth, eleventh or twelfth house, this final climax as Saturn passes over the ascendant is bound to be more significant in every way than the material climax when Saturn crosses over the tenth cusp.

As Saturn again passes through the first, second and third houses, there is a sense of new orientation as the self-preservation forces regroup themselves and dig deeper for the native's present needs and mature requirements As Saturn approaches the fourth cusp, preparatory to crossing into the second sector, the native tends to either fade away (the fourth house also representing the grave and the end of physical matter) or take hold and emerge again in a new cycle of responsibility and growth.

This is the natural flow of time as a seed develops into a tree. But each life pattern is subject to its own individuality, and this cycle could be cut off at any time for other reasons that will also be shown in the horoscope.

According to the structure of our present-day society, it would appear that the ideal timing of the Saturn cycles would be for the native to receive his first big push—the opportunity to externalize his life—somewhere after the twenty-second birthday, depending on the amount of formal education required for the goal he has in mind. Age twenty-two would be an average age for the completion of four years of college. If one had in mind to go out in the world earlier (or later), then that would be the ideal age for his Saturn to cross over the seventh house, beginning the climb toward the climax in the tenth house.

The decisive factor is the point of climax when Saturn goes over the tenth cusp. If this comes too early in life—before the native has finished his education or is really mature emotionally—then he has already gone into a "decline" in affairs and opportunities by the time he is ready (age-wise) to step out into the world. His best moments are, in a sense, wasted. For him, opportunities have stopped and he is soon faced with a necessity to reinventory himself and start all over again on a new level of reality.*

Of great importance are Saturn's contacts with its birth position—most notably the conjunction, squares and opposition. When Saturn passes over its own place at birth, a debt of long standing is dissolved. The native feels a sense of freedom that comes from solving long-term and difficult problems. Sometimes this is just a sense of long-needed relief and some people quit this life. But it can also bring a willingness to accept new burdens and to strengthen convictions for achieving new goals. This period is due approximately in the native's twenty-eighth year and again around his fifty-sixth year. Those fortunate enough to reach eighty-four are generally too old to undertake seriously a new direction, but it is not impossible.

When Saturn contacts the sun, there is generally a period of accountability like striking a balance sheet on the situation of the ego-force. If the native on the whole has met life squarely, these periods of accountability usually bring awards and payments. On the

—

*In Grant Lewi's book *Astrology for the Millions,* which is highly recommended, he traces the cycles of Saturn in complete detail through the lives of various great men of destiny.

conjunction of the sun not only great responsibility but also high position and honors can be bestowed. President Franklin D. Roosevelt first became president on a conjuction of Saturn to his Sun.

Saturn's relationships to other planets would depend on the importance of their relationship at birth.

A general rule for the effect of any transiting planet on a natal position is: THE POSSIBILITY OF SIGNIFICANT EVENTS DEVELOPING FROM TRANSITING ASPECTS IS IN DIRECT RATIO TO THE STRENGTH OF THEIR RELATIONSHIP AT BIRTH. If Saturn is in close aspect at birth, a transit of either planet reaffirms this relationship. If two planets are not in any close aspect at birth, a transit from either is of considerably less importance—often bringing nothing at all.

Saturn should be considered by far THE MOST IMPORTANT PLANET TO INFLUENCE ONE'S GENERAL FORTUNES AS IT TRANSITS THROUGH THE HOROSCOPE. Everyone should set up a timetable for Saturn's contact by aspect of all the important points in his horoscope and carefully note exactly what happens at these times. The real value is not in the nature of SPECIFIC EVENTS but in distinguishing a possible TREND or PATTERN by which these events are related. This is the importance of what Saturn is trying to teach us. . . .

The pattern that should be evident is the way in which we should be trying to solve our sense of self-preservation and extend the vision of our reality as outlined by our natal Saturn. In the:

First house: through our personality.

Second house: through our own ability to produce earnings.

Third house: by the concreteness of our thinking.

Fourth house: by the conservative allegiance to our true heritage.

Fifth house: by taking risks in extending the influence of our ego.

Sixth house: by working within the framework of duty and obligation.

Seventh house: by taking our lead from others.

Eighth house: by holding steadfast during times of great change and turmoil.

Ninth house: by furthering established molds of thinking.

Tenth house: by strict obedience to the rules laid down before us and seeing that they are carried out by those who come after.

Eleventh house: by seeking sympathetic understanding only from those older and wiser than ourselves.

Twelfth house: by reaching deeply within our subconscious selves for ultimate spiritual values.

Chapter 8

OTHER PLANETS

IN YOUR HOROSCOPE

MERCURY IN YOUR HOROSCOPE

Mercury in your horoscope shows the focus of your mentality as the instrument and reflection of the ego-force. Mercury is in fact never far removed in space from the sun—never more than 28° ahead or behind. The Sun's rate of motion through the "belt of space" (arbitrarily called the zodiac) is very constant—approximately one degree per day. When Mercury's motion is slightly faster than the Sun's, it moves ahead, and when it slows down a little, it falls behind the Sun.

When any planet's forward motion reduces to less than that of the earth, the planet (by comparison to the earth) is said to be in RETROGRADE motion. Astrologers are divided as to the significance (if any) that retrograde motion has on the planet's astrological significance.

In the case of Mercury it is generally advisable to note when this planet goes retrograde, which lasts from two to three weeks at a time and is shown in the current year ephemeris. All communication at that time tends to get fouled up, and individual mental efforts frequently have to be done over or later revised. One should never be too inflexible in any message transaction while Mercury is retrograde.

Mercury, as messenger, receives sensory stimuli, sorts them communicates them to the ego-center, receives back its instructions, and communicates these instructions to other centers. The function of Mercury should be distinguished from the content of thought, the patterns of thinking and the style of communication, all of which are shown by the condition of the third house. It should always be kept in mind that Mercury is only the ego's messenger, which reflects what it sees. It does not originate thought.

If Mercury as ruler of both Gemini and Virgo relates to your Sun, Moon or ascendant, then Mercury is particularly important to you. Your answer to all these matters (ego, emotions and personality) is a mental approach. If your Sun is in Gemini or Virgo, then Mercury (which may be in a different sign and house than the Sun) shows how you may help yourself fulfill your destiny. If your Moon is in Gemini or Virgo, then Mercury shows you how you will satisfy your emotional requirements. If your ascendant is in Gemini or Virgo, then Mercury shows you the key with which you can integrate your personality and control your immediate environment.

Where Mercury falls by house reflects your most instinctive mental capacities as they gather and assimilate stimuli. If Mercury is in the:

First house: then you gather stimuli from your immediate environment. Others sense and react to you as a highly perceptive being. Your personality image reflects a mental alertness that is obvious to others. You may even appear brilliant.

Second house: your reflective processes should produce ingenious ideas for making money and increasing your store of possessions. Much of your best thinking will be centered on these matters.

Third house: you should be noted for the quality of your delivery and your sense of style in communication. Since this is one of the natural houses of Mercury, all mental faculties should shine.

Fourth house: you have talents for self-analysis of your background, heritage and the subjective basis for your home security.

Fifth house: you have a mental approach in creative efforts to extend your ego, as well as a clever talent with children, primary education matters, romantic love-making and entertaining.

Sixth house: you have mental talents for collecting and categorizing details and assimilating knowledge about health, vocations, services, duties and obligations which are undertaken on behalf of others.

Seventh house: you have a mental facility for getting along with others, although you first have to take your cue from them, mentally. You may be able to read other people's minds and thoughts before they have even made their wishes known. This position suggests many mental contacts with all sorts of people. This is a very good position for dealing with the public.

Eighth house: there is an extraordinary mental alertness in times of crisis or emergency. There can also be insight into areas that lie beyond ordinary experience. There could even be some suggestion of the mind leaving the body to gather stimuli or sense data from a state of consciousness beyond the limits of ordinary time or space conceptions. In the language of the occult this is called astral projection.

Ninth house: this position is especially favored for intellectual pursuits in all realms of higher education that deal with principles and codes of thought rather than just specifics of thinking.

Tenth house: the native invariably knows how to adapt himself mentally to the prerogatives of administrative authority and to cater to those people in high position. Naturally this stands him in good graces and he receives the admiration of those higher up. His mental qualities contribute greatly to his rise in life.

Eleventh house: the native has the talent to sense and organize the essence of the hopes and aspirations that groups of sympathizers have in common. This talent would be very useful in gathering political information about a constituency or in catering to the desires of voters. The native would sense and voice what they want to hear (particularly if Mercury is in Cancer, Libra or Sagittarius).

Twelfth house: the native's reflective qualities are turned inward to seek the answers of "why" and "for what purpose" to the more distressing conditions in life. The native instinctively identifies with the underdog. This position is favored for research and very serious philosophical attitudes on the ultimate values in life.

For comments on the tempo of Mercury according to the sign in which it falls see page 332 under Chapter 22, "Astrological Analysis When You Don't Have the Time of Birth."

Particularly since Mercury's function is only a reflective quality rather then a creative element, it is most important how Mercury is strengthened in the horoscope by strong aspect relationships to other planetary forces. Mercury is encouraged by and easily assimilates stimuli from other forces that it aspects by soft angle. It is forced to consider and include the stimuli from those planetary forces that it aspects by hard angle. For further details on this see Chapter 9, "Aspects Between Planets."

MARS IN YOUR HOROSCOPE

Mars in your horoscope tells where and how you will initiate action, improvise corrective or adjustment measures, sally forth in competition, and aggressively fight for what you want. Sexually, it shows where you will act impulsively and spontaneously to satisfy natural instincts.

If Mars, as ruler of Aries, relates to your Sun, Moon or ascendant, then Mars is particularly important for you. If your Sun is in Aries, then Mars shows specifically how you MUST initiate the required aggressive action to fulfill your destiny. Mars always requires aggressive action. If your Moon is in Aries, Mars shows how you can best satisfy your emotional requirements which are strong and vigorous. If your ascendant is in Aries, Mars shows you in what specific direction you should turn your sense of competition with the best chance of winning.

Where Mars is by house triggers instinctive action in the affairs of that house and correspondingly in all other departments of your life *after* it has initiated the affairs of its own house.

If Mars is in the:

First house: the native has the power to trigger responsive action in order to engage competitively with all factors in the immediate environment. This is a self-generating position for Mars. All the Mars qualities are obvious in the personality.

Second house: the native will use his initiating force to increase primarily his earning powers and general source of supply. The presence of Mars in the second house indicates the native must fight to get the money that is due him from his labors.

Third house: the native will sharpen his mental capabilities for gaining advantage over others in thought, debate and communication. The presence of Mars shows that the native must seek at times to force his views on others.

Fourth house: the native will initiate action toward his subjective self, forcing formulation of effective techniques with which to attack or launch projects against that which is already established and inevitably aligned against him (the fourth being blocked by opposition from the tenth). The native must be prepared for this vigorous opposition to everything he tries to do. The chain of action is that the native must first get mad at himself in order to feel aggressively competent to fight others in getting what he wants across.

Fifth house: the native exerts himself by extending his ego influence in creative pursuits, including taking chances and assuming speculative risks. All fifth-house people are considered competitive to the native (including his own children).

Sixth house: the native tackles challenging conditions under which duties and obligations are assumed and discharged. This position indicates physical agitation over working conditions and subservient positions in life. The native fights with fellow workers and is angered by the limitation of his daily duties.

Seventh house: the native sees other people as invariably threatening him in some way. His primary response to this is a challenge to some form of competition. This position would be favored for compelling involvement in athletic competition. This is not a pattern for ease in social relationships, since relations with others tend to anger the native. The native, however, needs the sense of threat by others to turn him on to aggressive action.

Eighth house: the native energetically seeks the adjustment to important changes, mutations and developments where one situation or attitude is completely abandoned in favor of another newly born. The native has very intense sexual feelings, which at times may desire a certain amount of violence or excessive pitch. The native possesses talent for regenerative or recuperative powers, which may also have this effect on others as a pick-me-up or shot in the arm. Sexual awareness is more intense than with Mars in the fifth house.

Ninth house: the native energetically engages in contesting the veracity and up-to-dateness of certain codes of thought or principles of behavior currently implied in our institutions or laws or religions. The native does not wholly accept all the details or background on which his own principles are based. Certain points anger him. He will also take it upon himself to fight and defend actively such beliefs against nonbelievers or persons of opposing faiths or beliefs. The native fights and defends on principle rather than from a more personal conviction and independent appraisal of the rightness of certain issues. He follows what he believes is a sense of history or established tradition, even though by today's standards this may be outmoded or no longer a true reflection of the needs that gave birth to the institution.

Tenth house: the native actively engages in the overthrow or challenge of other people's authority over him or their right to subjugate or administer his affairs or ambitions. The native must fight for his place in life. He is likely to incur with some a dirty reputation which cannot be helped and must not be allowed to stand in the native's way or deter him from fighting. Whatever position the native seeks in life is already occupied by someone else who must in some way be unseated or discredited. The native's ambitions are such that he and the one already receiving most of the favor cannot both be right. The native must offer vigorous competition to get ahead.

Eleventh house: the native is a challenge to the common bonds of sympathy or collective hopes that certain groups champion together. The native enters into competition with close friends for the purpose of resolving certain cherished hopes and dreams which he has. The native would consider such argument or context as a mark of favor reserved for one's close friendships. He would not so engage himself in ordinary relationships that did not matter in his life. This makes, however, for stormy relationships with one's good friends because ordinarily one does not enter into such competition with friends. One usually feels that with good friends one doesn't have to prove oneself or suffer a challenge to one's cherished hopes. The native has many changes in friends. One by one they fall by the wayside as he gains advantage over them in some way. They last about as long as it takes to gain this sense of advantage, although the friend may be unaware of the reason.

Twelfth house: the native is challenged to seek vigorously a structure of ultimate values by which the apparent success or failures in life can be truly judged. This is a somewhat unnatural position for Mars, since the initiating force or instrument of instinctive action is forced into the background to work from within rather than to contest openly one's objective. The native is sexually drawn to those in unfortunate situations. Their very incapacity or failure sexually excites him. He is more willing to fight for their cause or rights than he is for his own. Outward action is considerably delayed by filtering through endless inner motivations and reflection thereon.

For comments on the tempo of Mars according to the sign in which it falls see page 332 in Chapter 22.

Mars is favorably assisted on occasion by those planetary forces to which it makes soft-angle aspects. It is forced into defensive action and attitudes by those planetary forces to which it is aspected by hard-angle aspects. For further details on these see Chapter 9.

VENUS IN YOUR HOROSCOPE

Venus, the symbol of beauty and the sentiment of affection, in your horoscope shows where you will relax, indulge your sense of comforts, improve the surroundings with color, ornamentation, music and romance. Where Venus is found, there is a condition of beauty—in the situation, principle, or in the native himself. As will be appreciated, this is a holiday kind of vibration, which in some cases is operative only with "weather permitting." The full benefits or "glow" of Venus' beauty may depend on a number of other considerations.

If Venus, as ruler of both Taurus and Libra, relates to your Sun, Moon or ascendant, then Venus is particularly important for you. Sociability and attractability are the key to your ego, emotions or personality. If your Sun is in Taurus or Libra, then Venus shows specifically how you can fulfill the beauty and material needs that are related to your destiny. If your Moon is in Taurus or Libra, then Venus shows you how your emotional needs along these same lines can best be realized. If your ascendant is in Taurus or Libra, then Venus shows the direction and best development of your attractive personality through your immediate environment.

Where Venus is by house shows where you are the most responsive to the effects of beauty, comfort and loving sentiment. If Venus is in the:

First house: it is the native who is beautiful and he knows it. He has the power to create beauty and attractive conditions immediately around him. This is always necessary in order to secure for himself the most desirable response from others. The world tends to see the native as a thing of beauty or loving sentiment, and they expect this from him BEFORE they will respond to him in the

way that was intended. Unless the world initially gets this treatment or satisfaction from the native, the native will be considered
a failure in ALL respects whether or not this is true. Natives who
have Venus in the first house must keep up the beauty and attractiveness of their image—this will always be important. It is the
"come-on" that fate has given you to enhance your drawing-card
ability.

Second house: the native usually has a pleasing and steady accumulation of possessions. This position is favored for enjoying the comforts and attractive things in life. The native has some talent which
beautifies and which can be turned into cash.

Third house: the pleasing influence is on the soothing effect and
sincere concern that the native shows in speech, mental patterns
and style of expression. This position is favored for socializing
with pleasure among those in the marketplace, brothers and sisters, and those in the near neighborhood. This position is favorable
for dealing pleasantly with customers and clients.

Fourth house: the native has talents around the home and for en-
hancing any aspects of family life or the background of his heritage. In the family circle is where the native flowers best and is
most pleasing and congenial. The native's beauty becomes subjective—more like a sense of beauty.

Fifth house: the native should have artistic or musical talents, which
are entertaining and can be used in a really creative way—especially with children.

Sixth house: the native's appreciation of the nicer things in life tends
to be diverted into situations where duties, obligations and services
can be made more pleasant and inviting. This pattern is favored for
the hotel and restaurant business.

Seventh house: there is a social charm in the native's manner of
handling other people which generally ensures instant success with
them. Others are happy to cooperate socially on most matters.

Eighth house: the native's charms are most evident in times of crisis
when he is confronted with significant changes. He has talent for
helping others over such situations. The native is inclined to exploit the sentiments of affection, as in prostitution or use of pornography. There will be peaceful conditions at the time of death.

Ninth house: the native will generally be well received around established institutions where all forms of higher learning are honored
and respected. This is a very favorable placement for enjoyment of
teaching. The native can contribute to the principles of art,

decoration, theories of design or music in an educational way. The native's sense of affection is enhanced by foreign effects or contact with foreign situations.

Tenth house: the native's ambition is favored in the arts that professionalize decoration, embellishment or music and ornamentation. The native's sense of affection is enhanced when directed toward people in high position.

Eleventh house: the native's social graces are attracted to group activities where he gains in stature and benefits through identification with group sympathies. The native is more affectionate among groups than on an individual basis.

Twelfth house: the native has a way of romanticizing and spreading cheer in a situation which most people find difficult, frustrating and depressing. This is obviously appreciated by those who are temporarily down and out, and the native is sentimentally drawn to such conditions. The native's sentiments are usually kept hidden and his sense of romance is better when conducted in secret.

In seeking outlets for the above Venus sentiments, the native's sense of beauty is encouraged by the affairs of the Taurus and Libra houses. The native's interest is also directed toward the affairs of the house related to the Venus house through the ruler of the cusp. This shows where one's artistic talents can be utilized both pleasantly and to advantage.

For comments on the tempo of Venus according to the sign in which it falls see page 332 under Chapter 22.

Venus is easily encouraged and strengthened by the planetary forces to which it makes soft-angle aspects. Venus is forced to compromise itself or forgo some of its joyous pleasures for more practical applications by the planetary forces to which it is aspected by hard angles. For further details see Chapter 9.

NEPTUNE IN YOUR HOROSCOPE

Neptune in your horoscope shows where and how you will respond to intuition and spiritual awareness. This is the planet of insight, idealization and inspiration. Neptune operates by subtle suggestions or vague and mysterious implications that are felt or sensed rather than seen or known. Since its domain extends perception beyond the ordinary five senses, it might be called the planet of extrasensory perception. Since most people rely chiefly on material causes, they tend to ridicule and fear what they do not understand. Others who are highly keyed to Neptune intuitively sense this power with great conviction and faith. Since Neptune is essentially a spiritual force, it tends to seem negative when coupled with situations that call for primarily material, physical or rational solutions. Thus Neptune can also suggest delusion, fraud, deception, intrigue and scandal. Unless utilized on its natural place (which is nonmaterial), Neptune is where you can get fooled and where you tend to deceive others.

If Neptune, as ruler of Pisces, relates to your Sun, Moon or ascendant, then Neptune is particularly important for you. The key in matters of the ego, emotions or personality is one of inspired vision. If your Sun is in Pisces, then your important solutions in life are essentially spiritual and inspirational. If your Moon is in Pisces, then you are naturally drawn emotionally to all that is mysterious, illusive, suggestive and idealistic about Neptune. If your ascendant is in Pisces, then the complete mastery of all the Neptunian tricks in the bag (including magic) is mandatory for you to develop your personality and mesmerize your immediate environment.

Where Neptune is by house shows where the subtle Neptunian forces will be the most suggestive in your affairs. If Neptune is in the:

First house: this is one of the positions where the native is more subject to self-delusion. Generally speaking, the practical demands of everyday living are better solved by more down-to-earth solutions. Neptune there indicates a strong reliance on spiritual qualities, which other people generally treat with some degree of skepticism. The native must be careful to be absolutely ethical in all matters lest he be considered a phony and a fraud.

Second house: Since Neptune dissipates and dissolves, its effect on this material house of supply is generally unsatisfactory. At best, earnings should come from Neptunian pursuits where the image is sold for the real. This includes movies, film making, television and all such expressions where images or masks are employed for effect.

Third house: this is a more favorable location for Neptune, since thought lends itself ideally to any expansion of boundaries or dissolving limitations on thinking. The native's best thinking is arrived at by intuition and possibly some form of extrasensory perception. The native should be able to inspire others by his thoughts or communication.

Fourth house: since this is already a subjective area of affairs, Neptune's presence tends to withold a realistic awareness of the native's true foundations. The path is open to many self-delusions which disperse rather than unify one's resolve on issues that should be clarified in order to face life. Neptune's effect on the foundations of life or the methods for seeking objectives does perhaps more harm than good.

Fifth house: the Neptunian inspiration can be nicely blended with the sense of creativity and show-business know-how where it is sometimes advantageous to make anything seem possible. The material aspects of gamble and speculation create something of a pitfall however. A touch of magic is used to gain any of the fifth-house pleasures.

Sixth house: Neptune can bring an uplift to affairs that often get bogged down in material details and crushing labor, where there is danger of losing sight of the real intent or purpose of the obligation. Neptune would tend to strengthen one's ability to carry or assume burdens by making them seem lighter or less irksome than they really are.

Seventh house: this is not a fortunate position for Neptune because it places all the native's relationships with others on an unreal or fanciful basis. The native is deluded by what he sees in others and others invariably fool the native in some way.

Eighth house: Neptune acts as a protective force that softens the fears of the unknown and extends insight into potentialities which lie beyond ordinary recognition. This can be a very lucky and fortunate position for the native. It favors strange inheritances and luck in finding new values in discarded objects or situations.

Ninth house: the native will be drawn to religious or mystical rituals which are already embodied in some kind of cult or coded framework of belief. The native gains much inspiration from the past and the sense of history involved with our principles of belief.

Tenth house: the native will assume a spiritual attitude toward material awards and ambitions. He will undoubtedly reject the more temporal judgments of life and find satisfaction primarily in justification of his own idealizations. His goals are essentially other-worldly. The native tends to be guided by certain inspired concepts or individuals who are nonmaterial in their attitudes or approach.

Eleventh house: the native has a spiritual affinity with others on a collective ideal which they cherish together. The native feels drawn to share his insights with others of similar sympathies.

Twelfth house: the native possesses a natural insight into many matters that most people find depressing and gloomy. There is a talent for helping unfortunate people with the magical touch or inspired thought that makes all the difference.

The spiritual import of Neptune (wherever it is found in the horoscope) is supported by the affairs and people of the Pisces house. The desirable application of this inspiration is suggested by the house where the ruler of the Neptune house is found.

For comments on the tempo of Neptune according to the sign in which it falls see Chapter 22, page 332.

Neptune is encouraged by soft-angle aspects to other planets that add to its inspirational coverage. It is forced into action by hard angles. It is more important for Neptune to be keyed to planets that get things done like the Sun, Mars and Saturn than to planets that emote, decorate, sympathize or just think about the matter.

JUPITER IN YOUR HOROSCOPE

Jupiter in your horoscope shows how you can apply your sense of optimistic expansion with the most profit. It also indicates where you will feel the most expansive and generous in material matters. It generally brings prosperity, abundance and fruitful conditions to the affairs and people of the house it occupies. While Saturn tends to close doors (to concentrate better the native's attention or certain fundamentals of his reality), Jupiter tends to open doors for expanding material potentialities and widening the native's horizon for further opportunities. Most people welcome the "forward" signal that Jupiter seems to release, just as they resent the time-out to check and refuel that Saturn imposes.

If Jupiter, as ruler of Sagittarius, relates to your Sun, Moon, or ascendant, then Jupiter is particularly important for you. The keynote (for ego, emotions or personality) is optimistic faith and invincible conviction in the rightness of your purpose. If your sun is in Sagittarius, then Jupiter points the way where the expansive spirit of your nature can best find an outlet in fulfilling its destiny. If your Moon is in Sagittarius, then Jupiter shows where your emotional nature will find some gratification in all that it aspires to feel. If your ascendant is in Sagittarius, then Jupiter is the key to how you can impress your immediate environment and let your personality shine forth as it yearns to do.

If Jupiter is in the:

First house: the native profits most by improving himself and keeping his personality image as bright and faultless and open-minded as possible. The native invariably appears successful and self-assured no matter what his actual material circumstances may be.

Second house: This is very favorable for abundant earnings and being well paid for any services rendered. The native would also be generous with his possessions.

Third house: Optimism and enthusiasm are evident in all the native's thoughts, speech and communication. Brothers and sisters are fortunate for the native. The native manages to live in prosperous surroundings.

Fourth house: the native comes from a fortunate background, and there are always conditions of abundance and reason to be thankful around the home.

Fifth house: This is a very favorable indication for profit from gamble and speculations; however the native may just naturally be successful in taking all kinds of chances, not just the chances of sport. The native's relations with children are fruitful and rewarding.

Sixth house: Jupiter brings favorable working conditions and profitable satisfactions from performing one's daily duties and obligations. The native profits from his vocation and through his fellow workers. He should be reasonably well honored materially for his services on behalf of others and should receive a title to indicate this.

Seventh house: The native is drawn to optimistic, outgoing people, and they tend to bring prosperity to the native. The material profits in life come through others.

Eighth house: Important changes in the native's life invariably turn out to be an improvement. There is some indication of inheritance or gain from property formerly belonging to others.

Ninth house: The native enthusiastically embraces doctrines and principles that extend his own thinking and justify his principles. Publishing and advertising are favored for success.

Tenth house: The native is assured of some degree of success and rise in position. There is ambition for fame and some probability of achievement in this direction.

Eleventh house: Success in dealing with groups is indicated, and the native has a fortunate way of lending his enthusiasm to collective ideals shared by others. This is a good position for a successful politician or spokesman for the people.

Twelfth house: the native's best success is acknowledged only privately by those in trouble whom he has helped in the possible reorientation of their spiritual values. Their protection may, in time of his need, help shield him materially from the world. The native feels richly rewarded in his spiritual evaluations, and this in turn endows his subconscious motivations in all matters with a sense of rightness.

In sowing the seeds to reap the harvest that Jupiter promises, the native is encouraged and directed in his purpose by the affairs of the Sagittarius house. The native should use this source of abundance to strengthen the moral purpose of the house related to the Jupiter house by the sign on the cusp. This suggests the use for which the abundance is given.

For comments on the tempo of Jupiter according to the sign in which it falls see Chapter 22, page 332.

Jupiter is aided in its sense of expansion and sense of right from wrong by those planets that it aspects by soft angle. It is forced to adjust its natural attitudes by those planets that it aspects by hard angle. It is naturally more effective when related to planets that get things done like the Sun, Mars and Saturn rather than the friendly persuasion of other planets that stand in the background.

URANUS IN YOUR HOROSCOPE

Uranus in your horoscope shows where you are likely to be the most independent and depart most obviously from the conventional way of doing things. The position of Uranus shows where you need to break away and cut out on your own because you strongly feel in this matter that you alone know what is best for yourself. If you are ever going to make a mark for individual and independent effort, you must do it in the area where you find Uranus. Uranus in some cases also shows the potentiality of genius, which is rare. It more often shows an indication of eccentricity, which is out of step with everybody else. Uranus makes itself felt by a marked deviation of movement or direction. Since any departure or break from the normal attracts attention to itself, the native must be prepared to defend himself, or his position in this area of life, if he wants to maintain his freedom of choice and the validity of his individual effort. The public is quick to close ranks against individual positions that threaten its solidarity. Usually the native is initially regarded as eccentric and ignored in this matter. If the native, however, persists and shows merit, circumstances seem to stack up against him until he can achieve a permanent breakthrough and get clear ahead of the crowd. Only time can prove the genius (or impossibility) of his action or work. There is something about the Uranian impulse against which we are helpless. It tends to push us unexpectedly into situations without preparation. Undoubtedly, if changes have to be made, sometimes this is the only way they can ever come about.

If Uranus, as ruler of Aquarius, relates to your Sun, Moon or ascendant, then Uranus is particularly important for you. The keynote for the ego, emotions or personality, is independence based on original insight. If your Sun is in Aquarius, then eccentricity becomes you and Uranus shows how this independence can conceivably be turned constructively into genius. If your Moon is in Aquarius, then chaotic emotions can best be focused in the direction which Uranus provides. If your ascendant is in Aquarius, then you need to know in what direction you can use your genius (such as it is) most effectively in the area that is tailor-made for your type of personality.

The disruptive force of Uranus is felt when in the:

First house: through the personality of the native himself. The native is eccentric and initiates sudden and erratic departures from ordinary channels of behavior. Most people readily note this unusual aspect in his nature and treat him accordingly. This usually does not deter him in the least from going his own way, since he is continually confronted with unusual challenges from his immediate environment that specifically call for just such behavior.

Second house: by upsetting the native's source of supply or state of his possessions. This position of Uranus is generally unfavorable since it places control of the earning powers in the hands of erratic forces over which he has little control no matter what he may feel he has rightfully earned. The presence of Uranus always indicates conditions over which the native has little control. The effect is the sweep or force of circumstances.

Third house: by unusual thoughts. The native's thinking follows the eccentric dictates of Uranus, and this sometimes leads to a very confused state of mind, which may however prove to be brilliant on one special subject or mental quirk.

Fourth house: by creating an odd state of subjectivity. The

eccentricity in one's life comes from one's background and natural heritage. If he is a nut, he comes by it naturally. One or both of the parents also share some eccentric quality. Uranus affects the native's sense of security in some way, usually in an upsetting manner. The native can devise ingenious programs with which to seek objectives. They may sound impractical in some ways, but they can at the same time achieve some astounding results if carried far enough.

Fifth house: by unusual attitudes toward pleasures, love-making, relations to offspring and creative pursuits. The element of unconventionality is present in all attitudes toward romance, sexual love-making and how to impress others with the individuality of your creative ego. The key word in all of these areas tends to be "anything goes."

Sixth house: by unusual conditions in the vocation. The everyday affairs of job, duties and health matters all are subject to sudden and drastic changes. The native seeks unusual employment. Also, the native suddenly takes up jobs and just as suddenly leaves them. Job-wise he tends to be here today and gone tomorrow, almost as though he had never been there at all even though he may have worked for years in one place. When something in this department is over, it always ends abruptly, even harshly.

Seventh house: by unusual relationships with the public. The native experiences unusual reactions from others—in general—seemingly unprovoked and generally unaccountable. The native, without being conscious of the fact, seeks unusual types in the crowd, multiplying these erratic relationships. All contact with outsiders tends to sweep the native off his feet, as though he were subject to every caprice in human nature. His type attracts this, and he contributes to it by his unusual attitude toward others.

Eighth house: sudden and drastic changes in the native's life. The native's important changes in life are always accompanied by unusual conditions, sudden upheavals and far-sweeping and unexpected results, generally beyond anything foreseen in the beginning. The native is also subject to sweeping passions of a sexual nature which have far-flung consequences. There will be many drastic changes in the native's life and dangerous exposures to life and property, but the native is advised to maintain a very independent and constructive attitude toward such matters. Although drastic at the time, the new life that is finally ushered in is potentially better than what was swept out of his life.

Ninth house: by adherence to unusual beliefs, principles and codes of thinking. The native has difficulty in fitting his ideas in with most beliefs already established or organized by others. This position indicates being mentally out of step in most areas of higher learning. Foreign contacts or travel produce astonishing results. The native is drawn to or tries to publicize organizations that are considered by ordinary people to be far out or beyond belief.

Tenth house: by unique goals that also impose unusual qualifications and strange conditions. The native is naturally drawn to unconventional matters that brand him as an eccentric of some kind. He must pursue these matters with much independence of thought. Time may eventually indicate that what he stood for has much merit and his interest was simply ahead of his time. He may have the satisfaction of being a pioneer in some matter, and it is possible that by some he may be acknowledged as a genius. The chances of his insights achieving the status they may deserve is highly problematical—depending a great deal on the condition of Uranus itself (by aspect), the Aquarius house and the sign and ruler on the cusp of the Uranus house (in this case the tenth).

Eleventh house: by unusual friendships. The native seeks unusual friendships and also experiences unusual reactions from those he selects as sympathetic comrades. Since the keynote of the native's best friends and that of himself toward them is one of extreme independence in attitude and behavior, this is bound to create unique relationships. Among them and between them anything goes.

Twelfth house: by devastating flashes of insight about inner motivations. This is generally an unfortunate position for Uranus because the native will suddenly be confronted with drastic conditions, which he must be subconsciously prepared for. The ordinary defenses in life will do him no good here. The native's inner life will be considerably upset from time to time, and the native will need a great deal of resources and inner fortitude to meet some severe test. Also, the uncontrollable and unpredictable quality of Uranus is in the twelfth house magnified by lying hidden under the surface or coming from behind or from the quarter least suspected and invariably at a time when one is least prepared to meet it effectively. Misfortunes may seem to compound other misfortunes in a way that is overwhelming.

For comments on the tempo of Uranus according to the sign in which it falls see Chapter 22, page 332.

In spite of the drastic and upsetting effect that Uranus brings, the native will be fortified and somewhat prepared for it from the direction of the Aquarius house. Such support is more or less denied when Uranus is in the Aquarius house. Circumstances are then completely taken out of the native's hands. He may unwittingly contribute to this, but he can't help himself. The probable outcome of the Uranian independence is suggested by the house where the ruler of the cusp of the Uranus house is found. Again this is in the hands of fate itself when Uranus is in the Aquarius house. In such cases the sole answer lies with the aspect condition of Uranus.

Uranus is encouraged by soft-angle aspects and forced to contain or modify itself (if possible) by hard angles. For more details on this see Chapter 9.

PLUTO IN YOUR HOROSCOPE

Pluto in your horoscope shows where you will most strongly resist conditions as you find them and will bend every effort (including violent revolt—if necessary) to bring into being conditions as you feel they should be. The Pluto nature always involves two sides: a destructive tearing down to get rid of outmoded forms—and a pointing toward a new potential of which Pluto only paves the way. The process is mutation, transition, death and rebirth. The method is invariably drastic and violent. The native would have to be very intimately keyed to Pluto, however, in order for him to sense this on a personal level. This would mean close hard angles to the Sun, Mars or Saturn. Usually the Pluto element manifests in our lives only as a more generalized social or political trend.

If Pluto, as ruler of Scorpio, relates to your Sun, Moon or ascendant then Pluto is ultimately keyed to you through the ego, emotions or personality image. The keynote is drastic upheaval and the necessity of starting changes from the bottom up. If your Sun is in Scorpio, then all social change and political events take on a personal implication in your affairs. The location of Pluto shows you where you can contribute to the future as you see it. If your Moon is in Scorpio, then your emotional upheavals need objectives where Pluto can focus your feelings. If your ascendant is in Scorpio, Pluto will show you how to control the volatile situation you feel is boiling all around you. You need to feel that your sense of identity becomes pivotal to instrumenting significant change rather than being trampled to death by the crowd as they sense the downfall of their situation.

The native's sense of revolt (such as it may be) is centered in the horoscope by the house position of Pluto. If Pluto is in the:

First house: the revolt is within the native as evident in his personality, which others can notice. The native is regarded as a potential revolutionary whether he is actively engaged in bomb throwing or not. Others respond to him on the surface as a reactionary malcontent, and he is forced to be on guard to protect himself.

Second house: the native wants to rebel in the worst way against the state of his financial affairs, which are sometimes reduced to rock bottom. The native sees a certain amount of injustice in this. In trying to make headway he tends to wipe out everything that went before to start with a clean slate. Sometimes it seems expedient that he is almost forced to take from others to supply his own needs. This seems justified at the time. In starting from scratch his material possessions tend to get eliminated, as though they were an added burden rather than a potential source of wealth. The Pluto impulse is always justified at the time in terms of the situation which forces the individual to drastic adjustments. Since Pluto always indicates two sides, the native should have several potential sources of earning money or two attitudes toward his possessions. There is a source of income realizable from some aspect of social change or conditions of the times.

Third house: the revolutionary tendencies come out in speech and general communication, since the native feels driven to drastic outbursts.

Fourth house: the native turns against his background and heritage and to some extent his family as the most immediate candidates for desired change. He tends to organize his subjective self in terms of the most desirable technique around the principles of "down with the old and on with the new."

Fifth house: the native experiences a violent need to create entirely new idioms as an extension of the creative individual. The ordinary conceptions most easily recognized by average people seem to the native totally unsuited for the creative message which he feels compelled to express. Romantic love attachments and their accompanied sexual expression especially come up for drastic overhaul. Iconoclasm becomes the slogan for all fifth-house matters, including children and their affairs.

Sixth house: the native turns his sense of needed reform against the duties and obligations that men usually assume in daily routine. The problems of labor in general and social reform in particular all are of interest. Radical attitudes about health matters are also evident. The native's own health is a matter of some concern because apparently very drastic methods are sometimes necessary to put it back in shape again.

Seventh house: the native tends to focus his attention on individuals whom he feels either favor or retard the progressive programs that he regards as necessary. This can lead to joint cooperative efforts with some people and open dispute and drastic reactions with others. Some kind of war is inevitable. This native is initially led or swept into social involvement by others to whom he is instinctively attracted. The native has dual attitudes toward other individuals and they in turn show two sides to him.

Eighth house: the native sees large-scale drastic change to be necessary and desirable as the only way to give birth to that which "must be." He is a born undercover agent who works best on secret and hidden assignments. Death is considered incidental (and somewhat unavoidable) to one's dedicated mission. If not the whole of him, at least some part of his nature has to die in order to face his emergencies in life.

Ninth house: the native's higher mental faculties are devoted to publishing, advertising or promoting those revolutionary ideas that are already channeled into movements and institutions formed for this purpose. These established institutions are considered natural positions from which to launch a reactionary attack.

Tenth house: the native's conscious goal is of a revolutionary nature. He will take by force if necessary to establish his position and authority over others. He is also likely to run into some fierce opposition from those in control, who will try and obliterate him if necessary. Those in authority seem particularly oppressive and intolerable to the native and his goals.

Eleventh house: the native joins with others of similar sympathies in order to put over their program, which is based on a desired new order. The native is naturally drawn to fellow revolutionaries for friends, but he is also likely to suffer drastic experiences through these same friends. Friendship among these comrades is considered expendable when necessary.

Twelfth house: the native's concern centers on those unfortunates who have been victimized by social injustices, which the native will feel as acutely as though experienced by himself. The focus is to give moral and spiritual support or to assist in intrigues rather than to suffer open confrontation with the roots of the evil. The native possesses a unique philosophy that enables him to see beyond the evils of the present, but he lends background assistance to any values that will rectify this sorrowful situation. When it comes to inner or subconscious motivations, the native has a dual or split conception even of himself (whether he recognizes or admits to this or not). This makes for some unfortunate mixup in his own affairs since he can conceivably support two programs at the same time that are contradictory to each other. What is needed in the subconscious is to strip things down to their base essentials and get the matter refunded on a more realistic basis. Sometimes a whole new life is needed to reflect these violent adjustments.

For comments on the tempo of Pluto according to the sign in which it falls see Chapter 22, page 332.

The native is supported and encouraged in this sense of rebellion by the affairs and persons of his Scorpio house. The ultimate outcome for the native of these attitudes is suggested by the affairs and persons of the house where the ruler of the Pluto house is found.

The forces that dynamically key Pluto to other elements in the native's character are shown by the hard angles which it makes. These are much more effective when keyed to the planets that get things done, the Sun, Mars and Saturn. Of less importance are the emotionally sympathetic ties shown by the soft angles. For more details on this see Chapter 9.

Chapter 9

ASPECTS BETWEEN PLANETS

Planets are considered to be in active contact when they stand at certain respective distances from each other. These certain points of contact are called ASPECTS. This angular distance is measured in degrees of the zodiac, the standard reference for all measurements in astrology. The effective points at which contact is made between planets are apparently determined by or follow certain scientific laws relating to other bodies or planes of electromagnetic force. L. Edward Johndro, a mathematician, physicist and radio engineer who later devoted his scientific background to the field of astrology, determined that the key relationship of bodies in electromagnetic contact was 15° or multiples thereof.

The primary aspects considered in this book are the spatial distances of 0° (together, called the CONJUNCTION), 60° apart (called the SEXTILE), 90° apart (called the SQUARE), 120° apart (called the TRINE), and 180° apart (called the OPPOSITION).

The difference or consequent effect of these various aspects is a matter of some controversy among astrologers. Some group the aspects into good or bad. Others feel the so-called bad aspects are the only ones worth considering and the so-called good aspects are relatively worthless in judging the horoscope.

The nature of the planets as elements or symbols of force are neither positive nor negative, masculine nor feminine, fortunate nor unfortunate. It is the position of the planets (at any moment of time) IN SIGNS that makes them seem in fortunate or unfortunate condition.

The same should be said in judging aspects between planets. It is incorrect to call certain aspects arbitrarily good or bad. The effect of aspects should be the combined nature of the planets acting in relationship. Whether this result tends to operate in a positive, constructive manner or a negative, destructive manner should be determined from the overall JUDGMENT of the horoscope, which establishes the character of the native. Those natives of sound character would tend to turn all aspects to advantage, while those of unsound character would tend to turn all aspects to disadvantage.

Perhaps a better way to approach aspects is to regard all HARD-ANGLE ASPECTS (conjunction, square and opposition) as A COMBINATION OF TWO OR MORE QUALITIES WITH ATTENDANT PROBLEMS INVOLVED.

SOFT-ANGLE ASPECTS (the sextile and trine) should be regarded as A COMBINATION OF TWO OR MORE QUALITIES THAT GENERALLY DO NOT CREATE ATTENDANT PROBLEMS.

HARD-ANGLE ASPECTS ARE PUT INTO EFFECTIVE OPERATION WITH DIFFICULTY. It takes more effort to operate with difficulty. Overcoming difficulty is said to develop character.

SOFT-ANGLE ASPECTS COOPERATE WITH EASE. It is a matter of luck to have things fall into place with comparative ease. However, too much such luck or good fortune without a struggle weakens the character.

Delineation of aspects between planets in this book will be confined to hard- and soft-angle aspects. The conjunction that is technically an angle of zero degrees (or no angle at all) is included under the category of hard angle because its effect belongs in the same group as the square and the opposition—that is, the effect is forcing. For all practical purposes the distinctions (if there are any) or the differences (which are subtle) within these groups serve no useful purpose. In fact there is some question as to whether such subtle differences as might be considered are genuinely effective. The respected research of certain astrological study groups has confirmed this to be true. Certainly there is no universality that certain aspects cause only certain results to the exclusion of any other. It was, they found, to be more significant that a relationship by ANY aspect occurred at the time of important events. They also found that unfortunate events occurred just as often under so-called good aspects as they did under bad and vice versa.

HARD-ANGLE ASPECTS ARE ALL FORCING.

THE CONJUNCTION: When two or more planets are together in the conjunction, the angular distance between them would be zero degrees. This relationship should be considered the strongest of all possible aspects. The result is to COUPLE the planetary forces together for better or worse. The involvement is absolute. There is no consideration possible of the one quality without the other. The outcome would depend on the individual natures of the planets that are joined together.

THE SQUARE: When two or more planets are in square, the angular distance between them would be 90°. THE ACTION OF ONE PLANET ALWAYS FORCES AN ACTION OR REACTION IN THE OTHER. The planets tend to work at cross-purposes but must somehow be forced to work in unison.

THE OPPOSITION: When two or more planets are in opposition, they are opposite to each other and the angular distance between them would be 180°. THE ACTION OF ONE PLANET ALWAYS BLOCKS THE ACTION OF THE OTHER. The planets tend to oppose each other but must also be forced to work in some form of unison.

SOFT-ANGLE ASPECTS ENCOURAGE EACH OTHER BUT DO NOT COMPEL ACTION. It is the forcing to action that makes the hard angles more effective in judging the character than the soft angles. Under soft angles, the action of one planet makes it easy for the action of the other IF THEY WANT TO ACT AT ALL. The difference in effect between the sextile and the trine is very slight. The trine is perhaps a bit easier (therefore said to be luckier).

THE SEXTILE: When the angular distance between two or more planets is 60°. This is a mild relationship said to offer opportunities but not without some effort on the native's part. In other words he can project these two qualities in his nature, if he feels like it, but not without some effort.

THE TRINE: When the angular distance between two or more planets is 120°. This is a relationship said to offer opportunities without any effort on the native's part. The effect is said to be lucky because the two qualities fall together (if necessary) without any effort or resistance between them.

It is well at this point to mention what is known as the ORB of influence or the allowable variation from exact aspect. Astrologers, in practice, differ widely on this point. Some allow a very wide margin, particularly with the Sun and Moon. I STRONGLY RECOMMEND A VERY CLOSE ORB. On the conjunction allow only 4° — possibly 6° involving the Sun. The justification for more allowance with the Sun is that the Sun's power is so strong that it draws planets into its orb. All other aspects should be restricted to no more than 3 or 4°. The closer the orb, the stronger the effect of the aspect in operation.

Since astrology is a system so complex and intricate, in order to make any sense out of it IN THE BEGINNING it is essential to stick to a few simple basic rules BEFORE you try to branch out and include the factors of lesser importance. In this book I try to emphasize only the PRIMARY CONSIDERATIONS so that you will be less likely to get off the track.

If there is any truth in astrological anaylsis at all, THE PRIMARY CONSIDERATIONS MUST ACCOUNT FOR THE GENERAL PICTURE OR THE OVERALL STRUCTURE. The secondary considerations (many of which are not taken up in this book at all) can provide only more details or further substantiation of the MAIN POSITION. No secondary consideration can substantially change the basic picture or else you have misjudged the primary factors.

When considering aspects, always bear in mind the following: The effect of the HARD-ANGLE ASPECTS is to FORCE CERTAIN QUALITIES TOGETHER, which invariably tends to arouse other people in a negative reaction AGAINST THE NATIVE.

Nevertheless, the native is still forced in this manner and MUST ACCEPT IT AND MAKE THE BEST OF IT REGARDLESS OF THE REACTION THIS CAUSES.

Many astrologers explain hard-angle aspects (which they call bad aspects) in such a way that one might suppose the native would be best advised to drop the pattern altogether because of the reaction invoked. This is nonsense. We are what we are, and whether the native wants to ignore it or not, CIRCUMSTANCES WILL ALWAYS FORCE THE NATIVE BACK INTO JUST THAT POSITION THAT IS NEEDED TO COUNTERBALANCE THIS SUPPOSEDLY UNFAVORABLE REACTION.

The solution comes not from CEASING TO BE WHAT ONE IS nor by exercising the "combined quality" in such a way that a naturally favorable reaction is received. That would only be possible through a soft angle, and YOU CAN'T TURN HARD ANGLES INTO SOFT ANGLES by applying them in a different manner. The only solution comes from accepting THE CONSEQUENCES of your real intent, making the best of it and going about your business regardless of what other people say or do.

You are in this life to develop your unique destiny no matter where it leads you.

The lesson inherent in hard-angle aspects is to HARD-NOSE yourself into being yourself, regardless of other people's opinions. If you are true to yourself, the others can't really stop you. But with hard angles others will always give you a hard time on the matter.

ASPECTS TO THE SUN

SUN-MOON

HARD ANGLE: Since the Sun (ego) is the polar magnetic opposite of the Moon (emotions), as well as symbolizing the typically masculine vs. feminine qualities, any hard-angle aspect emphasizes the difficulty of the two qualities WITHIN the native. The projection or gratification of the one always seems to be at the expense of the other. The native is always aware that half of himself seems to be sacrificed for the other half. This can be a severe test of character accompanied by much inner turmoil with a frequently unfortunate effect on health and vitality.

SOFT ANGLE: The ego and emotions tend to work easily together. Each becomes the complement rather than the contestant of the other. This promotes a general overall harmony, which is reflected throughout the entire system.

SUN-MERCURY

Mercury is never more than 28° ahead or behind the Sun in motion. Thus the only effective aspect that Mercury makes to the Sun is the close conjunction. Mercury is perhaps better situated when making no aspect to the Sun. This allows for some outside objectivity in the thinking.

HARD ANGLE: The ego experiences difficulty in expressing what it really wants. The native tends to think with his ego. There may be some disparity between what one thinks and what one ends up doing. The ego is forced to think about what it wants, which is an interruption of the will.

SUN-SATURN

HARD ANGLE: Saturn hardens the ego along lines that are fixed, rigid, inflexible, serious, conservative, practical and disciplined. There is a struggle within the self about all these matters when they come in conflict with the will, so others tend to suffer while the native goes about getting himself in hand.

SOFT ANGLE: The native adapts more easily to incorporating all the above qualities of Saturn into his general practices and methods. The ego does not resent the disciplines imposed by Saturn.

SUN-MARS

HARD ANGLE: Mars heightens the impulsive, aggressive, competitive and sensory aspects of the ego, which forces the native to override other people in a way that causes them to resist or fight back.

SOFT ANGLE: Even though the native uses all the above tactics, they do not seem to offend people or cause them to retaliate or backfire against the native. This is because the native was not forced to do things. He was able to act this way when opportunity permitted, or else he generally didn't do it at all. But here we see the ideal or typical difference between the strength of hard angles and the weakness of soft angles. Under the hard angle the native is forced and action results. Under the soft angle the native is not forced, and unless opportunities are ideal (which may not be frequent), no action is accomplished.

SUN-VENUS

HARD ANGLE: The Venus qualities of socializing, harmonizing, smoothing over, protecting and coloring up are recognized to be somehow essential to the native's projection of himself, yet they tend not to have the same effect in which they were intended. However the native is forced by circumstances to act this way whether he feels like it or not.

SOFT ANGLE: The native easily incorporates all the above attributes in his manner and approach (when he feels like it), which smooths all interpersonal relations. Because the native isn't forced, he only projects himself when he feels like it, which is to say in a socializing, pleasing manner. The result is that he projects himself less.

SUN-NEPTUNE

HARD ANGLE: The Neptune qualities of idealization, inspiration, extended vision and extrasensory perception are strong when in hard angle to the ego-force or will power, although they seem at times to get in the way of the native's presentation of himself. This has to do with the nature of the self and the nature of ideals. Here the native is forced to present the two together. Most people (because they are not keyed to the ideality of Neptune) tend to react initially to the side of Neptune qualities which they see as delusion, intrigue, insincerity or fraud. Unfortunate as this may be, in some cases the native has to stand up to this and bring others over to his position plus the positive side of Neptune, which stands for ideals and inspiration and spiritual values. The native simply has to outride the negative reactions and stand on positive idealism.

SOFT ANGLE: The native is able to incorporate the better side of the Neptune quality with a more immediate inspirational effect. This is because he is not forced to present himself inspirationally, so he is able to bide his time until such opportunities present themselves when this can be done more effectively, as above. In the meantime the native is primarily engaged in those presentations of himself that may have been forced on him by any hard angles to the Sun.

SUN-JUPITER

HARD ANGLE: The Jupiter qualities of optimism, expansive vision, eternal hope and constructive uplift seem to sit on the native in an unnatural fashion, which forces him to justify or prove the sincerity of his intent.

SOFT ANGLE: The native combines the above qualities in his nature (on occasion when he feels like it) so naturally that it readily convinces others.

SUN-PLUTO

HARD ANGLE: The native is forced to incorporate the Pluto qualities of revolution, drastic reform, instigation of violent changes and disruption of outmoded conditions in such a manner that he faces constant resistance on all levels to everything that he tries to do in these directions.

SOFT ANGLE: The native still (on special occasions when he feels like it) incorporates all the above qualities in his approach and generally escapes the worst consequences which might be directed against him personally. Because he is not forced into these attitudes by hard angles, he can incorporate them or leave them out as he chooses. Under hard angle it always has to be Sun-Pluto; under soft angle only sometimes or practically never if the consequences could be turned against the native.

SUN-URANUS

HARD ANGLE: The native is forced to step out of line, away from the crowd, in order to tune to his special wavelength, which gives him an independent perspective. This special viewpoint is generally ahead of its time because of its tolerance and exceptionally broad-based values which ordinary people might consider unconventional, eccentric and peculiar.

SOFT ANGLE: The native, on occasion when he feels like it, finds himself acting in an unusual manner, which does not seem to attract attention to himself in a negative way.

ASPECTS TO THE MOON

MOON-MERCURY

HARD ANGLE: The native is forced to consider constantly his emotional reactions from a detached mental standpoint, as though he were an outsider passing judgment on himself. The responsive emotions of the Moon here are fettered or shackled with a mental reaction, at times unwelcome, but always necessary. The native always has to ask himself what he thinks about his feelings. He can't feel spontaneously without first reviewing his mental reactions.

SOFT ANGLE: The native's emotional nature seems a natural outgrowth and consequences of correct or fortunate mental attitudes. When he feels like it, his feelings are thoughtful or his thoughts are full of emotion, but he can feel something independently of mental reactions or think something independently of his emotions.

MOON-SATURN

HARD ANGLE: The native's emotional nature is forced to restrain itself for more serious considerations, which tend to harden and discipline the emotions out of proportion to their normal feelings. Other people consider or experience the native as emotionally cool, hard and unsympathetic.

SOFT ANGLE: The native, when he wants to, can cool his emotions and hold them in disciplined control so that he is fully aware of all the practical implications involved. He will at times actually enjoy a certain amount of emotional denial. He finds it easy to feel favorable toward difficult efforts required to get things done.

MOON-MARS

HARD ANGLE: The native's emotional nature is forced to feel aggressive, competitive and hot-tempered, which invokes unfavorable reactions. Circumstances invariably force the native to strong feelings. He can seldom, if ever, feel dispassionate about anything. It is either a strong, hot feeling or none at all.

SOFT ANGLE: The native's emotional nature can quickly rise to heated fits of passion when he wants to, or he can cool it and let it pass. He likes to feel heated about things but doesn't believe it is always necessary to feel this way. The native is generally admired for his emotional sense of competition and aggressive excitability.

MOON-VENUS

HARD ANGLE: The native is forced to compromise his emotional attitudes for social purposes or to better engage the effective co-operation of others. The native realizes the desirability of social cooperation but is frequently unwilling to compromise his feelings for that purpose. However the native has talent for putting himself in contact with others, even though public sentiments invariably tend at first to run against him.

SOFT ANGLE: The native easily adapts his own emotional requirements to those expected of him by others with whom he is in social contact. He seldom, if ever, finds it difficult to adjust emotionally to social requirements.

MOON-NEPTUNE

HARD ANGLE: The native finds it difficult to adjust emotionally to inspirational attitudes that he feels tend to lead him astray rather than lead him on to higher things. Yet he is constantly challenged to become or feel himself to be a better self in spite of many false starts. Eventually this leads to a more realistic view of emotional inspiration which is bound to be workable. Emotionally he has to feel inspirational or it won't satisfy him emotionally.

SOFT ANGLE: The emotions, when he feels like it, lend themselves almost too readily to any sort of inspirational catchall. This doesn't earn the native certain misunderstandings about his emotional idealism; rather they tend to peter out or dissolve for lack of real nourishment. The soft angle simply does not provide the emotions with the constant source of inspirational raw material that the hard angles would do. Also, feeling inspirationally only when you want to or when the occasion seems to permit it doesn't supply the test reactions that would insure that one's feelings were sincerely inspirational as opposed to being flights of private fancy.

MOON-JUPITER

HARD ANGLE: The native's emotions are challenged for some sort of balancing factor between real and unreal factors, material and spiritual matters, common sense and high-flown theories of moral uplift. The difficulty arises when the native's emotional focus tends to personalize itself rather than to consider the wider horizons and broader potential in the outside world. The native is forced to place his feelings on a higher plane of reference than his own gratifications.

The problem here is not only to feel but to feel about things in the right way rather than a wrong way. The balance of Jupiter introduces this concept of right and wrong to an otherwise personal sense of emotional gratification.

SOFT ANGLE: The native's emotions, when they want to, can reach out to broader horizons, which may or may not put him out of his normal depth. The emotions are diffused with expansive longings (sometimes unattainable) which are easily justified. If the native were forced to do this all the time, whenever he reacted emotionally to anything, he would eventually establish a sense of balance in his emotional perspective.

MOON-PLUTO

HARD ANGLE: The native's feelings are challenged by the necessities for improvement or change in surrounding conditions. The native's feelings are given to violent upheavals against his wishes because he cannot resist the wider implications impinging upon his sensibilities. Emotionally he is forced to consider the underside of situations and the degree to which possible change is indicated. This supercharges the feelings with psychic forces that make the native acutely aware of the spiritual responsibility of his emotional reactions.

SOFT ANGLE: The native's feelings are easily drawn to unfavorable conditions in the world around him that call out for correction and sympathy. The native is emotionally more sympathetic to unfavorable conditions but is less prepared in the long run actually to do something about them beyond extending his heartfelt sympathy.

MOON-URANUS

HARD ANGLE: The native's emotions are continually thrown out of joint by some sudden factor that he overlooked in his efforts to effect an independently unique approach. After many deep regrets on the erratic outcome of his independent, if not to say neurotic, behavior the native comes to restrict his independence of sympathy to the more outstanding potentialities. The native is forced to feel different from others. What he must learn to accept is the consequence of this independence.

SOFT ANGLE: The native all too easily is encouraged to emote in an erratic and unconventional manner. This may give him personal gratifications, but they are less likely to lead to constructive utilization of unique insights that he feels but may not wholly believe.

ASPECTS TO MERCURY

MERCURY-SATURN

HARD ANGLE: The native's thinking is restricted to practical solutions on serious subjects, which all tend to have material objectives. Whenever his thinking gets out of this mold or pattern, difficulties arise and then the native is forced backward. The native is forced to discipline his thoughts and think in absolutely realistic and factual terms.

SOFT ANGLE: The native naturally leans to more serious subjects and easily disciplines himself to some sort of scientific approach or laboratorylike analysis on even simple matters. The serious cast to the thought patterns is considered more important than the seriousness of the content. The native likes to think about frustrating situations and conditions, which restrict the individual rather than release him for lighter tasks.

MERCURY-MARS

HARD ANGLE: The native is prone to explosive expressions, which startle others and get their guard up for immediate defense. The native invariably uses harsh tactics in springing his objectives, but this very shock treatment is essential for some important purpose that the native finally comes to recognize. In the meantime the fights and repercussions make the native a mental fighter. The native is forced to seek mental advantages over his competition. He must accept the consequences and advantages of this attitude.

SOFT ANGLE: The native is a little more diplomatic in his use of aggressive expressions, which still have shock treatment effect. But the native uses this technique only when he wants to or feels the confronting situation will accept it. He is less likely to sharpen this technique to its highest since he does not experience or test it on all occasions. As a perfected battle weapon it would need more test reactions to guide him than just those of favorable response.

MERCURY-VENUS

HARD ANGLE: The native speaks first and then has cause to rephrase himself in more soothing, pleasing terms, initially killing the best effect of either. Eventually he should learn that the two must be indulgently styled from the beginning and thus he develops an effective mode of expression which properly conveys the sentiments he is forced to express. The native is forced to tone down his style of communication. What he thinks and the style in which it is expressed must be pleasantly combined.

SOFT ANGLE: The native is given to sweet, soothing speech, thoughts and expressions, which are generally pleasing but apt to be forgotten soon. Flattery seldom has the same lasting impression as truthful comments.

MERCURY-NEPTUNE

HARD ANGLE: The native resists a desired inspirational quality in his expression or else resorts to a phony jargon that fools no one but himself. After much trial and error he learns to combine the two in such a way that the more desirable and inspirational effects of Neptune are pleasingly combined in a style of thought and expression. The native is forced to think inspirationally. Since most people aren't keyed to Neptune, they may regard his expression as phony in some way. The native must accept this reaction and go ahead in his own style, trying to eliminate the vagueness or unreal qualities and accent the true ideals that Neptune suggests.

SOFT ANGLE: The native's thoughts wander in unusual channels not easily followed or understood by others. There is much inclination to other-worldly attitudes and high-flown flights of imagination of a mystical nature. The native is less likely to bring this down to practical application or sound idealism because he primarily indulges himself for his own gratification. He is not forced by circumstances to come to terms with the real and the phony side of Neptune.

MERCURY-JUPITER

HARD ANGLE: The native finds it difficult to think expansively and at the same time keep to some kind of personal orientation that pleases him. Whenever his thoughts take flight, they tend to get out of balance and just shoot aimlessly for the wild blue yonder. Eventually through some sort of compromise (because he is jerked back to reality often enough) the native learns to formulate his own position and at the same time align himself with progressive, forward movements in established channels of thoughts.

SOFT ANGLE: The native's thoughts easily seek flight and to some extent sound impressive enough, so he is not reminded or corrected or learns to see for himself how ungrounded or totally without reason some of his thinking might be. The main thing in this pattern is that his style impresses others—almost too easily.

MERCURY-PLUTO

HARD ANGLE: The native desires to pursue his own inclinations of thinking and yet at the same time he is constantly channeled to reflect on those matters immediately around him which require violent overhaul and corrective changes from the ground up, even at the expense of certain people's thinking that stands in his way. The native is forced into progressive thinking at all times. This gives his thoughts a psychic awareness of the conditions and potentialities of change.

SOFT ANGLE: The native's thoughts naturally run to all sorts of wild and revolutionary schemes, which somehow leak out and yet do not turn the world upside down or against him. The native is less likely to get his unusually strong thought patterns behind some cause where it will do some good because he pursues these channels only when he feels like it or when opportunities present themselves that won't backfire on him. He has a way of saying any old thing (at times) and getting away with it.

MERCURY-URANUS

HARD ANGLE: The native's thinking is erratic and unconventional, yet because it gets him into unfavorable situations, he fights within himself as to whether he is right or justified in such wildly independent mental behavior. Eventually he comes to realize that he is being challenged on his independent positions just to strengthen his creative genius in this line. He has to find a way of putting things together mentally that is uniquely original.

SOFT ANGLE: The native's thinking and expression are frequently erratic, but because they don't have much effect on others, he does not learn to improve his style and self-consciously find out for himself just wherein he thinks so differently from others or how he might capitalize on some potentiality of mental genius. One needs the reaction value (both the good and the bad) provided by the hard angles to sharpen any tool one has and put it into effective operation.

That which flows too easily, erratic or otherwise, is more apt to fall on barren ground.

ASPECTS TO SATURN

SATURN-MARS

HARD ANGLE: The native is consciously pulled two ways: forward toward expansive action and backward to careful deliberation. this often builds up inner tension, which ends in some kind of an explosion or ACTION WHICH HURTS. Through endless unfortunate reactions from others the native learns to adjust this in such a manner that it becomes action that builds constructively because it is so realistic from the beginning. Anything less ends in a fizzle, which burns both the native and those around him. This is a difficult pattern to control and requires much skill to get it right finally. But this aspect is potentially one of the strongest combinations of possible planetary force. Usually this technique is perfected only late in life when it is also designed to work best. Anything connected with Saturn works this way.

SOFT ANGLE: The native's impulses easily give in to restrictive and disciplinary forces which guide his sense of security. This makes the native shrewd but also more prone to commit cruel acts on others because circumstances in his favor so often let him get away with it. One might be said here to be lucky in getting away with many petty acts that hamper or restrict others.

SATURN-VENUS

HARD ANGLE: The native's sentimental nature is hardened by his inadequacies in achieving a certain maturity of feeling. The native tends to be overly loving and then excessively harsh. Since this invokes many unfavorable reactions, the native learns to temper his sentiments until they can be expressed in a mature manner or toward a mature individual who can understand the depth and seriousness of what the native really feels. The native's sentiments for affection are forced to be realistic and serious.

SOFT ANGLE: The native's feelings easily run to matters beyond his years and are directed to older people who seem to understand better his intentions and be more gratifyingly appreciative. This tends to lead to that which is merely old and narrow rather than to uncover new depths of feeling in matters that are less easily suppressed or more rigidly fixed. Under hard angles one seeks wiser reception and not just necessarily older models.

SATURN-NEPTUNE

HARD ANGLE: This is a complex pattern involving two qualities that normally have little to do with each other. Saturn involves carefully laid plans, firm foundations, careful measurements, sound attitudes and practical material objectives. Neptune, on the other hand, suggests dissolving borders and lines of distinction, the disregard of measurements, espousing spiritual rather than material values, and introducing inspiration as the guide rather than the more limiting practical considerations. The native is challenged to combine the two in a way that makes sound principles inspirational, breathes hope into reality, redesigns the practical so that it is more adaptable and less oppressive. There is some suggestion of the art of alchemy, which was said to turn base metals into gold. Whenever the native sets out to do the practical thing, his course is directed toward something more inspirational. And whenever he sets out to do something inspirational, he is reminded of practical values. This frustration must be utilized to keep trying until he has found an ideal solution where both can be satisfied and the IDEAL WILL BE WORKABLE. The native is forced to be realistic about his ideals. This is a strong constructive key for Neptune, as it is whenever related to one of the planets that get things done like the Sun, Mars and Saturn.

SOFT ANGLE: The native is not faced with a conflict between the ideal and the practical, as he sees all practical matters as ideals and all ideals as practical. This sets him apart as one who sees more or puts more into things than others do. In short, he may make some progress, but he has lost those who might eventually widen both the practicality and the ideality of what he is working for. He moves in a closed circuit of practical ideals instead of gaining from the reaction value of objective resistance.

SATURN-JUPITER

HARD ANGLE: The native is confronted with application to expand and contract at the same time. One voice says to raise his hopes and have faith (not in spiritual value as with Neptune) but in the ideal balance which is in nature itself. And the other voice says to hold back, recheck and proceed with caution, keeping your eyes on the ground. This also tends to build up explosive reactions in the native, strangely breaking new ground in both directions at once. The native gets on firmer footing and also gains some recognition or breakthrough to higher purpose. Rewards and admission of basic considerations go hand in hand like good news and bad news, but somehow both are welcome. The native's ambivalence for going first forward in one direction and then backward in another does not earn favor with those around him. Every step forward is at the expense of a half step backward, which is a very trying and difficult way to get ahead. This can make for solid advancement however painfully slow. The native is forced to reach for reality and lift his sights at the same time.

SOFT ANGLE: Since Saturn is much tougher than Jupiter, one's expansive attitudes are usually compromised to the demands of more practical and fundamental issues. The native is accustomed to retreat and accepts it with good grace. However, the native at the same time is rather more prepared to step forward with sound procedures that invariably work rather than frustrate himself by having to retrace steps. This position is favorable but less likely to hit the "big time" because it takes the explosive setbacks to force the native over the top and way out in front as obviously a winner. For this, hard angles in the long run are better.

SATURN-PLUTO

HARD ANGLE: The native's best efforts and particularly his own sense of security are forced into matters dealing with social situations in need of change and overhaul. There is much inner debate as to how well the native feels he can afford to put his own security on the line in order to instigate social reforms that apply to or benefit many others besides himself. Ultimately the native finds he has no choice. He has to play along with the larger issues no matter what it may cost him personally. This may not ensure an altogether favorable spot for him, but it does provide a channel of application that has far more importance than just individual rights or selfish attitudes. The native is forced to bring his sense of reality to bear on the psychic necessities of change.

SOFT ANGLES: The native easily lends his work efforts to causes that some people would consider destructive or socially undesirable merely because they want change rather than the status quo. The native is less likely to innovate approaches than he is to lend practical efforts to push something already going because he is not challenged to examine his intentions or sharpen his attitudes or particularly sacrifice his sense of security for what he is engaged in. When one is challenged every step of the way, then one tends to be more cautious and to be eventually in a cause that is perhaps more sound and desirable rather than just crackpot reactionary.

SATURN-URANUS

HARD ANGLE: The native is challenged to be progressive, independent, realistic and practical at the same time. This is no small trick. The native eventually comes to see that his only chance for a fundamental breakthrough and one which affects his whole security setup is to proceed independently and fabricate for himself some ingenious approach that will answer all requirements at once. The native proceeds slowly on his own to teach himself tricks that will eventually provide some whole new approach to some matter of serious importance. The native's greatest difficulty is in getting started on his own, since others feel that he is beginning at the wrong end. He has to rely on his own intuition as to which end to start with, and this takes a great deal of independent self-assurance. The native is forced to be realistic and ingenious at the same time.

SOFT ANGLE: The native seems to get started easily doing important things in a strange manner, which allows him to get far afield and leave everyone else behind before they know what he is up to. This generally works fine as long as the native has other qualities that keep him on a sound operating level, otherwise he is apt to let things run wild and is less apt to remain sound because others do not challenge him or force him to inventory what he is doing.

ASPECTS TO MARS

MARS-VENUS

HARD ANGLE: The native has difficulty in properly satisfying his sexual love interests. He is either too physical or too sentimental. Since this is a problem to him, it takes up a considerable amount of his time and effort to find a satisfactory solution. Romantic attitudes about sexual matters dominate his motivations. He has to be forced to combine passion with the sentiments of affection. This may not seem like a problem to some people, but it is to this native.

SOFT ANGLE: Sexual love-making comes easily to the native, and he generally pleases himself and others in this matter. Consequently his activity does not take up a disproportionate part of his time or interest. He has no hangups here. This is the pattern of an active lover.

MARS-NEPTUNE

HARD ANGLE: The native's energies are diffused, deflected or perverted in some way from a physical basis to an idealistic or unreal motivation. The native acts in a strange and somewhat unnatural manner. Sexual deviation could be a problem or matter of concern. The impulse of one always forces the other into the picture. The native cannot ignore this pattern or behavior manifestation in his life or affairs. He must in some way come to terms with it so that both urges are satisfied. The native is forced to put his passions on a more spiritual plane, which at the same time denies a certain physical application.

SOFT ANGLE: The native considers it just as natural to take indirect routes of expression as direct ones. He takes either with ease. There is no psychological hangup, as there would be with hard angles. Deviation of energies comes naturally to the native. There is some suggestion of bisexuality or looking upon bisexuality as perfectly natural.

MARS-JUPITER

HARD ANGLE: The native finds it difficult to initiate action that is at the same time fair, just and takes all desirable factors into consideration. His actions lack balance and desirable intent. Because this causes him so much trouble, he finally learns to concentrate only on those activities that are productive and desirable. The native is forced in his actions to do what is traditionally right.

SOFT ANGLE: The native naturally acts in a way that seems as though it should be successful from the beginning, but the burden of the correctness in his programs rests entirely on his own faith. The native will lack the benefit of test cases and trial reactions from others on the effectiveness of his schemes by which he might better improve his methods and his batting average other than by test of his own faith. Faith is great, but test reactions and actual results are better for seeing if you are indeed using the right program With a hard angle aspect the native will see at once if he is not using the right program and be forced to make the necessary corrections. With soft angles the native's faith assumes he is right and he goes right ahead in spite of results. Reality does not force these results on him. Rash impulsive acts might tend to be right, but the results may be something else.

MARS-PLUTO

HARD ANGLE: The native has difficulty in starting anything that does not lead to trouble or blow up in his face because it is too controversial for those around him. This forces the native to be more careful and secretive about what he is up to. The native's best actions will eventually be those that clear ground for new projects or make sure that any present projects which are no longer serving their intended purpose (as he sees it) are called to task on the matter. The native is forced to action that is progressive.

SOFT ANGLE: The native easily lends his initiative and energetic forces to activities that are reactionary to public interest (public interest being invariably aligned with ongoing established institutions that cover the majority of cases). The native is more acutely aware than most of the true relationship of public policies and true human needs. This is particularly so when times have changed and the policies in effect no longer serve their original needs. This leads the way for him to instrument any desired changes as he sees it. Since these involvements generally meet with little resistance from others, he is apt to get involved with a more personal application of the changes that he sees as desirable. A hard-angle aspect would force one to the more fundamental issues at stake rather than just pleasing one's own sense for needed reform. This is a strong relationship to Pluto in either case, for it keys Pluto to one of the planets that gets things done.

MARS-URANUS

HARD ANGLE: The native has difficulty in feeling independently sure of his own ingenious approach to energetic action to get started effectively at all. Initially he moves in spurts and jerks, coming suddenly to a halt and then erratically starting off in some entirely new, unrelated direction. Eventually, due to being constantly taken to task for the seeming craziness of his behavior, he learns to trust in the "genius" of himself and act in his own unique way and the hell with what other people think. The native is forced to energize suddenly and without apparent provocation or reason. The best that can be hoped for is short-lived ingenious action.

SOFT ANGLE: The native naturally takes to odd behavior and doing crazy things that momentarily catch his interest. He is less aware of the possible lack of advantages in not concentrating on more enterprising programs rather than just doing everything differently. As usual, the challenge of the hard angle is potentially more productive of sound solutions than the initial encouragement of the soft angles, which primarily pleases the native but is less interested in results which work out with others. With the hard angles the native is forced to make all his actions ingenious. On the soft angles he need act in this way only when he feels like it.

ASPECTS TO VENUS

VENUS-NEPTUNE

HARD ANGLE: The native has difficulty in adjusting his affectionate nature and sense of love toward those objects that are genuine and at the same time truly rich in spiritual intent. Because he so often attaches himself to something that turns out to be phony or otherwise falls flat on its face, the native gradually acquires enough maturity to align himself with the really finer objects in life (people or situations). The native's sentiments are forced to concentrate on a higher plane, which at the same time denies a certain physical element of expression.

SOFT ANGLE: The native easily seeks objects for affection that inspire him; whether this is of sound spiritual substance or not, it satisfies the native. The soft-angle enticement, because it lacks the test results or concrete proof forced by the hard angle, is more apt to be less effective and somewhat more phony because the satisfaction of the native is the only yardstick used.

VENUS-JUPITER

HARD ANGLE: The native's love nature seems constantly off balance because the native does not sufficiently consider the fruitful advantages of a more moderate approach. The sentiments are challenged to be more expansive and to consider all the possibilities which are available if the native will only look for them The native continually settles for an immediate gratification only to be made aware of the poverty of his choice. This awareness soon breaks up the glow of romance, and the native is forced to look further for a better and more uplifting solution. The native's baser instincts in gratifying love sentiments are gradually purified and improved through trial and many errors. The native is forced to combine sentiment and uplift in his sense of affection.

SOFT ANGLE: The native's faith in his own infallibility to grow roses in ash heaps overly sustains him beyond the point where it is still possible to be a little more realistic about his love sentiments. The native settles for something above average but invariably less than he might otherwise attract to himself if he tried harder. The soft angle doesn't force him to try harder.

VENUS-PLUTO

HARD ANGLE: The native's love nature is challenged to include a more fundamental application such as the unsatisfied needs of unfortunate people who for one reason or another have far fewer advantages than he has. The native is so acutely aware of the pitfalls of love sentiments that he is hardly able to satisfy his own in a personal way. Broad-scale satisfaction of affectional needs becomes a hangup that the native is challenged to resolve. Eventually this has to lead to some sort of solution or extensive concentration on the matter. The native is forced to consider the sentiments of love in the same context as the psychic potentialities of rejuvenating change. One solution is to forgo personal gratifications in favor of warm feelings for persons caught in the web of social changes.

SOFT ANGLE: The native feels naturally drawn to becoming sentimentally and affectionally attached to those who are peculiarly situated in life due to some disadvantage, limitation or impairment of some kind. The native is more encouraged to satisfy his own needs for self-sacrifice than he is to do something about unfortunate people other than to use them as the object of his individual affection—that is, love them.

VENUS-URANUS

HARD ANGLE: The native has difficulty in controlling the unconventional trend of his affections and sentiments. He assumes a very independent and unique viewpoint on the matter, which sets him apart from others and involves problems. This only causes more outlandish behavior by the native. Eventually the native sees his right to satisfy his affections as related to a new attitude of behavior or moral code that must first be established so that others who share his sentiments can enjoy the same for themselves. The nature of his affections become a cause to be won for cases similar to his own. The native is forced to forgo personal gratifications of an affectional nature in favor of some form of liberation along unusual lines.

SOFT ANGLE: The native naturally satisfies his love nature in unconventional ways, which others do not seem to notice or resent. This develops a special kind of selfishness in the native's nature because the erratic behavior of his affections can hardly lead to settled satisfactions in others. This does not, however, stop the native from indulging himself as independently as he pleases.

ASPECTS TO NEPTUNE

NEPTUNE-JUPITER

HARD ANGLE: The native has difficulty in adjusting his sense of inspiration along lines that follow the sensitivity patterns of others who have indeed been faced with much the same material. The path of Jupiter is always along lines laid down by others in such a manner that a code or law is established which represents the formal mode of many contributions. Every time the native feels inspirational or divinely inspired he seems to run counter to established forms or codes of firmly entrenched bodies of belief. Eventually the native comes to see that what he senses is not fundamentally different from what certain others also sensed and thus the intensity of his idealism (because it was held back so long) makes a real contribution. The native is forced to adjust his idealism to certain principles of moral uplift.

SOFT ANGLE: The native's awareness of spiritual values easily follows the lines of expression already laid down by established sects such as religious orders. There is no awareness that what he feels is different from what others so inspired also feel. This makes for considerably less originality of vision or lacks the spiritual intensity that being out of step creates under a hard-angle aspect.

NEPTUNE-PLUTO

HARD ANGLE: The native experiences much difficulty in reconciling spiritual insights with unfortunate conditions where others seem to live in spiritual darkness. The native cannot freely pursue his ideals without considering the ideals of others and why they are not as free to feel or sense things as he may be. Eventually the native is inspired to champion attitudes that bring help to change the conditions which darken the spiritual qualities in other people's lives. The native is forced to channel his own sense of spirituality along lines of spiritual force that encourage or instrument significant sweeping social changes.

SOFT ANGLE: The native naturally identifies his own spirituality with all those unfortunates who seem lost, defeated or trapped in some way. His interest is more in sharing their burdens than in focusing his inspiration on doing something drastic about their conditions.

NEPTUNE-URANUS

HARD ANGLE: The native feels peculiarly isolated in the uniqueness or the strangely upsetting quality whenever he gives in to spiritual flights of inspiration. While he might want to pursue the matter further, an erratic uncontrollable factor in his nature seems to prevent him from getting closer to the situation. His sense of inspiration (such as it is) is swept in and out of his consciousness in an upsetting way. He becomes psychically agitated and a little queer in his be-havior. The native must somehow come to believe in the authority of his own insights and not be confused by comparing them with others who are not on his same wavelength of inspiration. The native is forced to be inspirational in ways that differ widely from ordinary channels of feeling.

SOFT ANGLE: The native's sense of ideality naturally leaps from context to context and entertains all sorts of wild propositions which the native finds exhilarating. The probability of this heightened sense of awareness leading to valid insights is considerably diminished by the erratic and uncontrollable qualities of Uranus that dash in but fade out of his attention too quickly.

ASPECTS TO JUPITER

JUPITER-PLUTO

HARD ANGLE: The native finds it difficult to adjust his aware-ness of the desirabilities of change in certain conditions around him to the coded beliefs that he also tries to follow. Apparently the principles which generally guide him do not adequately account for or provide for the wide disparagement between existing conditions and the traditions of which they are supposed to be a fair reflection. This deeply disturbs the native to the point where he makes war on his principles because they do not properly reflect conditions or needs as they really are.

SOFT ANGLE: The native naturally follows principles and codes that have reactionary or revolutionary aims. The degree to which this leads the native astray or interferes with the rest of his affairs is something else.

JUPITER-URANUS

HARD ANGLE: The native has difficulty in adjusting his sense of right and desired expansion to a unique and independent slant which he has and which others consider eccentric or unconventional. He feels in some way that his best efforts should be channeled to pro-moting his certain ingenious insights. Yet every time he tries to do something progressive in this direction he falls flat on his face. What is needed is to believe more firmly in the uniqueness and individuality of his views together with the unquestioned desirability of his right to push the matter further—a special kind of self-assurance, plus almost a religious faith.

SOFT ANGLE: The native suddenly pursues expansive programs with absolute conviction and positive action. The fact that this program may be completely out of step with others or even be headed for disaster does not turn the native from his objective. His pursuit of the unattainable is somewhat doomed to misguided faith and careless flaws.

ASPECTS TO PLUTO

PLUTO-URANUS

HARD ANGLE: The native is forced to reconcile his independent and unique slant on things with bringing about desirable changes in existing conditions which no longer reflect the needs or circumstances which gave them birth. This is an awareness of a combination of social forces which are essentially reactionary and revolutionary and at the same time suddenly and unexpectedly brought to a head in the native's affairs. The native is apt to be picked up and swept into social problems that influence the whole course of his life. The native is forced to combine his potentiality for ingenious originality with the forces and desirability of social change.

SOFT ANGLE: The native's sense of social needs naturally takes unusual forms of adjustment, which, while natural to the native, make him rather unadaptable to the rest of society. His sense of need for social change takes an unconventional form.

Chapter 10

THE SOURCE OF

MONEY IN YOUR LIFE

THE 2ND, 4TH, 5TH, 8TH, & 11TH HOUSES:
THE SIGNS ON THEIR CUSPS & PLANETS THEREIN

The native has five sources of money in life. That which he earns himself is shown by the condition of the second house. That which should come to him as part of his heritage—normally inheritance through the parents—is shown by the condition of the fourth house. That which he gains from gambling, speculation and pursuit of other pleasures is shown by the condition of the fifth house. That which comes to him by accident (as finding something) or inheritance from partners or friends is shown by the condition of the eighth house. That which comes to him by gift or honors of his profession or state of life is shown by the condition of the eleventh house.

The second, fifth, eighth, and eleventh all are fixed positions, being the inevitable consequences of some aspect of the angular houses which they follow. Earnings in the second result from capitalization of the self in the first. Speculative gains in the fifth result from assurance to take risks following the subjective acceptance of one's real security in the fourth. Inheritance in the eighth results from some relationship with others in the seventh. Benefits in the eleventh result from recognized achievement of the self in the tenth.

Whatever inheritance we receive from parental background in the fourth is somewhat different. It is considered ours from the beginning. It is not the result of something we did.

ARIES on any of the five potential money houses is not favorable for financial wealth. For one thing Aries follows Pisces—the sign of disappointment—on the angular houses. The results in Aries are likely to be starting from scratch. Since Aries is ruled by Mars, rather than gain, one is more apt to lose money by impetuous behavior. It may be frequently necessary to take by force money that is rightfully due. With Aries the identity of the personality is more important than monetary gains and the native's pride keeps him from asking even when in need. Aries on the second shows that the native's financial resources are largely up to his own initiative. He will have to fight for it. On the fourth the native comes from pioneering stock where effort counts. Even though there might be money in the family background, it is seldom available to the native when he wants it. He is instead encouraged to seek his own. On the fifth the native is naturally daring but seldom lucky in speculative ventures. All financial gambles should be avoided. On the eighth the native is considered too self-sufficient for others to provide for him. Inheritance is very doubtful. On the eleventh the native as a leader in social groups is considered above the need of assistance. Aries is too proud to accept gifts. He will turn them over to some friend whom he feels needs it more than he does.

TAURUS on any of the five potential money houses is always favorable for some kind of material benefits. Taurus is the natural money sign of the zodiac and is talented in accounting for comforts. Following the Aries personality on the angles, it should certainly have something outstanding to capitalize or fall back on. On the second it should give a natural sense of how to earn money and to look after it. On the fourth the native is brought up in a money-conscious background. This should certainly provide him with a comfortable inheritance eventually. On the fifth it would channel even one's pleasurable pursuits along profitable lines. On the eighth it suggests accountability of joint funds, which presupposes funds to be accountable for. On the eleventh it leans toward friendships with those who have means and resources.

GEMINI is not favorable for attracting money. The riches here are of the mind rather than the purse. Following the fixed sign Taurus on the angles there is not much left to extend from. On the second it means that one must seek earnings by one's wits—not the soundest of commodities or the easiest to sell. On the fourth one's heritage may be more in the mind or the way you look at it. On the fifth it is very dubious as a sure winner in gamble. The surface is apt to be more impressive than what lies underneath. On the eighth the native makes many contacts with the beyond but mainly to satisfy his curiosity. It is not favorable for material gain. On the eleventh there are many contacts with stimulating friends who mainly give each other ideas rather than material advantages.

CANCER is very fruitful wherever money is concerned. The maternal instinct has a sixth sense about financial ways to enhance security and protect the family assets. Following Gemini on the angles, which draws attention by showing off, Cancers busy themselves collecting the admission for the show. Cancer on the second makes the native sensitive to what the public needs, wants and will pay for. On the fourth the native carefully nourishes his birthright and watches it multiply. On the fifth there is little wasted effort where his sensitivity to the public ensures a market or audience even before he begins to extend himself creatively. On the eighth his sense of protection and conservation is rewarded by those he has "mothered." On the eleventh the adhesive quality so necessary in keeping groups responsive to their common sympathies is fondly acknowledged. Some people seek in friendship a parent substitute, which they will pay for.

LEO is a quasi money sign in that it presupposes an abundant treasury with which to impress others with their generosity and kingly display. The money must come from somewhere in order for Leo to spend it so lavishly, but it most often does not come from the native himself. Following the protective Cancer on the angles, their sense of security centers more in their vision of identity in preference to a sense of finance. Leo on the second makes one generous and egotistical in the way he squanders his resources. On the fourth it makes one highly conscious of the advantages of a grand-scale background. A strong sense of imperial pride will always flavor the home atmosphere, but the money to pay for it will generally have to come from some source other than the native. The fourth house reflecting the general conditions at the close of life suggests, however, that some degree of "state" is achieved and maintained in mature years. On the fifth there is far too much ego and self-assurance involved with the game of chance and taking risks to ensure even a minimum chance of gambling luck. On the eighth it is somewhat favorable for receiving inheritance by the gracious gratitude of princes. On the eleventh it is also favorable for the privilege of friendship with strong personalities who are naturally generous.

VIRGO on the whole is an unfavorable sign for productive wealth, except as an opportunity for hard work and labors of love. Following the prideful Leo on the angles, there has been little provision for material abundance since the self under Leo has been too busy creating an impressive image. Virgo on the second indicates earnings through subordinate services or routine jobs. The native is unlikely to be extravagant about money that he earns. He would in fact be very exacting, fussy and detailed. On the fourth the background is limited due to the pressure of many obligations and responsibilities. On the fifth the ego is too critical and objective to be purely speculative or find pleasure in gambling. On the eighth the native seldom meets those in life who could provide a generous inheritance. Following Leo on the seventh, those he does meet are too concerned with their own vanity to reward those who serve them well. On the eleventh one's friends are too faultfinding and thrifty to enjoy being expansive. The best one could expect from these friends is another burden to carry, or a piece of constructive advice.

LIBRA is another quasi-money sign, since it implies security, comfort and a general ease of financial conditions. However, it favors others as the source of financial resources rather than the native himself. Following the limited horizon of Virgo on the angles, the self, which is humble in spirit, is disinclined to produce riches in resources. With Libra on the second the native should be able to live on a comfortable income as a result of industrious labors, but some help would be indicated through inheritance from the parents (Sagittarius on the fourth) or the generosity of friends (Cancer on the eleventh). On the fourth some inheritance from parents might be expected, since the inherited background suggests comfort and attractive surroundings. On the fifth there is average luck in gamble and speculation but not abundantly so—certainly not enough to consistently rely on. The native is more apt to bring luck to others in this regard. On the eighth only minor inheritances are indicated which comfort but do not supply independence. On the eleventh, while very favorable for social popularity, it is doubtful that these friendships will ever be a source of gifts of money.

SCORPIO is a good sign for money, usually having been earned or created by someone else. Of particular importance is the profit realized from restoring life or attention to objects or situations left for dead by others. This would involve finding or dealing in antiques, artifacts, junk, lost property or affairs of the dead. Following Libra on the angles, the native has already established a connecting link with others which leads to these potential restorations. With Scorpio on the second the native has many secret sources of supply which sometimes may not always be on the up-and-up. The native may sometimes have to resort to taking what he has rightfully earned. On the fourth the native comes from an interesting background full of many potential values which should someday stand him in good stead. There are apt to be problems over the family inheritance in which the native seldom gets an equal share. He may get less or he may take more. On the fifth there is a native shrewdness about gambling and taking risks, which are usually profitable. He might be advised to be in the business of gambling, however, rather than as a gambling customer. On the eighth is very favorable for an unusual inheritance which may have to be appropriated from the heirs originally intended. The native is usually not averse to this with "me first" Aries on the ascendant. On the eleventh there is some chance of honors which come from wide social participation that can be turned into ready cash. This is a likely position for politicians.

SAGITTARIUS is another quasi-money sign that is not always associated with material wealth, as is popularly assumed by its relationship to Jupiter. The principle involved with Sagittarius and Jupiter is one of spiritual wealth which comes from the harmonizing balance of material values against higher principles. This gives one a release, a joy, an enthusiasm and an optimistic faith, but it does not necessarily bring material abundance. Sagittarians are usually people whose faith is content to find their abundance in heaven. Like Leo they assume the affluence of wealth but for a different reason. Following Scorpio on the angles (IN CONSIDERING EACH MONEY HOUSE ONE MUST REMEMBER WHAT SIGN IS ON THE ANGLE HOUSE IMMEDIATELY PRECEDING), the personal magnetism is not concentrated on financial resources but on some intense aspect of the self. Sagittarius on the second should provide an above-average source of income, or at the very least the native is able to live as though he had a good income. On the fourth the native's best source of money would be what he might inherit from his parental background. On the fifth this would be generally favorable for luck in gambling if the native speculated. Usually the native prefers only very sure bets and playing it safe all the way, which is really not speculation. On the eighth this is somewhat favored for inheritance, but there may be some fluke involved, as though the inheritance were not originally intended that way. For example, inheritance passing to someone else who turned it over to the native. On the eleventh it is generally unlikely to produce financial gifts, but it will produce many enthusiastic friendships.

CAPRICORN must be considerd a money sign since it inevitably wins in one way or another through persistence and seeing things through to the bitter end. It is hard under these circumstances not to achieve some kind of profitable return on one's investment. Following Sagittarius on the angles, goodwill is already established, so many opportunities that could pay off are provided. On the second are indicated steady earnings, which may be slow or limited at first but will definitely increase in time. On the fourth the native comes from an established background which is bound to include substantial assets of some kind. The native may be a long time receiving his parental inheritance since the parents may live to a ripe old age. Capricorn on the fifth may be favorable for a very cautious and long-range kind of speculation like investing in undeveloped land in neglected areas. It is not favorable for the in-and-out situation geared to quick turnover. On the eighth there should be some eventual inheritance which may not be sizable, but it may prove a lifesaver at the time. On the eleventh there should be some honors of financial value during the lifetime but not enough to be jubilant about.

AQUARIUS, in spite of its uncertainty and erratic behavior, should be favorable for money. Following Capricorn on the angles, there is bound to be something of substance and character about the native in spite of the unexpected and sensational aspects connected with his money affairs. Aquarius in the horoscope shows where one should behave with the greatest sense of independence—as though you didn't need it. Although this display of independence may get one in hot water from time to time, only full confidence in the spirit of this independence will solve the challenge in that area of your life. With Aquarius on the second house there is much uncertainty in one's financial affairs. Earnings are at times subject to every caprice of fate, but one must persistently pursue one's course (with Capricorn on the ascendant) independent of the state of one's resources. On the fourth (the preceding Capricorn is not on the angles here) there is bound to be something unusual in the family background which is most unlikely to be money. This would undoubtedly encourage the predatory aspects of the Scorpio ascendant. Parental inheritance is most unlikely. On the fifth the native is unlikely to gamble or speculate, but occasionally, when the native is very sure of himself, he will assume large risks which could ultimately pay off. The results are bound to be surprising. On the eighth an unsuspected inheritance is favored. The time and amount are very unpredictable.

On the eleventh there could also be unexpected benefits resulting from unusual friends who are attracted to this gifted destiny.

PISCES like Aquarius, which it follows on the angles, can also provide unexpected financial conditions. At the very least there should be an illusion of wealth, if not entirely the actuality. Just as one must be independent where Aquarius is concerned, one must go forward with complete faith where Pisces is concerned. People who are closely keyed to Neptune behave with an inner conviction that very often comes true. One has to proceed on faith as the only possible way. Pisces on the second shows that there is something unusual or different in the way the native earns his living. There is some degree of magic required or manipulated illusion, where the native capitalizes on the image rather than the material reality. On the fourth the native is blessed with a divine kind of protection which should, if needed, also provide some financial assets. What is important is that whatever is REALLY NEEDED is what will be provided by parental inheritance. On the fifth the native may have some rare luck in gambling and speculation, but he should not push his luck too far and he should be guided exclusively by his own intuition and not other people's advice. On the eighth an inheritance is favored which should also provide a spiritual uplift. On the eleventh there could also be financial benefits through the intervention of one's friends, even though inadvertent on their part or not specifically intended that way.

As always in synthesizing the factors in the horoscope one must look for the condition of the key or ruling planet which unlocks the sign on the door of the house in which you are interested. The location of planetary rulers by house position is described in general terms in Chapter 4, page 83.

Next, one should consider any planets that are in the money houses and their condition as they relate to other planets in aspect.

SUN IN THE HOUSE establishes a very basic concern with the affairs of that house because this involves the very character of the native's destiny. In general the presence of the Sun establishes a lifelong struggle of some kind. What is called for is individuality of effort and dedication to purpose. For more details on this see Chapter 4 "The Character of Your Destiny."

MOON IN THE HOUSE points up that this is the focus of all the

emotional reactions. This is not especially favorable for money results because the native has many changes of attitude which cause
tension and strain. The native blows hot and cold toward the affairs
of this house. There is much sensitivity but little or no consistency.
Such financial benefits as might arise would do so through some
performance or contact before the public or related to women or
women's interests. For more details see Chapter 5, "The Focus of
Your Emotions."

MERCURY IN THE HOUSE is not so favorable, although it shows
that this subject occupies a good deal of the native's thoughts and
interests. The native must use his wits to gain profit. He should
develop some good ideas on the subject, which, however, is not the
same as ready cash. Much depends on the aspect relationships to
Mercury. Mercury in the second or fifth house indicates that writing
or communication is a possible source of income.

SATURN IN THE HOUSE immediately shows material limitation,
which in this case makes the native acutely sensitive to the lack of
money, and how seriously this retards him in other departments of
life. Conditions in the beginning of life are apt to be severe where
money is concerned. This will to some extent leave a permanent scar
on the native's personality—particularly in the second or fourth
houses. However, money conditions are bound to improve with age.
With the maturity and common sense of old age there will also be
more money available—particularly in the second house. For further
details see Chapter 7, "Saturn in Your Horoscope."

MARS IN THE HOUSE immediately indicates that a fight or competitive effort is required. Money matters are not on a peaceful basis,
to say the least. It is generally up to the native to initiate or invent
his own money resources. There is some indication of waste or im-
provident use of money with Mars around.

VENUS IN THE HOUSE is fortunate. This cools things down, and
while it may not indicate great wealth, there is generally sufficient
money to supply comforts and make things attractive.

NEPTUNE IN THE HOUSE brings a question mark. There could
certainly be the appearance of money if not the real thing. Someone
is apt to be fooled about money. It could be the native or the native
could be fooling others. Sharp practices are around somewhere either
in view or under the surface. Money could mysteriously float in or
just as easily fade away in dissipation or declining values on a losing
market. Much depends on the aspect relationships of Neptune.

JUPITER IN THE HOUSE is favorable. It generally indicates some kind of abundance which may not all be material. But in any event there should be enough money to sustain the native's position as prosperous. Money conditions are easy or are associated with honors which are heaped on the native or with his title. One would have to look further into the aspect relationships to other planets to see the real substance of this apparent abundance.

PLUTO IN THE HOUSE is not altogether unfavorable. There is some suggestion of a power struggle which throws one in and out of favor. Since there is a heightened intensity and an acute awareness of all the angles involved, the native is less likely to let golden opportunities where money is involved entirely slip through his fingers. There is something around that is definitely profitable. The native may have to learn to adjust his moral code to take advantage of what might be possible. The presence of Pluto always indicates a double standard or money from two or more sources that are somehow related.

URANUS IN THE HOUSE represents unexpected conditions usually beyond the native's control. In a money house this is usually the proverbial foot on a banana peel. The native should watch his step. But this could also indicate a sudden windfall. The important thing is that the native must never appear too anxious about the money from this house. He should at all times appear as though he did not really need this factor. The more independent he becomes, the more likely money is liable to fall into his lap by URANIAN MESSENGER. This should not, however, apply wholesale to dealing with other considerations in this money house which may require different tactics. This would only apply to the Uranian part of the deal, which always acts independently of everything else. Anything from Uranus could be characterized "by the hand of fate."

Chapter 11

CREATIVE EXPRESSION

IN YOUR LIFE

THE 3RD, 5TH, & 9TH HOUSES
& THE SIGNS ON THEIR CUSPS

The factor of expression and creative effort in your life is shown in several different houses of the horoscope according to type and emphasis.

How the native thinks, speaks, writes and his general style of communicating directly with others is shown in the third house. The third house is the instrumentality of all expression and communication.

The type of creativity which becomes an extension of the ego-force is found in the fifth house. There the native might pour himself into some artistic format such as music, art, entertaining, or acting because it gives him pleasure. With fifth-house creativity there is usually an object created which is separate and distinct from the native.

The projection, promotion and publication of ideas, principles, codes, and rituals is shown in the ninth house.

The native's thoughts are reflected in the third, his creative actions in the fifth, and the principles on which he stands in the ninth.

The ninth house involves the publication of or publicity connected with whole structures of thought. It is the intellectualization or formal pattern of advanced thinking that has become a code, a law and sometimes even a religion. In the ninth house one's thinking becomes involved with the same channels of thinking of others in the past. This is what establishes a pattern of thinking or a basic principle.

The third house implies an immediate audience in speaking or writing directly to others—an exchange of communication in THE MARKETPLACE. In the fifth the native creates something which stands on its own—a new entity—a child, a work of art, a piece of music, or a theatrical role. In the ninth house one's thoughts have advanced to a state of intellectuality where they merge with a whole system of thought and become part of a larger framework of meaning and reference. This can involve teaching or promotion of ideas or publishing material intended for a wide and possibly unknown or foreign audience.

One's creativity tends to take one of these three directions, although one may lead to the other or each can stand independently.

If the native has a strong third house, he learns early to deal effectively with those in his near neighborhood in an exchange of news and views. This begins initially with brothers and sisters but soon extends to the marketplace—an office, shop or place of business. Often the native feels no need to go beyond this immediate contact. He has no necessity to create something that stands on its own or preach to those beyond his immediate contacts. If one has in mind to deal with customers on a direct basis—no matter what he may be selling or expressing—a good third house is mandatory. With a poor third house one will never have a good flow of clients in the marketplace. This goes as well for lecturing and trying to throw a personal sales pitch.

If the native has a strong fifth house, he needs a larger audience than those immediately around him. He needs to reach out to groups and strangers. It is not necessary that he feel intimate with the audience. He may sense them but in an impersonal, artistic way. The fifth house shows one's probable chances for success in certain of the arts and fields of entertainment.

When we get to the ninth house, the native needs an even wider audience. He has generally become involved with the universal principles or theories behind what he is trying to express. This often leads to publishing, propagandizing, teaching in institutions of higher learning and preaching, all of which are engaged in stuffing the desirability of certain positions into the common picture.

In order for the native to have a real creative interest, the house in question must be occupied by one or more planets. The house could still be important to the native (as, say, the Capricorn house is always important in everybody's life), but this importance will not be obvious to the native unless he has planets there to make it so. Factors of importance would be the Sun, Mars or Saturn, which are planets which get things done, or the ruler of the ascendant (which unlocks the native's personality) or the ruler of the tenth house (which unlocks the native's ambitions and probable recognition for success). The Moon lends emotional support but may mean nothing more. To be really important for the native there should be a heavy concentration of planetary force directed toward these houses—preferably the Sun or Moon and several others.

If the house of interest is unoccupied, then the affairs of that house cannot be considered as being of primary importance in the native's life.

The nature of the sign on the house in question has much to do with the native's attitude toward the affairs and people of that house.

If the sign is:

ARIES: the native is more desirous of using the affairs of that house as a convenient coat hanger to carry the persuasive qualities of his personality or impress others with the unique individuality of his efforts. His involvements are likely to be pioneering, and he is certainly advised to work on his own rather than to string along with others. Often the native must first find himself through applying effort to the affairs of this house. It is not often that one has time to integrate himself sufficiently to go on and produce something remarkable. The ego would have to be strongly fortified to push beyond self-awareness. It usually is if the Sun happens to be in Aries.

TAURUS: the native is not particularly creative, although he may enjoy the results of attractive efforts. Taurus is not an innovator, being more interested in the material advantages and physical comforts which the affairs of that house will provide. Taurus is interested in counting out such advantages and looking after them to see that everything is in reasonable order and on deck for convenient assignments. Whatever creative efforts the Taurus/Venus talent will produce are largely for his own convenience and will stop right there.

GEMINI: This is a favorable sign for communication and reflecting a variety of angles which may coexist simultaneously. It is an ideal tempo for a quick brushup. It is not satisfactory for prolonged efforts or reaching beneath the surface. Gemini is always more interested in covering the broadest area rather than any concentrated penetration. Gemini always implies an audience or exchange situation. This would be most effective on the third (its natural house), slightly less so on the fifth (which has too many egotistical and superficial qualities), and least desirable on the ninth where the force of substance is required to weather the long pull needed for larger audiences, where little or no personal contact is usually available. Gemini, on the other hand, needs this personalized sensory stimulation which is lacking in the ninth house.

CANCER: This is always a fruitful, productive sign which is well placed on any creative matter. The Cancer sensitivity gives a sense of the potential public response—valuable talent when trying to be creative. Public recognition and approval is the best encouragement to go on and do something better. There is also a sense of timing which is most important if the native cares about the reaction to what he is creating. Cancer is about equally placed on the third, fifth or ninth house. There is some danger of moodiness and tuning out on a situation before the job is finished. Much would depend on the condition of the Moon.

LEO: This is certainly a creative sign, being the natural ruler of the fifth house. The native is well advised in this matter to proceed as though he had all the right in the world to undertake whatever he tries. There can be no hanging back or indecisive false starts. The native must take over from the beginning and see it through with a kingly prerogative. The native will seldom be inclined to back down on any of the affairs of his Leo house, for this is where he has a natural birthright to rule and BE HEARD. The native will defend his prerogatives with all the force of his integrity. The final result may prove to be disappointing, but you may be sure the native will give it all he has and will impress some people.

VIRGO: This is not a creative sign, but in certain mental occupations it does give a capacity for infinite patience and an inordinate passion for details and painstaking refinements. This is excellent for research and scientific applications which are not technically within the category of creativity as such. The Virgo house is where the native will work hard and apply himself diligently, even without compensation or recognition.

LIBRA: This is a creative sign and one which immediately involves others with any possible enjoyments or satisfactions. "To please" and "win over" are always uppermost in the Libra mind. The Libra house always shows some special talent which the native has in dealing with other people. It is therefore always good to have Libra out in front on a house that counts and not buried on a back road or a hidden path such as the fourth, sixth, eighth or twelfth house. The presence of this sign indicates that other people in some way form the content or material out of which the native fashions his product. They may not be aware of the use to which they are put in this regard. And it really doesn't matter. But it takes the sense of others to feed or fill the affairs of the Libra house.

SCORPIO: This is a creative sign. In the first place it always suggests mobility and the hidden potentials of change and the mysterious allurement of the unknown. However, it is also mandatory that the native wear a mask in all dealings with the affairs and people of this house. He will never be as effective without some shield or wall to stand between him and others. He especially needs this fortification in the affairs of the Scorpio house. The Scorpio attitude always treads on somewhat dangerous ground and one slip may kill the whole effect. The dynamics of Scorpio are best when the audience is bedazzled from all sides at once and the focus of their reaction is unlikely to strike the native. Scorpio always suggests more than is currently available, and no one knows this better than the native when it comes to the affairs and persons of that house. He must allow himself alternate escape routes in case of an emergency.

SAGITTARIUS: This is a promotional sign more than a creative one. It picks up and promotes what has gone before, which just happens to coincide with what the native would have done. In this case it saves the native a certain amount of groundwork, and he is happy to give an added push with the ring of his hearty endorsement. The native always projects an unqualified endorsement of the affairs and persons of his Sagittarius house, and he enjoys preaching to others about the obvious advantages of their seeing the matter through his convictions. Sagittarius would be most favored on its own house—the ninth. It is less favored on the third, which would tend toward dogmatism and less independence of thought. It is least favorable on the fifth where it is too uptight to easily slip into the swinging pleasures of life.

CAPRICORN: This is not a creative sign. It is favorable for persistent struggle toward one material objective, but the very factors that isolate and discipline the native toward his goal at the same time kill the real fires of creative expression. Capricorn would be favored for moving in and organizing a business situation for profit after the creative product has been born. It would usually not know where to begin to fabricate something primarily out of inspiration, imagination and colorful effects. The native entertains only the most serious attitudes toward the affairs and people of his Capricorn house, which he initially distrusts in terms of any personal profit. Eventually he comes to see that he must in some way come to terms with the realities of this house if he is to develop a sense of self-preservation and settle his emotional security so he can get on with the business of life. The Capricorn house is always of vital importance—supporting as it does the disciplinary effect of Saturn in the horoscope. But the native is usually reluctant to tackle effectively or even get started on the affairs of this house until he has reached a certain maturity and realized its importance to the foundations of his life. Sometimes this comes only very late in life after many false starts or pathetic setbacks. This is when he finally comes to terms with the realities there. The Capricorn house is always inescapable, but it may take years for the native to even look into the matter. This is particularly true if the Capricorn house is unoccupied or the native has no planets (or conscious talents) in Capricorn.

AQUARIUS: This is a quasi-creative house in that it lives on revelation and unusual insights which may begin and end within the native's private life. Unless the native is otherwise directed, he may feel no necessity whatsoever to reveal to others what he perceives. It is often enough just to have made the discovery. And this discovery may be quite unrelated to anything else in his life, let alone the need to pass it on to others. The erratic forces of Uranus are much more at home in the fields of science or dealing with impersonal social issues than in concentrating and filtering the native's personal creative efforts. The tempo is more that of shock treatment, which is more of a technique than a creative object. Undoubtedly many artists, writers and even entertainers are indeed patterned to the projection of shock treatment tactics only thinly disguised as creative effort. Their value lies in the instrumentality or function of what they do rather than the thing itself. To me this is not creative in the artistic sense, even though it is considered creative by the native.

PISCES: This is a creative sign which requires a certain background or special glasses in order to read between the lines of what is intended. The beholder also has to be keyed to this special idiom in order to receive the message. This elevates the quality or tone of the creativity but limits the audience and fields of application where this product can be enjoyed. Exclusiveness is achieved at the expense of general circulation. The native is inclined to accept on faith and inner conviction the affairs and people of his Pisces house. He does not consider this area open for examination or general discussion since it is his subconscious motivations which guide him there rather than logic or practical consideration. It is generally impossible to shake the native's professed attitudes to this area. He considers this off limits and a matter of private concern. As long as it measures up to his inner requirements, that is all that is necessary. From a strictly commercial point of view or ready exchange value, the native's efforts in this direction are not as much creative as inspirational. He employs the Neptune/Pisces brush for spiritual reasons rather than for artistic effects. This may be even more compelling, but with all the above qualifications Pisces would be more effective on the fifth house, where it has greater freedom for suggestibility. It would be less so on either the third or ninth, where it would be more apt to refine the native's ideas and principles out of ordinary reach.

For contributory factors regarding the placement of the ruler of the sign on the cusp of the creative house, see Chapter 4, page 83.

Any planet in the house is encouraged by the soft-angle aspects but is forced to adjust itself by the hard angles. For more details on this see Chapter 9, "Aspects Between Planets."

Chapter 12

THE SECURITY FACTOR:

YOUR SUBJECTIVE SELF

THE 4TH HOUSE

The fourth house of the horoscope reflects HOW THE NATIVE SEES HIMSELF. Naturally this is a subjective valuation. And we see ourselves as we inwardly feel ourselves to be. We usually consider this more important than any surface impression we seem to make through our personality image (shown in the first house). In fact, some people seem totally unaware of their personality image.

How we regard ourselves becomes the hub of our emotional security. When this is upset, we feel endangered. It is at such times that we feel the need to draw upon all the resources of our background, heritage and the format of our present self to meet this challenge.

How we go about securing objectives involves the way in which we see ourselves—as a REACTIVE BEING reaching for something. We first seem aware of these reactions as we deal with the focus of our background through our parents and their relation to our patterns of behavior. The fourth house, then, also represents the home and our relationships to parents. This tends to revolve around the parent who dominates the parent/child relationship.

The fourth house also represents the native's own home after he establishes one for himself. This would include the daily routines with members of the immediate family who also live in the home. The partner as an individual is represented by the seventh house, and the children as individuals are represented by the fifth house. As a family unit they are reflected in the conditions of the fourth house.

As an area of material the fourth house also represents real estate and fixed assets. Portable assets, cash and general resources are shown in the second house.

The fourth house is also said to symbolize general conditions toward the end of the native's life—the mature years—and the grave after his death.

The conditions and character of the fourth house are a matter of the native's private concern. The public is usually not aware of what goes on there.

If there are no planets in the fourth house, the native has no problems in the way he sees or accepts himself. He goes about his business, and his subjective self remains his private, but untroubled, concern. There are no particular problems with parents or with members of his own family. While his techniques for getting things done may not be the world's greatest, he see nothing particularly wrong with them, and in general he gets out of them what he puts into them. There is no psychological problem causing introspective analysis. The general tempo of this subjective reaction to the self is shown by the sign on the cusp. If that sign is:

ARIES: The native sees himself as a strong-willed individualist whose personal identity and sense of self-worth must never be defeated. It will probably be challenged often. He tends to see himself as a self-made person who has to fight aggressively for everything he wants. He enjoys competition and the opportunity to test his mettle and get the edge on someone or something. He has little time for analyzing others since he is so preoccupied with himself. To him this is the only natural way to be. He probably comes from a background of strong individualists and was encouraged in this "me first" philosophy from an early age by parents. His sense of personal integrity is his strongest virtue. He values his ability to dominate others and regards himself as ardent in love and brave in battle. His home life is apt to be full of strife as he tries to impose his will on the family unit. Everyone else must generally play Indian to his "chief" or else there will be war and blows. He tries to be fair and just, but he can only see things his way. This may be a better vision than some people have, but it is still his tune to which the rest of the family must dance. The only security he will ever know or feel he can really count on is what he creates for himself. He will never be content with what others may provide for him. With Libra on the tenth house his conscious ambitions (out in the world away from the family) are to be well liked and to be a part of the social scene. He is not a loner. He starts everything with a push, but this is only to get a larger share of love and affection. The Aries subjective appraisal is more suitable for a man's horoscope than a woman's, although women today seem more and more to be taking aggressive attitudes and pushing their way to the front. The woman with Aries on the fourth house will always consider her efforts more important no matter what kind of a mate she has. The native actually enjoys a good battle or else he doesn't feel he is really alive. In mature years life is still apt to be strenuous and active with little let up from battle. Conditions at the close of life will be demanding, and his grave may stand alone and distinguished.

TAURUS: The native regards himself as dependable, competent, down-to-earth, realistic, practical and generally able to meet most situations in life. He will always have time left over, or take time, to see to the comforts of life and to beautify his surroundings. His background is one of peace and solid comforts, and the home he makes for himself will also be like this. The main topic of interest around the home will center on practical considerations and how to make life more comfortable for all members of the family. There is a strong earthy quality in all his family relationships with a healthy appreciation for back-to-earth attitudes. The pursuit of accounting for money is a major consideration. The native regards himself as a money-conscious person. Conditions at the end of life will be comfortable and serene. The grave should be an object of beauty.

GEMINI: The native regards himself as singularly well informed on almost everything that catches his interest. The techniques which he comes to employ are apt to be versatile, adaptive, open-minded and phrased in terms that others can readily understand. He tends to see almost everything in life as a communication problem which, when solved, automatically gets the job done. It is natural for him to gather others around him and involve them in his projects. The home will be a center of activity, comings and goings, news events and a marketplace of information. One or both of the parents should be talented, expressive and well connected with customers and clients. Conditions at the end of life are apt to be lively, fleeting, effective (but not necessarily substantial). The grave would follow the vogue of the moment and be easily accessible for everyone to see. The inscription should reveal more than just the bare facts.

CANCER: The native has deep sensitive moods about himself which are highly responsive to public reactions. The native is not independently aware of his subjective self. He is aware of his basic self by the manner in which the public reacts to him. This is the part of his nature which he then comes to consider his primary or better self. He would discard or ignore any elements of his nature to which he seemed unable to get a response or significant public reaction. This type of attitude (especially about himself) would keep the native responsive and alive to the changing scene around him and the potentials of working with the tide of affairs rather than in any way against them. The Cancer attunement draws from outside conditions and builds these qualities into what he may already have to supply the current need. Conditions at the end of life would be sound and well protected. In general they will provide the native with all the nourishment he may require for whatever he has in mind. The grave should exhibit some sort of distinction or public fame over and above the private circle of his family.

LEO: The native sees himself as a resourceful personality of indominatable will power who initially believes he can make most things come to pass by just willing them into existence. This may prove effective as long as the ego is well supported and happens to be blessed favorably with material advantages which can buy what the ego wills to be. If the native is not fortunately placed in life, nor has the material resources to pay for his schemes, it may become increasingly difficult to substantiate fully the scale which the native regards as mandatory for his best efforts. The native regards himself as the only one qualified to make decisions for himself and this prerogative is directly related to his ego. Personal integrity and unblemished character is the general framework within which the native conceives all his programs. The location and condition of the Sun is most important to see what supports the native's subjective self and how it will focus best in effective operation. General conditions at the close of life are apt to be marked with a certain distinction, and the scale of surroundings should be somewhat impressive. The grave should be distinctive and styled considerably superior to average mortals.

VIRGO: The native assumes a humility toward life because he senses a need and service which he must somehow fulfill in duty to others. Whether this is exactly true or not is beside the point because this is how the native sees it. He is fussy, meticulous and overly detailed in all his undertakings. He comes from a demanding background where standards of perfection were much in evidence from one or both of the parents. General conditions at the close of life will be very well organized with little or nothing left to chance. There will be a place and an appointed time for all things. Some people might consider such a tight schedule as more of a limitation or confinement, but the native will be happy in working within his elaborate plans. The grave would be plain, unobtrusive and set back rather than standing out from its surroundings.

LIBRA: The native sees others as playing an important role in shaping the formation of his character. To some extent he will try to include all their wishes and make them his wishes if possible. He does not try to stand alone on matters, being predisposed to find and digest the reaction of others before he feels entitled to take a stand of his own. It will be somewhat difficult to get him to take a position of his own because he is much given to procrastination—especially about himself. Often he will put off decisive action in order to gather opinions and then fail to formulate any stand at all. Procrastination and overindulgence in social involvements tend to retard the native's character. His methods become a conglomeration of all the people to whom he responds. He sees himself as an arbiter of differences rather than a champion of any of his own. The native is a born peacemaker. Conditions at the end of life will be pleasant, friendly, comfortable and attractive. The grave should be an object of beauty.

SCORPIO: The native is preoccupied with discovering new depths and possibilities in his own nature. He would most often find conditions around him insufficient to warrant his best efforts, and therefore this leaves him free to indulge and pursue his own gratifications. He tends to be a loner and remain aloof from the crowd. He may take some interest in a reactionary cause or movement. To him all dissent is a natural right. He will always regard himself as able to handle even the most extraordinary of situations should conditions demand it—which they seldom will. He prefers the independent approach and to poke around in out-of-the-way places as though hunting for something lost in the past. The native is not sure what he is looking for, and of the moment his curiosity is sufficient justification for whatever he may be doing. He wants to keep his private life to himself, and whatever he finds he is unlikely to spread around. Conditions at the end of life are apt to be uncertain and radically different from the rest of his life. The native will desire these changes. The grave is apt to be hidden, lost, or hard to find.

SAGITTARIUS: The native naturally regards himself as an undying optimist with an urgent message to be impressed on anyone who will listen. He sees himself as his brother's keeper and equally responsible for his faults and his virtues. This makes for somewhat of a busybody or naïve do-gooder who is convinced that only his way will work out properly. His sense of personal faith is enormous and unlikely to be shaken by facts or persuasion. The native comes from a family of positive thinkers who take it upon themselves to set the world straight in certain respects. The approach is essentially mental and intellectual and tied to established codes of behavior which have been proven over and over again. The native sees a place for himself in a long line of marchers who are well organized and already getting things done. Conditions at the close of life are apt to be insulated and entirely built around his own code of behavior. Regardless of whether the trend is actually up or down, the native will still be enthusiastic about it and assume an air of success which he feels is indisputable. The grave should be rich and impressive.

CAPRICORN: The native will be very set in his ways and given to self-discipline from early childhood. He sees himself as a plodder who is stubbornly determined to make something of his life and he is prepared to work hard and make any personal sacrifice which may be necessary. He comes from a family whose members are used to looking after themselves with a shirt-sleeve reality. The native is hard on himself since he has been schooled in tough realistic attitudes from early childhood. He will also be very firm toward his own family and demand disciplined attitudes and down-to-earth methods. There is a firm sense of ambition at the root of all efforts, and the native feels it his duty to make a mark in the world. Conditions at the end of life are bound to be better than they were in early childhood, but the native is so accustomed to harsh disciplines that it is doubtful as to whether these lifelong habits of economy and denial will allow him much enjoyment of any material success he is sure to have achieved.

AQUARIUS: The native does not see himself as a direct link with the traditions of his past. He is more apt to regard himself as a radical departure from such limitations with a license to pursue his own inclinations in some ingenious and independent way. His relationships with parents and family are apt to be eccentric and based on some advanced frame of thinking which grants considerable freedom and individual rights. There may be some lack of consistency, although the native doesn't sense this. The native is bound to be especially gifted in some special way. It is up to him to discover this for himself and exploit it in the best way that he can. With Leo on the tenth house there is a great deal of ambition where originality and inventive genius are mandatory for what the native has in mind. Conditions at the end of life are apt to be unusual and generally out of step with others and what might have been expected by others for the native. Whatever unique conditions are involved, the native is unlikely to be too upset about them since he has a way of focusing on (for him) more important matters. Something about the grave is apt to be a surprise. There may be no real grave since the native may desire to have his remains scattered to the winds or he may have been lost in the wild blue yonder or otherwise have met with some freak ending.

PISCES: The native is blessed with a certain introspective insight which enables him to be more conscious of the inner motivations behind his purpose and methods. He sees himself as a person with a mission—a special destiny—which he accepts with a certain philosophic detachment. He does not require of life the usual material goals. Although he may be blessed with material abundance, he will consider these riches as tools or objects to further some spiritual or charitable purpose. The native will have a certain emotional and spiritual maturity and an idealized way of regarding things. He is unlikely to be thrown off balance by any lack of specific method, since he feels that somehow (as if by fate) whatever he needs to do a job will be provided or shown in due course. He accepts this without any problems. He assumes that everyone could do the same for himself if he only felt as he does. This isn't true of course because the Pisces approach in method is very specialized and takes the magic of Neptune to materialize. Conditions at the end of life are apt to find the native considerably withdrawn from the main currents of material life. The native will probably be satisfied with these conditions, however they appear to others. The grave should be inspiring and have a haunting, ethereal kind of beauty. In itself it may be simple and unobtrusive, but from certain angles or in a certain light or at certain times of the day there will be an atmosphere that is quiet, peaceful and rather special.

Check the section at the end of Chapter 4, page 83, for the supporting factors of the subjective self as shown by the house position of the ruler of the cusp.

If there are one or more planets in the fourth house, the native has cause for self-conscious concern in the way he sees himself. He has reason to reflect subjectively about a difference which marks or distinguishes him from his background, heritage or parental influence. Because he is subjectively different, he must first test the validity and reliability of this difference so that he may use it as an asset rather than let it defeat him as a liability. Whatever shows up in the fourth house is something that the native has more of than his immediate family (especially his parents) anticipated. Circumstances will require that the native use these special planetary forces in dealing with all his fourth-house problems, including relationships within his family. It is up to him to make the most of what he has. Because this is a family difference, it may make him closer (and more beloved) or set him apart (with criticism and disapproval) from the family scene. This is not an easy problem to resolve because the native must both evaluate and appreciate the potentiality of what is given to him as a special talent to use in formulating his techniques against the world (his worldly ambitions in the tenth house). Regardless of the opinions of others (particularly the family), the native must incorporate whatever planetary force he has in the fourth house as the only right way for him to secure that which he wants most in the tenth house, as well as deal effectively with his own family relationships. Remember that the placement of a planetary force (or talent) is a two-way street. The native both receives and gives out experiences in that tempo.

If that planet is the:

SUN: the native's whole destiny revolves around some solution within the subjective self. He is destined to shed light on what makes us all tick and how the human spirit can best adapt itself to meeting worldly problems. The Sun here shows that this will be a lifelong problem. For more details on this see Chapter 4, "The Character of your Destiny"—Sun in the fourth house.

MOON: the native is blessed with a certain intuitive rapport with his subjective self which gives him a talent for drawing public attention and understanding toward the formulation of ways and means in which the individual can present himself more effectively to the world. For more details on this pattern see Chapter 5, "The Focus of Your Emotions"—Moon in the fourth house.

MERCURY: the native is gifted with a mental sparkle and the ability to understand and communicate the importance that the native's regard to his subjective self holds to the other departments of living. The native thinks best when applying himself to self-analysis. The results of this study in depth can be handed on to others to help them in their subjective problems.

SATURN: the native is initially depressed and restricted by some material or physical condition which focuses his whole sense of self-preservation on this subjective appraisal. Eventually the native will work out some solution that will ultimately bring him profit and prestige but only after long, hard effort and painstaking self-discipline. The conditions of life are harsh, but apparently this is needed to bring the native to his highest potential.

MARS: the native is impulsive and rash in the way he goes about obtaining his objectives. Inevitably this draws antagonistic reactions from those in authority who regard the native as an aggressive upstart. However, for what the native wants in life (shown in the tenth house) only by such aggressive acts will the native be able to win his point. It would be fatal to launch any programs without a strong Martian trigger or knife thrust. The native must come to see that this is his birthright in spite of any family troubles that such procedures might have caused in the past or present. The native must fight to win, and he must accept the implication that whatever he does to rise in the world will start a fight in some quarters. With this pattern the native must first fight with himself to convince himself to go to war to secure his birthright.

VENUS: the native must employ sweetness and affectionate interest for others in all his techniques for securing objective goals. The native is loving and warm in relationships within the family circle. He will correspondingly be less loving and warm in relationships outside the family circle, except as an impersonal means to achieve his ambitions. What we have by way of planets in the fourth house is used with the family circle, to protect and secure emotional security, against the subjective self and to launch programs to secure our ambitions in the tenth house.

NEPTUNE: the native is unrealistic and visionary when it comes to seeing himself, dealing with the family circle, evaluating his emotional security and securing his ambitions in life. But he also has a rare gift of inspirational magic, which may move mountains on occasion and ultimately be far more effective than all the material or physical effort in the world. The native must let his feelings be the judge and not the effect that these visionary attitudes have on others. It is very important as to the condition and support which Neptune receives from other factors in the horoscope as to exactly how effective or how phony the Neptune magic will be. The native may be reduced to some kind of fraud in order to fulfill the subjective demands of the fourth house. It is hard for others to judge fairly the propriety of this because the situations and people whom the native meets in life must apparently call for this Neptunian touch.

JUPITER: the native has a richness of faith and an abundance of positive optimism that he must stick with in order to persuade others and secure all his fourth-house functions. The native finds riches within the self and within his family circle which he must incorporate in his attitudes toward tenth-house goals. At the same time it must be appreciated that this position generally denies him riches from other sources. His abundance in life is a private matter.

PLUTO: the native is forced to instigate a radical departure from his background, his heritage and possibly even his parents and family. He will feel it necessary to destroy or nullify something and at the same time bring to life another side of himself that is in marked contrast to everything else. The native is likely to undergo sweeping changes—particularly in his inner-subjective self and family relationships. There is a dual nature present—a double attitude which is somehow mandatory under the circumstances, which only the native knows best. The native's efforts to secure his ambitions are sure to run into trouble and dissent. Some degree of violent undertone is also possible. Certain things have to die in order for other things to be forced into life. The native's private life is tempestuous and uncertain.

URANUS: there is an unpredictable quality which may blow up many carefully laid plans, but the ultimate outcome will surprisingly be found to have been possible only by such unpredictable techniques. The native is never sure what he can expect—either of himself or of those who should support him within the family circle. Standard techniques will never work right for the native. He may have to start off that way, but sooner or later he will have to take an independent stand and invent some ingenious method for catching others by surprise. Above all the native must independently view things—especially his subjective appraisals.

Naturally the so-called pure essence of any of the planetary forces in the fourth house may be considerably altered or qualified by the significant aspects which that planet makes to others in the horoscope. For such possible modifications see Chapter 9, "Aspects Between Planets."

Perhaps a comment should be added, although it should be obvious, that if the house in question contains several planets (which may not be linked together by angular aspect unless it be the conjunction), the effect of these planets on the affairs of that house must be considered even though contradictory. It is further pointed out that since each planet rules or controls its own house, the concern of that planet in the affairs of the house where the planet falls is supported or influenced by a distinctly different department of life and experience (namely, the house which it rules).

Chapter 13

CHILDREN, SPECULATION

AND GAMBLING

THE 5TH HOUSE

The fifth house of the horoscope is essentially the area where the ego EXTENDS ITSELF IN CREATIVE EFFORT. These activities include the so-called pleasurable pursuits. Under normal conditions this would be a period of relaxation during which the native would reach out in some way to broaden his sphere of influence. It follows the fourth house, supposedly after the native has secured some degree of emotional security by his acceptance of his subjective self and resolved the techniques or methods by which he will seek his goals in the tenth house of ambition.

The first efforts involve some form of romancing, falling in love, and the sexual side of love-making. The area of pleasure is extended to include entertainment, engaging in games of chance, speculative adventures, and projecting the ego in some objective manner as a creation of artistic form—art objects, musical idiom, imaginative writing and begetting children. It also includes the native's primary education as opposed to his higher education in the ninth house.

The creation of, or indulgence in, all these directions is supposed to give the native sensory gratification. This is an area where the individuality of the ego dominates, and this domination is accepted and blended with the satisfaction of others. What is created is an extension or projection of the native's ego image.

By implication the fifth house is also said to include the native's early education and beginning introduction to the tools of life.

All the houses represent areas of activity and interest, as well as persons or objects associated with these interests. As the fourth house represents the home, it also represents the parent or motherly aspects of the home. The tenth house usually represents the father; the third brothers and sisters; the seventh one's partner; and the fifth one's children; and so on.

A very interesting factor about the houses which has not been mentioned before is the relationship which they bear to each other, when any house is considered in the first or ascendant position.

For example, if one wants to study in more detail the effect ON THE NATIVE of his mother (a fourth-house subject), then move or consider the fourth house in the position of the ascendant. The fifth house then becomes the second house of the mother's earnings; the sixth house becomes the third house of the mother's brothers and sisters; the seventh house becomes the fourth house of the mother's reflective, subjective self and her own mother; and so on.

Any person symbolized by a house can be studied in this manner. But it is pointed out that this information is filtered through the native. It is that person's effect on these matters as they relate to or touch upon the native's life. This is not to deny that the person being studied does not have a somewhat different condition as it touches on someone else's life. As far as the native's relationship with his mother goes, the mother tends (in his eyes) to see herself in this way or react to any of the departments in her life as they affect the native's life. Another child in the same family may see and experience his mother in an entirely different way, as indeed the mother reacts differently to each person in her life.

As the fifth house represents the native's children, by turning or considering the fifth house in the first position, the ninth house then represents how the children as a whole see that parent (the native), regardless of whether the native is the child's mother or father. The other parent, by doing the same thing in his horoscope, could see how the same children regard him.

As might be supposed, all sorts of fascinating insights can be obtained through the horoscope in this way.

One of the questions with which most people seem obsessed in life is their potential to gamble and win. The desire to get something for nothing is fascinating. The answer to this is irrevocably shown in the condition of the fifth house—its sign, the condition of its ruler and any planets within the house. The fifth house shows not only the native's attitudes toward speculative risks but the probability of their outcome.

IF THE NATIVE DOES NOT HAVE A VERY FAVORABLE FIFTH HOUSE, THEN HE HAD BETTER AVOID ALL GAMBLING; HE IS PROBABLY GAMBLING TO LOSE. This is a well-known psychological condition found among many compulsive gamblers. Gambling in the losing sense is more from a guilt complex and a sense of self-destruction. They do it because it gives them pleasure to punish themselves, as would any fifth-house activity or indulgence.

If there are no planets in the fifth house, one may assume that all fifth-house matters are no special problem to the native. It is not to say that such pleasures as may be derived have no place in the native's daily life, but they do not have any SPECIAL PLACE in his overall perspective.

The general tempo of fifth-house matters in the native's life is set by the sign on the cusp. If that sign is:

ARIES: the native gets exhilaration out of fifth-house affairs, which he tends to enter into impetuously, rashly and with a certain foolhardy abandon. All pleasure figures in some way in getting him started. Pleasures tend to come first, but this is apparently necessary and desirable (in his case) to get the native launched in constructive work projects. In a physical and competitive sense everybody is somewhat best when engaged in Aries/Mars projects, for this is where the Mars trigger takes hold and energetic physical action tends to formulate in their affairs along original lines. However, it is only a point of beginning, and the native must go on from there to confront whatever his particular challenge. Relations with children are energetic, competitive, volatile and tempestuous.

TAURUS: there is a money aspect or a potential source of material comforts that can materialize from some aspect of fifth-house matters for the native. It is necessary to look further to see how this relates to the FOCUS OF HIS SOURCES FOR MONEY. This Venus-ruled sign primarily shows a condition of ease, comfort and satisfaction from earthly pleasures and an attractive addition to one's background. Relations with children should be gratifying, sensible, regular and well organized. There is a feeling of mutual responsibility.

GEMINI: the native's approach is primarily mental and communicative. He thinks and talks about fifth-house matters a great deal but may not necessarily partake of them physically as much as might be suggested. It is generally enough for him to be mentally occupied. This may prove very productive if this area otherwise figures prominently in the horoscope. But under Gemini no one particular area of pleasure will ever occupy his thinking for long. The native rapidly loses interest and wants to go on to something new and different. Relations with children are stimulating, noisy and superficial.

CANCER: the native feels great sensitivity and emotional rapport about fifth-house matters. He has a certain talent for anticipating the probable appeal or public reaction to such objects as his creativity might produce. His sense of timing is very good, which is a favorable factor for any speculative ventures. The native would be naturally cautious and conservative about all speculations, but his intuition would also tell him when a situation is both sound and ripe to move on. His interest in fifth-house matters will not be steady or constant, being given to moods and periods when he feels definitely turned off on that subject. Much depends on the condition of the Moon as to how much actual profit or tension the native will realize in this direction. Relations with children are tense, strained, overly possessive, excessively protective and highly emotional. However this very combination of attitudes also lends itself to close and deep understanding on both sides.

LEO: the native is apt to be overly confident and too self-assured to be really aware of all the pitfalls that might ensue because of overextending the ego. He naturally feels self-assured on all fifth-house matters and is disinclined to take anyone's advice but his own, which to him becomes a matter of pride and personal integrity. This pattern is favorable for daring and courageous undertakings but can be foolhardy and unwarranted in certain high-risk areas of speculation and gamble. Relations with children are imperious, generous, proud, self-rationalizing, overly sensitive to criticism from outsiders, nonobjective and intensely loyal.

VIRGO: the qualities of critical perfection and hair-splitting details are somewhat out of place in the general area of pleasure, entertainment and speculative ventures. The native's relations with his children are apt to be uncomfortable, burdensome and unrewarding. The native is too critical and demanding of perfection, which may be very difficult for others to live up to or live with. He is unlikely to get much pleasure from gambling even if he should win. The worry and anxiety would outweigh any profits that might develop. Any creative efforts would be highly detailed, exacting and specialized. Relations with children would be demanding on both sides. The parent may well expect too much of the child since these are the parent's standards and may be far from the child's talents.

LIBRA: this pattern is very favorable for romantic attachments and the social side of pleasures, although the controlling factor tends to pass to others. The satisfactions of the other party become rather more important than the native's. This is not especially favorable for speculative gambles, except as they should develop through contacts with others or as a by-product of such social involvements. Relations with children are satisfying and comfortable. There is a real warmth of understanding among all parties involved. The native is naturally affectionate and understanding with others but is also highly susceptible to a variety of people—not just a limited few.

SCORPIO: all the native's involvements with fifth-house situations or people are surcharged with an undercurrent of sexuality and hidden implications. There is always a potential for trouble with the native's fifth-house affairs which, when considered with a certain predatory forethought, will generally prove profitable or exploitable for the native, regardless of how things turn out for the others involved. The native may have to take or appropriate fifth-house matters for himself from a somewhat selfish standpoint in order to make them work in his life. A certain bedrock realism and stripping situations of all superficialities is mandatory. The native is supposed to come on strong in fifth-house situations, play his cards close to the chest, and keep his real motivations to himself. One might say that others who get involved are asking for what they get. This is not a favorable tempo for dealing with children because what is called for is too sophisticated for children to handle effectively.

SAGITTARIUS: the native brings to fifth-house matters a natural optimism and undying enthusiasm, which may be both impressive and a lot of hot air. If the native's positions are well grounded and if Jupiter is well situated in the horoscope, the native stands to find most fifth-house matters profitable and proof for his enthusiasms. The native tends to follow established modes of thinking and behavior on these matters and is therefore unlikely to get out of line or introduce particularly earthy considerations into the picture. Where Sagittarius falls is where the native has his head in the clouds and is rather unworldly and not particularly physical. Relations with children are impressive and on the up and up.

CAPRICORN: the native is apt to assume very serious attitudes about all fifth-house matters as something not to be taken lightly or to be tossed about carelessly. In fact in some way the native senses that his outcome in fifth-house matters in some way affects his basic sense of self-preservation. It can become a life-and-death matter. His reputation and general position are dependent on how he conducts himself in this area. Conditions are generally more favorable toward the close of life than in early years, when things are apt to be restrictive and limited. Relations with children are apt to be burdensome and a heavy responsibility but also a material necessity that eventually has great influence on the native's life.

AQUARIUS: the native's attitude is unconventional, perhaps farsighted but definitely out of step with most people's views on fifth-house matters. This pattern is indicative of a real free swinger on fifth-house pleasures. Responsibility is much less of an issue, and independence and eccentric behavior is far more favored. Relations with children are apt to be odd, sporadic, changeable and inconsistent. One's children are apt to give much concern and provoke conditions in the native's life which bring about major turnabouts.

PISCES: the native may be either exceedingly inspirational and capable of magic in fifth-house matters or off the beam and insincere to the point of phoniness. Even at his worst, however, the native may gain some sort of valuable insight into subconscious matters which has lasting value. There are factors implied or suggested that do not reach the surface. Much of the best that is possible lies submerged and surrounded in mysticism or strange symbols. The native may not be sure himself (or even want to be) of what his real intentions are. Relations with children are apt to be idealized, unreal and reacted to as images rather than concrete realities. This is not to say that this in itself makes them any less satisfying than any other kind of relationship, but it does make them different. There is a rare luck factor which may be favorable for gamble under special circumstances.

For the potential profit that can be realized from fifth-house matters we look to the position of the ruler of the cusp. For this see the section at the end of Chapter 4, page 83.

If the house is occupied by one or more planets, this gives added importance to the affairs of this house and the people connected with it. If that planet is the:

SUN: this is of primary importance, and the native must work out the pattern of his destiny within the framework of fifth-house matters. For more details on this pattern see Chapter 4, "The Character of Your Destiny"—Sun in the fifth house.

MOON: this becomes the focus of the native's emotions and he feels great sensitivity and rapport toward all fifth-house matters, although he may not actually engage in them physically. His feelings run hot and cold and are generally too inconsistent or moody for steady dependability. For more details on this pattern see Chapter 5, "The Focus of Your Emotions"—Moon in the fifth house.

MERCURY: the native has many good thoughts on fifth-house matters which contribute to expressive creativity and the tools for general communication. There should be a talent for witty remarks which are both entertaining and generally persuasive. In speculation this favors the "in and out" situation with quick turnover and not too much commitment at a time in any one place.

SATURN: there are chronic responsibilities which tax and limit the native, so he gets little real pleasure out of fifth-house affairs. Nevertheless, he is bound to these matters in some meaningful way, since his whole sense of self-preservation is tied to a successful handling and dogged determination to see these fifth-house matters through to their bitter end. For more details on this pattern see Chapter 7, "Saturn in Your Horoscope"—Saturn in the fifth house.

MARS: this pattern is favorable for active participation in all phases of the entertainment business, including con games and carnivals. If involved in gambling, the native is advised to be in the business end rather than as a customer or player. It is natural but risky for the native to gamble. Much depends on the condition of Mars (by aspect connection) and the Aries house and the other general conditions of the fifth house itself (sign and ruler).

VENUS: this is favorable for good fortune and artistic benefits from fifth-house matters. The native feels a natural warmth and affection for all people in his fifth house, and they in turn are comforting to him.

NEPTUNE: this is an indication calling for pause and caution. All may not be what it seems both for the native and for others involved with him in fifth-house matters. Someone is liable to get fooled, or defrauded. Still others may be highly inspired and saved by this planetary force. Much depends on the condition of Neptune and other factors such as the Pisces house and the sign on the cusp of the fifth and its ruler.

JUPITER: this is mostly favorable for benefits and profits if pursued with a mature sense of proportion and a careful observance of all the rules of propriety and tradition. One has to be spiritually right in one's objectives in order to reap the abundance of Jupiter, for all the profit is not material. The native will most often be vindicated for his rightness, although this may not always mean cash in the pocket. The feeling of higher assurance should be considered more important. The native should generally have a feeling of a green light to go forward when soundly on the right track of creative effort. The feeling to go forward and expand in this direction is very strong. The native should be willing to take chances in all matters—not just in money gambles. The native may be luckier for others than he is for himself.

PLUTO: this is rather a danger sign when found in the fifth house. Trouble is usually around, and the native is forced to assume a double standard or use a two-edged sword when going about his fifth-house objectives. There is also a social implication in all creative efforts and a predatory sense of retribution which may be too strong for most people's sense of romance. The factor is more that of high drama or the overwhelming sweep of circumstances which force or compel the native to do things he might never have done on his own. Pluto represents the focus of psychic forces which may be necessary in order to handle this department of life. The results may be devastating and require beginning again in a new direction.

URANUS: this is also an upsetting element in the romance situation which introduces the unexpected and a hint of fate. The native must think and behave independently of what is expected of him by others in this area. He must work on some ingenious approach to creativity which is ahead of the crowd. The unconventional approach is favored over following the footsteps of others.

Always look to see in what way these planetary concentrations are fortified or challenged by other planets as they affect the potentials of the fifth house of speculative affairs.

Chapter 14

YOUR JOB, HEALTH

AND OTHER DUTIES

THE 6TH HOUSE

Your obligations, including that which you owe yourself or which others may owe you, are shown by the condition of the sixth house. Responsibilities to yourself would include care and maintenance of your body. Your obligations to others may take the form of a service or labor which you undertake in their behalf.

If the house is unoccupied, it means primarily that you are not consciously burdened by any of these problems. You take what comes and do what you must when the situation demands it without any emotional hangups. If you owe somebody for something, you pay it. If someone owes you something, you collect it. If you have a job to do, you do it. The settlement of debts which arise from daily routine do not enter into the more important perspectives around which the meaning of your life takes shape.

The natural condition of the body such as basic constitution—sound or weak—is shown in the first house. The conditions of sickness or malfunctions which develop along the way are shown in the sixth house as routine health matters.

The general tempo of all these matters is shown by the sign on the cusp. If that sign is:

ARIES: the native must take the initiative to actively correct or restore certain factors which aggressively intrude upon his daily routine. There are many personalities involved in and around one's vocation. It will frequently be necessary to put down forcibly (Mars fashion) certain intrusions or infringements which would appear to intimidate you or challenge your identity. It is apparent that you must energetically exert yourself in all matters connected with obligations which you assume. Nothing in this department of your life will be handled with ease. It will take strong measures and undoubtedly cause friction, which can't be helped.

TAURUS: money and sound housekeeping are factors. Since this Venus sign leans toward comforts and soft living, there may be some need to keep from getting spoiled or overpampered, including these attitudes toward yourself. Routine and pleasant surroundings are mandatory for good health and efficiency on the job.

GEMINI: ideas and mental attitudes are key factors for getting through the day's routine. Do not spend too much time on any one factor. Skim along the top picking out the highlights and cover as much ground as possible as quickly as you can. Nothing will ever be so bad that right thinking won't solve the main problem. Talk things over with others, particularly with fellow workers. Ask for advice and exchange views and opinions. Your sixth-house problem will always be solved in this manner.

CANCER: involvement with the public is indicated—a situation in which many people constantly come and go, particularly women and sensitive types who are seeking protection, subjective support, a kind word, comforting thought and a MOTHERLY GESTURE on your part. In daily routines the native is called upon to "mother" people along. There is much sensitivity about other people's needs and particularly their daily wants. This sign is favorable for nursing or any function that becomes a MOTHER SUBSTITUTE. The native must sometimes consciously "tune out" to insulate and conserve his psychic as well as his physical energies. This is a very productive sign for sound accomplishments in this area of life.

LEO: what is needed is complete self-assurance and even a certain arrogance and assumption of imperial prerogatives. Even though you may not feel you are fully prepared for what is always demanded of you (from duties, jobs, obligations and health routine), you must take the bull by the horns and act as though you were in fact an authority on all these matters. Impressive postures are somehow needed to pull off what must be done. Don't hesitate and don't balk; just wade right in and think about it later.

VIRGO: naturally this introduces limitless details, backbreaking labors, faultfinding criticism, thankless tasks, hair-splitting refinements and a thousand other details that crop up. Extreme care and deliberate measurements and concepts of perfection are objectives to be kept in mind on all sixth-house matters. With Virgo you are well prepared for this and do not mind. In fact, you enjoy doing all these things in your daily work.

LIBRA: reaching out to others and getting them involved in what you are supposed to do is the answer. People in some way become the *material* which you are supposed to work with. This may not necessarily mean the actual physical person, but it is something that has to do with people, what they represent, or how they figure in some equation you are presented with. Being a Venus sign, you need attractive surroundings and peaceful attitudes to get anything done. You need to feel happy and loved. It is also important that you be very fond of your daily work or you will not be able to do it. You should avoid any tasks which you do not enjoy, as they may make you sick. There are plenty of jobs that are enjoyable, so why bother with something that is distasteful? This native usually has Taurus on the ascendant, so there are many clerical talents available which are always in demand. With Libra on the sixth you should always keep looking around—turning the coin over to see what is on the other side. Social life is good for the constitution.

SCORPIO: first, you should seek a situation which fascinates your curiosity. You will often find yourself picked up and swept into situations through force of circumstances—usually fortunate for you, although it may mean misfortune for someone else. You should avoid routine and seek instead a situation that gives you a great deal of freedom. Nothing should be considered fixed or inflexible. The rare good fortune that could result from this pattern lies in the potential of change and your willingness to catch opportunities on the crest of the wave rather than waiting until any advantages are obvious to everybody. It is particularly advisable to avoid what most people are currently exploiting and seek one's fortunes among dead issues. You have the talent for rediscovering or restoring values to dead situations.

SAGITTARIUS: You should look for traditional values and develop a sense of history which would seem to align you to the current leader of an ongoing situation. Big business, corporations and large institutions, which stem from the contributions of many individuals, are indicated. The challenge at hand is not to strike out on one's own but rather to fall in line behind something already well grounded with proof of its workability. The task at hand is not to criticize or harbor self-doubts but rather to march forward and gather the abundance while it lasts.

CAPRICORN: careful selection of one ambitious goal at a time and following through to the bitter end is worth more than all the switching back and forth or opportunistic enticements that may occasionally attract you. Your opportunities in life are somewhat limited and, once offered, are seldom repeated. The challenge for you is straight and narrow, hard and rough, with little time for self-pity or sentimental distractions. Fortunately you have been given either a sound constitution for the task ahead or the will power and discipline to force yourself over the hump. There are many obstacles to be overcome. You may have a chronic health condition which in some way limits you, but this very limitation is necessary in order to keep you in the direction which is best for you. You may be reluctant in youth to see things this way but will eventually in maturity come to see that in your case this is true. All sixth-house conditions are generally unsatisfactory in early years but improve with age. What seemed impossible in your youth is not only possible but desirable in mature life.

AQUARIUS: what is needed is an attitude of complete independence and a reliance on the ingenuity of your own solutions to whatever presents itself in the way of sixth-house matters. Most often you are the victim of circumstances beyond your control. You should not dwell on this as a sign of poor luck or waste time blaming destiny for what befalls you. You are naturally drawn to unusual situations where independence of thought—if not the talent of genius—may be necessary to lift you up and get you going again. Whatever happens to you in this department of life comes about unexpectedly—both the good and the bad. While you may be struck down one day, you may be blown sky high the next. This is the department of your life where almost anything goes and the unconventional approach is always advisable over ordinary methods.

PISCES: you are divinely guided to those obligations and situations where you are required to labor. The point is that you should follow your intuition and allow yourself to be guided rather than to force issues or dictate your own terms. The saying "Those who stand and wait are also served" very much applies with Pisces on the sixth house. The challenge is not so much a matter of faith but rather opening up the sensitivities so that you actually feel what is best for you. This intuitive guide will never fail you. With Aries on the seventh house and Libra on the ascendant this guidance may well involve following an outstanding individual who will go out of his way to help you. You are sure to have abundant social contacts for finding this individual. It is up to you to be willing to follow.

Refer to the section at the end of Chapter 4, page 83, for details on the house ruler of the sign on the cusp—in this case the sixth house.

If the house is occupied by one or more planets, the affairs of the sixth house naturally gain in importance and concern. If that planet is the:

SUN: this of course establishes the sixth house as the setting through which you will unfold the character of your destiny. You will have a definite amount of inner resolve to be considered on all sixth-house matters. The Sun indicates a lifelong struggle or concern over these matters. You will be supported in your tasks and labors by the affairs and persons of the Leo house. The purpose or direction of these labors is indicated by the location of the planet that rules the sixth-house cusp. For more details on this placement of the Sun see Chapter 4, "The Character of Your Destiny"—Sun in the sixth house.

MOON: the sixth house now becomes the focus of your emotional responses. You suffer much tension and inner turmoil on the affairs and people of this house. You are supported and fortified in your anxieties by the affairs and people of your Cancer house. The emotional advantage of this involvement in sixth-house obligations is indicated by the location of the ruler of the sixth cusp. For more details see Chapter 5, "The Focus of Your Emotions"—Moon in the sixth house.

MERCURY: you have many original thoughts on how to meet and handle all sixth-house matters. Basically you see all problems in this area as a mental challenge which requires clear thinking and sound views. You have many mental contributions to make on these subjects, and your first thoughts always arise from some connection in this area. Some aspect of your ideal vocation has to do with writing or the expression or communication of ideas. For the supporting source of your mental stimuli see the affairs and persons of your Gemini and Virgo houses. For the most useful application of these ideas see the location of the ruler of the sixth cusp.

SATURN: you have very serious considerations to make about sixth-house matters, which are essentially vital to your entire welfare. None of the affairs of this house is to be taken lightly. Indeed the very development of your sense of self-preservation must stem from tasks and duties arising out of sixth-house matters. Conditions in early life are bound to be difficult but always improve with age. Health matters may be a permanent problem. Wherever Saturn falls more or less creates permanent problems or chronic conditions. Even after the problems are not so pressing, you never feel secure about these matters and long years of fear have formed basic habits of thrift which are impossible to overcome or toss aside. You must look to the affairs and people of your Capricorn house to know who or what will most help you meet the challenge in the sixth house of duty. For the direction of the immediate step forward after you have somewhat solved your security problems, look to the location of the ruler of the sixth cusp. For more details on Saturn in the sixth house see Chapter 7, "Saturn in Your Horoscope."

MARS: you are very impulsive and rash in your handling of sixth-house matters, which gives rise to misunderstandings, arguments and trouble. You must inevitably face some sort of aggressive competition from situations and people of the sixth house (servants, fellow workers, your employees, health administrators, etc.), and you must somehow get the competitive edge on them in order to solve the problem. You will have to fight in order to hold your own. You should have good regenerative powers, but it is wise to ease off every once in a while to recharge your batteries because you can't push Mars every minute. Saturn is the steady pusher; Mars is only the trigger. The force of Mars is EXTRA ENERGY when you need just that one bit more to get over the line.

VENUS: this is a very favorable placement which ensures that your job, duties and daily affairs are usually pleasant, attractive and gratifying. The keynote for Venus is conditions of cooperation and that which is pleasantly agreeable. There should be social possibilities connected with work, and you are destined to find peace and contentment in your vocation. The affairs and people of your Taurus and Libra houses are always willing to help this along. The reason why you are given this pleasant lift in your labors is indicated by the location of the ruler of the sixth-house cusp.

NEPTUNE: this introduces certain conditions or attitudes which are not altogether realistic. It may be necessary to pretend to be somewhere else or be someone else, or wear a mask, or assume a carefully contrived image of what is expected of you in order to meet these problems. Since the sixth house is the area of everyday routine, it means you cannot afford to let others see your real nature in everyday matters. This could also suggest that your everyday life revolved around conditions where the image was considered the real and the reality was dealing with contrived images. Movies, television and the theater are like this. Much depends on how well fortified the Neptune is (by being keyed to planets which get things done like the Sun, Mars and Saturn) in order to determine how personally inspirational you may be. The challenge here, of course, is to be inspirational and idealistic in all sixth-house matters and not phony or contrived. Look for the affairs and people of your Pisces house for what spiritual guidance they can give you to dissolve the labors of the sixth house. This would be your source of "magic" to be used. The constructive purpose for this magic touch (which may have to be learned) is shown by the location of the ruler of the sixth-house cusp.

JUPITER: this planet always brings some material benefits and lightens the burdens so that you feel enthusiastic, optimistic and very righteous about your sixth-house routines. This may not be a steady flow or the abundance you might prefer, but you will never be entirely wanting or utterly without cause and encouragement for hope in the affairs of this house. The affairs and people of your Sagittarius house will always confirm this good fortune for you. The reason or possible application of this good fortune (such as it is) is indicated by the location of the ruler of the sixth-house cusp.

PLUTO: this is a disruptive element in the conduct of your duties and responsibilities. Conditions of the sixth house may on occasion get down to absolute rock bottom before they can show any improvement, and then it is likely that a turn of events will change everything so completely that you are made into an entirely new person. The going may get rough, but the outcome could be astounding. When Pluto does something, it does it from the ground up by transforming people into new characters. The past may seem unrelated to the potentials of the new situation. You are advised to prepare yourself for sweeping changes throughout your life in all sixth-house matters. In jobs this will call for complete new beginnings or carrying on two jobs at once. In health it means drastic confrontations with death but not necessarily fatal. It can mean the death of old conditions. In relations with fellow workers, servants, employees and those who are working out obligations for you or you with them, it means violent reactions and regenerative changes. If Pluto is in the sixth house, you are already aware of this potential threat and instinctively allow for the consequences. The affairs and people of your Scorpio house contribute to these changes and social implications in your obligations. The desirable aftermath of such adjustment to change is shown by the location of the ruler of the sixth-house cusp.

URANUS: this erratic element produces sudden and unexpected events or conditions. You have already prepared for this by assuming an air of independence and allowability for the intervention of fate itself. You may have some unusual talent which, if otherwise well supported in the character, may approach the quality of genius. You will tend to behave oddly in your daily life and fellow workers may think you a bit queer. The source for this talent comes from the affairs and people of your Aquarius house, which is the storehouse for your forward thinking, which finds focus through Uranus in the sixth house of labors and routine. The best direction in which this potential genius can be used or projected is shown by the location of the ruler of the sixth-house cusp.

Chapter 15

OTHER PEOPLE IN YOUR LIFE

THE 7TH HOUSE

The importance of other people in your life is shown in the horoscope by the condition of the seventh house. The world of course is a gigantic complex of infinite variety. But each of us, as we view the world outside ourselves, is geared to select and concentrate on one specific type which for us holds the most interest. The type or quality that it suggests is identified by the sign on our seventh house.

When we say "type," we are referring to the quality that the type suggests, whether this is found in the personality image (a surface impression), the more inner manifestations of the ego-drive (related to the Sun), or the emotional focus (related to the Moon). Our sensibilities are able to detect this quality no matter which planetary force reflects it.

These are the general qualities that catch our eye and interest:

ARIES: We always notice outstanding individualists who are forcing their way above the crowd by some distinguishing characteristic. All the general Aries characteristics are what we see first in others when we look around us. Those who do not in some way have the Aries characteristics do not hold our attention in the same way. We tend to pass them by, since we do not include them as potential for either cooperative partnership or engaging competition.

TAURUS: The type we notice is physical, earthy, practical, rugged, dependable, and he gravitates toward conditions of comfort and attractive surroundings.

GEMINI: This type is witty, charming, mentally stimulating, full of ideas and opinions, outspoken in his criticism—and he flies from subject to subject!

CANCER: This type is home-loving, gentle, protective, motherly, sensitive, sympathetic and seems conscious of great potentialities if we can get his attention.

LEO: This type is flamboyant, impressive, patronizing, self-assured, gay, entertaining, enthusiastic and self-motivated.

VIRGO: This type is very much the perfectionist in everything, fond of refinements, hair-splitting distinctions, and careful choice of details, meticulous in speech and manner, somewhat subservient or condescending and humble, not particularly interested in pushing himself forward, more anxious to get things right than to impress others with his talents.

LIBRA: This type is social, always seeking others out or trying to turn them on to test their views or reactions, and if possible draw them out so they see themselves to new advantage. They make us feel good because they are interested in us.

SCORPIO: This type is secretive but highly suggestive of hidden depths and possibilities. There is always a hint of sexuality and the possibility of a quick pickup or shot in the arm that comes from contact with this type. There is also some hint of danger lurking and the thrill of the unknown.

SAGITTARIUS: This type has his head in the clouds and speaks with all the assurance and authority of God's chosen messenger. They preach a lot and often convince others with the sweep of their enthusiasm and optimistic views. They seem to have an inside track to all the obvious advantages that anyone in his right mind should want. They want you to see the world through their eyes.

CAPRICORN: This type is slow, mature, unruffled, doggedly persistent, and gives the appearance of being his own master, making his own rules and absolutely sure of knowing what he wants and getting it.

AQUARIUS: This type is friendly yet detached and seems to open doors in relationships or extend the boundaries of one's thinking, or to suggest new possibilities or improved methods of doing things. They seem to be in touch with all sorts of marvelous possibilities that seem to be there if one has the insight to see things differently as they do.

PISCES: This type is rather quiet, unassuming, preferring to drift to the background and observe what others are about. When approached, they are always warm and comfortable and willing to invite you in to share their special perch. But you have to look hard to see if they are real or just a dream because things they do or say suggest some sort of unreality or being in touch with things that ordinary people do not see.

Next we look to see what planets are in the seventh house. If there are no planets in the seventh house, other people in general do not play an important role in your life. You can take them or leave them alone. They drift in and out of importance in your affairs according to the immediate circumstances. You do not take your daily cue from general contact with others. Other people do not control or dominate your affairs. It is more likely that you, instead, dominate others—one or many, as the case may be.

If there are one or more planets in the seventh house, other people in your life become correspondingly more important in your daily affairs. Each planet in the seventh house refers to some cue which you take from others in respect to that quality in your nature. If that planet is the:

SUN: this of course is of major importance. Other people dominate your ego, but it is only through others that you can fulfill yourself or your destiny. The presence of the Sun indicates a lifelong problem in adjusting to this interference of others in your affairs. For more details on the importance of this pattern see Chapter 4, "The Character of Your Destiny"—Sun in the seventh house.

MOON: your emotions are entirely focused through others and they have the power to turn your feelings on or off as they wish. Emotionally nothing is entirely up to you. Your emotions run hot and cold about the desirability of cooperating in partnerships or openly contesting others in competition. For more details on this pattern see Chapter 5, "The Focus of Your Emotions"—Moon in the seventh house.

MERCURY: your thinking is keyed to others for stimulation and any opportunity to express yourself. You need other people to pull your thoughts together and make any sense or purpose. This position would ensure much mental intercourse with others on all subjects. It is not, however, a very independent or desirable position for one's "thinking box." The mental contributions which you make to others are shown by the Gemini and Virgo houses. The effective presentation of this joint expression or competitive debate is shown by the location of the ruler of the seventh house.

SATURN: your sense of security comes from others. You generally find others depressing or restrictive, and they sit on your personality development. Saturn in this position inclines you to accept a certain amount of discipline and/or punishment from other people. What in your nature needs this discipline and guidance is shown by your Capricorn house. The first step forward in realistic cooperation is shown by the location of the ruler of your seventh house.

MARS: makes you feel highly competitive with everyone. This creates very scrappy and argumentive relationships, even on a casual level. Relationships are never equal or even. One or the other seems to be sparring for position or aggressive domination. However, others are favored to win out over you, for which you are secretly prepared and actually somewhat enjoy. Relations with others always imply physical or even sexual contact, although, of course, this may not be consummated. The reason you feel impelled to fight with others is to establish the affairs of your Aries house which need an aggressive push in order to formulate the individuality of their character. The purpose that this pioneering effort can have in the rest of your life is shown by the location of the ruler of the seventh house.

VENUS: this makes for very loving relationships with others because you initially feel loving toward them and they in turn seem to return this warm affection. You are extremely dependent on others for any emotional expression or balance. There is little possibility of any emotional balance if unsupported by others. This is not a very healthy pattern. The sense of happiness and contentment, having hardly any self-sufficiency at all, is far too vulnerable. The qualities in your nature which make it possible for you to feel so affectionate toward others is shown by your Taurus and Libra houses. The contentment which this can spread to other areas of your life is shown by the location of the ruler of your seventh house.

NEPTUNE: there is a certain amount of deception involved in your relations with others. In some cases, depending on the importance of the Pisces/Neptune axis in your life, this could be considered a source of inspiration. In most cases it will involve some form of playacting, pretentious attitudes or exaggerated conditions of imagination. Your relationships with others would tend to dissolve under everyday pressures. You will idealize others in such a way that makes it almost impossible to see them clearly as they really are. All your relations with others will tend to become disappointing if put to any kind of a practical test. You are encouraged by your Pisces house to take this imaginative position. The consequences of this magical relationship are suggested by the location of the ruler of your seventh house.

JUPITER: other people stimulate your sense of conviction and corresponding spirit of expansive optimism. Your relations with others will tend to bring out the best in you with a corresponding feeling of goodwill all around. This is a very favorable position for Jupiter in the horoscope, giving ideal balance in all interpersonal relationships. The conviction for this sense of rightness in dealing with others is supported by the Sagittarian house. The extension of this joint goodwill is suggested by the location of the ruler of the seventh house.

PLUTO: you tend to run up against the worst side in other people or at least catch them somewhat at their worst advantage. You invariably experience two sides of other people's nature or a split or dual attitude on their part. You also show two sides to others. Other people have the effect on you of wiping out certain accomplishments in the past, causing the need for you to start over again. You are drawn into or brought face-to-face with social implications by contact with others. A potentially violent and disruptive element in your makeup is brought to light by contact with others.

URANUS: like Pluto this pattern creates disruptive and chaotic conditions which upset normal reactions with others. First, you have a very independent and unique view of others, and any possible influence they might or should have in your affairs tends toward unconventional results. All contact begins and ends suddenly without explanation, which is generally due to uncertain circumstances beyond your control. Other people have a strange effect on you because the chain reactions that they set off seem to be the opposite of what they may have intended. The source of this independent attitude toward others is found in matters of the Aquarius house. The explosive effect that this is likely to have in other departments of your life is shown by the location of the ruler of the seventh house.

The focus of these cue points by which you take your green light from others is further modified by strong aspects that planets in the seventh house may make to other forces. For more details on this see Chapter 9, "Aspects Between Planets."

COMPARISON OF HOROSCOPES

The comparison of horoscopes to see how one person relates to another is fascinating and involves many subtle factors. Eventually (if warranted) every major element should be considered in turn. This is especially true when dealing with members of the same family, who are already tied by bonds of responsibility.

CONSIDERATION OF THE RELATIONSHIP BETWEEN THE TWO EGOS should be the basic framework around which any further details can be developed. As the Sun is the symbol of the ego-force, first study the implications shown by THE HOUSE IN YOUR HOROSCOPE WHERE HIS SUN FALLS. This shows the primary POTENTIAL HE WILL HAVE ON YOU. As a refinement of this it is also equally valid to test your Sun in his horoscope to show your potential effect on him.

However, before you make this test it is most essential that you already recognize the importance that the affairs of EACH OF YOUR HOUSES plays in your own life.

A key of great value in this study—which does not always stand out as obviously a matter of importance—is THE SIGNIFICANCE IN YOUR AFFAIRS OF THE HOUSE INDICATED BY THE NATURAL ORDER OF THE SIGN ON YOUR ASCENDANT. For example, if Libra (the seventh sign of the zodiac) is the sign on your ascendant, this indicates that your seventh house is an area where meaningful relationships are very important to you. If Capricorn, the tenth sign, were on the ascendant, it would indicate your tenth house. If Taurus, the second sign, were on the ascendant, it would indicate the importance in your life of people whose Sun fell in your second house. When you think about this, it should become more obvious, since the sign on the ascendant has everything to do with the manner in which the native fulfills his personality development and makes initial contact with others. And the basic nature of this sign is related to the house which it naturally rules—that is, its order in the zodiac. What may not be fully appreciated is the further implications which this fulfillment of the personality has in bringing to flower the other departments of life.

To make this analysis of ego relationship, we rotate our own horoscope to bring the house in question to the ascendant position. This puts the affairs of that house in the focus of the immediate environment, which is the subject that the two of you have most in common. You will now see that between the two of you this places ALL

YOUR AFFAIRS IN AN ENTIRELY DIFFERENT PERSPECTIVE. For example, if his Sun falls in your fifth house, we move your horoscope around so that your fifth house now becomes the ascendant. Your sixth house is now in the second house position. Your eighth house is now in the fourth house position, and so on. When his Sun falls in your first house, there is no need to move the horoscope. His effect on you leaves your own affairs in the same perspective as they normally have been.

A word here about the fact that you may already know that you do not like persons whose Sun falls in certain signs of the zodiac. Unless your horoscope happens to have zero degrees of each sign on the cusps, it is more correct to realize that it is certain areas of the zodiac which you may not like rather than certain signs in their entirety. You may have noticed that invariably you do not like Aries types or Virgo types and so on. If this is so, the reasons for this will be found by the above method of rotating certain portions of that sign to your ascendant position. For example, if you have 10° of Scorpio on the fifth house and you move this up to the ascendant position, only 20° of Scorpio will fall in this category and the first 10° of Scorpio will fall in the prior category (or in this example, a fourth-house influence).

HOW MUCH COMPETITION CAN YOU TAKE?

If his Sun falls in your FIRST HOUSE, this introduces an element of competition in all your affairs because of your respective egos. Depending on how strong your own ego requirements are, this may be acceptable to you or utterly intolerable. If you are the type who does not mind domination by another (the extreme example being your Sun in your seventh house), then you will accept this person quite naturally. In many instances you may feel that someone else can do things better than you could yourself and be grateful rather than resentful. It is impossible for you to ignore this person when he is around. The danger is that you are inclined to overreact. You take what others say or do too seriously or make too much of it, as though this were some kind of personal challenge. You can always learn something from this party which can strengthen your own sense of self-worth, but it may be at some expense to the ease or cordiality of your social relations. His presence should force you to better yourself in order to top him. It is generally impossible for you to completely accept this reason without reservations. Most important in dealing with this person, do not tell him your troubles or give reasons for any possible indecision. This person will always take you at your face value, so it is important that you maintain "face" no matter what may be going on inside. This is an entirely open man-to-man relationship. This person can help you or force you to better YOURSELF in some way. He is not, unfortunately, in a position to help or change any of your other affairs since your perspective on these' matters is still the same with or without his influence. Those areas in your life which are a problem will still be a problem and those areas in which you have talent and success will still seem that way.

COULD YOU USE A LITTLE HELP?

If his Sun falls in your SECOND HOUSE, this person stands in some way to help improve your source of supply or earning power. In some cases and at certain times this person might be a drain on your resources, but eventually he will be in a position to contribute substantially to your financial welfare. This is one of the most favorable positions for warm human relationships. You—in some way without knowing why—are able to open up something for the other party which otherwise might never have been possible for him. And he will always want to help you in any way he can to better yourself and realize your full potential, particularly for you to be paid for your real worth. In his eyes you can do no wrong. With your first house in the twelfth position HE KNOWS ALL YOUR SECRET FAULTS BUT THIS MAKES NO DIFFERENCE. Nothing you say or do will turn him against you. He will always stand ready to help you improve some personal skill you may have. With your twelfth at the eleventh position YOUR SUBCONSCIOUS MOTIVATIONS BECOME A HOPE. With your eleventh at the tenth YOUR HOPES BECOME POSSIBLE OF RECOGNITION. With your tenth at the ninth YOUR AMBITIONS BECOME A LAW. With your ninth at the eighth YOUR PRINCIPLES BECOME FLEXIBLE. With your eighth at the seventh OTHERS HELP YOU MAKE CHANGES. With your seventh at the sixth OTHERS BECOME YOUR SERVANTS. With your sixth at the fifth YOUR DUTIES BECOME PLEASURABLE AND CREATIVE. With your fifth at the fourth YOUR EFFORTS TO EXTEND YOUR EGO CREATIVELY BECOME PART OF

YOUR NATURAL TECHNIQUE. With your fourth at the third YOUR SUBJECTIVE SELF CAN BE OPENLY REVIEWED IN FRIENDLY CONVERSATION. With your third at the second YOUR IDEAS BECOME PROFITABLE.

THE TROUBLE WITH BROTHERS AND SISTERS IS . . .

If his Sun falls in your THIRD HOUSE, you should enjoy a congenial mental rapport. Each should prove mentally stimulating to the other. This will be similar to a brotherly or sisterly relationship which with time tends to fade away as each matures and follows his own life. By revolving your horoscope we find: With your second in the twelfth IT IS BETTER TO KEEP YOUR RESOURCES TO YOURSELF. With your first at the eleventh YOUR IDENTITY, INSTEAD OF STANDING ALONE, BECOMES ONE OF A GROUP. With your twelfth at the tenth YOUR SECRETS LEAK OUT IN PUBLIC. With your eleventh at the ninth YOUR PRIVATE DREAMS SEEM HAMPERED BY CODES AND PRINCIPLES. With your tenth at the eighth THERE IS A TENDENCY TO KILL YOUR AMBITIONS OR BE FORCED TO ADJUST THEM. With your ninth at the seventh OTHER PEOPLE DICTATE WHAT PRINCIPLES YOU SHOULD BELIEVE IN. With your eighth at the sixth THE SPIRITUAL IMPLICATIONS OF WHAT YOU DO BECOME A MATTER OF DUTY. With your seventh at the fifth YOUR CREATIVITY AND EVEN YOUR PLEASURES ARE CONTROLLED BY OTHERS. With your sixth at the fourth YOUR DUTY TO FAMILY AND HERITAGE IS HEAVILY STRESSED AT ALL TIMES. With your fifth at the third YOUR PLEASURES AND ROMANTIC PURSUITS ARE MUCH DISCUSSED BETWEEN YOU. With your fourth at the second YOUR LOYALTY TO FAMILY BECOMES A MATTER OF DOLLARS AND CENTS.

WHO NEEDS ANOTHER PARENT?

If his Sun falls in your FOURTH HOUSE, the relationship is definitely that of "him" as your parent or guardian to "you" as the child. As with all parents, they must be obeyed, and what they consider as best for your own good is accepted without question or there is trouble. As long as you are willing to accept this parental authority, things run smoothly. And you will always find that you definitely do take more from these people than you ever will from others. The bond is close, but as with parents, it can become oppressive and suffocating. As one matures, he should be able to make it on his own without a parent continually watching over him. One may feel indulgent from time to time, as one would to a parent's interest, but in the long run it is pretty much of a "you under their thumb" position—or "Look, Ma, I would rather do it myself." It is interesting how this accounts for older people allowing themselves to be dominated by certain young people or how a young man can be attracted to a much older woman (the mother domination). With your third at the twelfth YOU ARE BEST ADVISED TO KEEP HOW YOU REALLY THINK TO YOURSELF. With your second at the eleventh YOUR ABILITY TO EARN IS CONSIDERED A HOPE OF PRIMARY IMPORTANCE BETWEEN YOU. With your first at the tenth YOUR SELF-WORTH IS AUTOMATICALLY ACCEPTED TO BE OF OBVIOUS VALUE WITHOUT QUESTION. With your twelfth at the ninth YOUR INNER MOTIVATIONS MUST SUPPORT YOUR PRINCIPLES WHETHER THEY CAN BE PROVED OR NOT. With your eleventh at the eighth YOUR PERSONAL HOPES ARE CONSIDERED THE THING ABOUT YOU MOST IN NEED OF CHANGE. With your tenth at the seventh YOUR AMBITION AND POSITION IN LIFE SEEMS WHOLLY DOMINATED BY WHAT OTHER PEOPLE WANT. With your ninth at the sixth YOUR PRINCIPLES MUST GIVE WAY TO DUTY. With your eighth at the fifth YOUR OWN SOURCE OF REJUVENATION SEEMS TO BE IN SEEKING PLEASURE OR TAKING GREAT RISKS. With your seventh at the fourth OTHER PEOPLE'S INFLUENCE AND DESIRABILITY SEEMS SUBJECT TO PARENTAL APPROVAL. With your sixth at the third YOUR SENSE OF DUTY IS CONSTANTLY UNDER DISCUSSION. With your fifth at the second YOU ARE REMINDED THAT IDLE PURSUITS OF RELAXATION FOR PLEASURE WOULD BETTER BE SPENT TRYING TO EARN MONEY.

THE JOYS OF LIVING

If his Sun falls in your FIFTH HOUSE, this is usually a most happy relationship, although not entirely free from pitfalls. You may want to enjoy yourself with this person, and many serious considerations are willingly put aside to do so. The danger is that too many important considerations may have to be sidetracked for this relationship. Your desire is to give to and protect him as you would a fond child. Yet any sense of real responsibility between you would only spoil the fun. In order to get the most of this relationship you must be indulgent and at times childish and playful. With your fourth at the twelfth PARENTAL RESTRICTIONS ARE PUSHED INTO THE BACKGROUND. With your third at the eleventh YOU SPEAK MUCH OF THE DREAMS YOU SHARE IN COMMON. With your second at the tenth YOUR FONDEST AMBITION IS TO HAVE MORE SO YOU CAN GIVE MORE. With your first at the ninth YOUR PERSONALITY IS ESTABLISHED RATHER THAN CHALLENGED. With your twelfth at the eighth YOUR REAL MOTIVATIONS ARE KEPT SECRET OR EVEN CHANGED. With your eleventh at the seventh YOU ALLOW WHAT YOU DREAM FOR TO BE DICTATED OR CONTROLLED BY OTHERS. With your tenth at the sixth YOUR OWN AMBITIONS ARE SET ASIDE FOR DUTIES TO OTHERS. With your ninth at the fifth ALL YOUR PRINCIPLES SEEM CREATIVE. With your eighth at the fourth CHANGE SEEMS POSSIBLE IN ALL THINGS THAT WERE PREVIOUSLY CONSIDERED FIXED AND IRREVOCABLE. With your seventh at the third EVERYONE SEEMS TO STIMULATE YOU. With your sixth at the second EVEN YOUR OBLIGATIONS SEEM PROFITABLE.

THE SLAVERY OF DEVOTION

If his Sun falls in your SIXTH HOUSE, this is similar to two ships who pass in the night. In the morning they may be out of sight. The sole purpose is to repay a service or debt of some kind. The controlling factor is a sense of obligation, which one or the other may feel without knowing exactly why. At the same time the coming together is somewhat inevitable. If you accept assistance from this person, he must eventually be paid back IN FULL. You may be well loved and well served, but somehow you will pay for it and only you can know what the price is. Service and discharge of obligation are the things that bring you together. With your fifth at the twelfth PLEASURES AND JOYS ARE MINIMAL OR FRUSTRATING. With your fourth at the eleventh THE STRENGTH OF YOUR SUBJECTIVE SELF BECOMES A BOND OF MUTUAL SUPPORT. With your third at the tenth YOUR THOUGHT BECOMES HIS COMMAND. With your second at the ninth YOUR POSSESSIONS BECOME SACRED. With your first at the eighth YOUR PERSONAL IDENTITY IS FORCED TO CHANGE IN SUBTLE WAYS. With your twelfth at the seventh YOUR SECRET BURDENS ARE AT LEAST PARTIALLY SHARED BY ANOTHER. With your eleventh at the sixth YOUR HOPES BECOME HIS DUTY. With your tenth at the fifth YOUR AMBITION IS SHELVED IN FAVOR OF PLEASURE AND RO-MANCE. With your ninth at the fourth YOUR PRINCIPLES AT TIMES SEEM MORE IMPORTANT THAN YOU. With your eighth at the third YOUR THOUGHTS SEEK CHANGE. With your sixth at the second YOUR DUTIES SEEM ENTIRELY MONETARY.

THE PITFALLS OF PARTNERSHIP, OR ONE SOUL AS TWO

If his Sun falls in your SEVENTH HOUSE, you must either co-operate completely or else go your separate ways to avoid becoming enemies. There is no in-between possible in this relationship. There seems to be a certain ideality and obvious advantage to your becoming partners. But there also seems to be a certain natural antipathy of attitudes, which could lead to total disagreements. There will always be a tendency to pull in opposite directions, which must be over-come if the partnership is to survive. Uppermost at all times must be the slogan: For the good of both. As will be noted from rotating your horoscope, placing your seventh in the first position reverses all the natural order of your own horoscope, which in a sense delivers you completely into the control of others. With your seventh at the first OTHER PEOPLE BECOME MORE IMPORTANT TO YOU THAN YOU ARE TO YOURSELF. With your sixth at the twelfth ALL YOUR DUTIES AND OBLIGATIONS BECOME DEEPLY IM-PLANTED IN YOUR SUBCONSCIOUS. With your fifth at the eleventh ANY THOUGHT OF PLEASURE MUST BE CONSID-ERED A SHARED THING. With your fourth at the tenth THE FOUNDATIONS ON WHICH YOU STAND ARE PUT ON THE TABLE FOR BETTER OR WORSE. With your third at the ninth YOUR PERSONAL THINKING MUST SOMEHOW ASSUME THE STATUS OF A GENERAL CODE OR PRINCIPLE. With your sec-ond at the eighth YOUR EARNINGS BECOME JOINT PROPERTY. With your first at the seventh YOUR IDENTITY IS IRREVOCABLY TIED TO ANOTHER. With your twelfth at the sixth YOUR INNER

MOTIVATIONS BECOME A DEBT. With your eleventh at the fifth THE DREAMS YOU SHARE WITH OTHERS BECOME A SOURCE OF PLEASURE AND CREATIVITY. With your tenth at the fourth YOUR REPUTATION, INSTEAD OF BEING A RESULT OF YOUR METHOD, BECOMES THE METHOD BY WHICH YOU REACH A POSITION. With your ninth at the third YOU TEND TO INVENT YOUR OWN PRINCIPLES. With your eighth at the second JOINT PROPERTY BECOMES ENTRUSTED TO YOUR CARE.

THAT ONE STEP FURTHER ON

If his Sun falls in your EIGHTH HOUSE, this is a touchy relationship with many secret undertones. This person is capable of bringing about great changes in you or helping you discover significant things about yourself. In any event you will seldom be the same again. What probably brings you two together in the first place is some impending need or desire for change which you may feel is somewhat overdue. The eighth house is the area of secret implications, and there will be plenty of them in your relationship with this person. It depends on your own chart how well you can handle this sort of thing and whether you can afford this person in your life. This person will set about to change you in some way for which you may not be at all prepared. The best that he can do is to bring alive or rekindle something which you may have long ago given up. With your seventh in the twelfth WHAT OTHER PEOPLE THINK ABOUT YOU OR THEIR GENERAL REACTIONS TO YOU WILL BE PUT OUT OF YOUR CONSCIOUS THINKING. With your sixth in the eleventh YOU WILL REEXAMINE YOUR DUTIES AND OBLIGATIONS AND SEE HOW THEY MEASURE UP TO YOUR DREAMS AND HOPES. With your fifth at the tenth YOU ARE BOUND TO BECOME MORE AMBITIOUS ABOUT YOUR SENSE OF CREATIVITY AND YOUR CHANCES TO WIN. With your fourth at the ninth YOU ARE BOUND TO RECOGNIZE MORE EFFECTIVELY JUST HOW YOUR OWN SUBJECTIVITY FITS IN WITH THE ESTABLISHED CODES OF OTHERS. With your third at the eighth YOU WILL BE FAR LESS HESITANT ABOUT CHANGING YOUR THINKING, EXPLORING NEW POSSIBILITIES, AND REVIVING SOME FORMER IDEAS WHICH NOW SEEM WORKABLE. With your second at the seventh OTHER PEOPLE SEEM MORE WILLING TO CONTRIBUTE TO YOUR

FINANCIAL WELFARE AND PAY YOU FOR YOUR TRUE CON-
TRIBUTIONS. With your first at the sixth YOU WILL APPLY
YOURSELF MORE ENTHUSIASTICALLY TOWARD YOUR OB-
LIGATIONS WHICH SEEM NEWLY IMPORTANT. You now see
your duties in a new light. With your twelfth at the fifth YOU
BRING YOUR INNER MOTIVATIONS MORE IN LINE WITH
ANY CREATIVE EFFORTS OF YOUR EGO. With your eleventh at
the fourth YOUR DREAMS AND HOPES BECOME MORE CLOSE-
LY ASSOCIATED WITH THE METHODS AND TECHNIQUES
THAT YOU PRACTICE. With your tenth at the third YOU ARE
ABLE TO SEE AND TALK MORE CLEARLY ABOUT WHAT
YOUR REAL AMBITIONS ARE OR USED TO BE. With your ninth
at the second YOU ARE BETTER ABLE TO STRUCTURE YOUR
HIGHER THOUGHTS INTO PRODUCTIVE AND PROFITABLE
CHANNELS.

YOUR BEST ADVERTISER

If his Sun is in your NINTH HOUSE, this person will always
promote you and champion your thoughts as though they were his
own. This person will advertise you and publish your good points to
the world. He likes you and wants to stand behind you in every way.
The relationship is best kept on a lofty, inspirational level. It is not
entirely designed for the everyday routine demands of living. Once
he has established his goodwill with you, then it will be easy for you
to let this person become your teacher. With your eighth at the
twelfth THOUGHTS OF CHANGE OR FEELING THE NECESSITY
TO MAKE FURTHER CHANGES ARE PUT OUT OF YOUR CON-
SCIOUS MIND. With your seventh at the eleventh YOU ARE WILL-
ING TO MELD YOUR DREAMS AND HOPES WITH THIS
PERSON. With your sixth at the tenth YOU FEEL A NEW SENSE
OF DUTY TO REALIZE YOUR BEST AMBITIONS. With your fifth
at the ninth YOUR SENSE OF CREATIVITY SEEMS TO FIND
TRAILBLAZERS WHO WILL MAKE THINGS EASIER FOR YOU.
With your fourth at the eighth THE IRREVOCABLE INHERI-
TANCE OF YOUR PAST SOMEHOW SEEMS NOT SO FIXED;
INDEED A SHIFT OF ACCENT AND SOME THINGS CAN SEEM
TOTALLY DIFFERENT. With your third at the seventh YOUR
SENSE OF COMMUNICATION SEEMS TO FIND A NEW AUDI-

ENCE. With your second at the sixth YOU ACCEPT A GREATER RESPONSIBILITY TOWARD REALIZING THE REAL WORTH OF YOUR EFFORTS. With your first at the fifth YOUR SELF-WORTH SEEMS MORE INVINCIBLE AND WORTHY OF CREATIVE EFFORTS. With your twelfth at the fourth YOU ARE ABLE TO REEXAMINE YOUR INNER MOTIVATIONS AND FIND THEM MORE IN LINE WITH YOUR BACKGROUND THAN YOU IMAGINED. What you are seems more in the line of a natural development than a step out of line. With your eleventh at the third YOU ARE BETTER ABLE TO EXPRESS YOUR HOPES AND DREAMS. With your tenth at the second YOUR AMBITIONS SEEM TO PAY OFF AS NEVER BEFORE.

THE HEAVY HAND OF AUTHORITY

If his Sun is in your TENTH HOUSE, this, as with all the angle positions, creates a touchy relationship. This person can undoubtedly do a great deal for your reputation and position in life IF HE REALLY WANTS TO. Unfortunately he does not always want to. Many of them would prefer to keep you in a subordinate position where they remain your boss or commanding officer. This person has the edge on you with regard to where you desire to be. There is a definite envy involved which you either have to forget about or challenge this person on the matter. It is generally not favorable to have other people's Sun sitting in your tenth house of ambition. THEIR EGO CHALLENGES YOUR RIGHT TO BE RECOGNIZED. The best that can be said is that their challenge to you may help you make your best effort to get what you REALLY WANT.

With your ninth at the twelfth YOUR PRINCIPLES MUST BE DRIVEN UNDERGROUND AND KEPT TO YOURSELF. With your eighth at the eleventh YOU MAY HAVE TO SEEK THE FRIENDLY SUPPORT OF OTHERS IN ORDER TO EFFECT THE CHANGES WHICH YOU MAY CONSIDER NECESSARY. With your seventh at the tenth OTHERS SEEM TO BE PERSONALLY DICTATING YOUR GOALS AND CONTROLLING THE AMOUNT OF RECOGNITION YOU SHOULD RECEIVE. With your sixth at the ninth YOUR SENSE OF DUTY AND RESPONSIBILITY IS FORCED TO BE CONSIDERED AS LAW. With your fifth at the eighth YOUR IDEAS ABOUT PLEASURE AND THE PLACE OF ROMANCE

WILL HAVE TO BE CHANGED IN SOME WAY. With your fourth at the seventh YOU AND WHAT STANDS BEHIND YOU WILL BE THE SUBJECT OF OTHER PEOPLE'S REVIEW AND/OR JUDGMENT. With your third at the sixth THE FREEDOM OF YOUR EXPRESSION MUST STAND ASIDE FOR DUTY AND OBLIGATION. With your second at the fifth YOUR REAL EARNINGS SEEM RISKY AND IN DANGER OF BEING SPECULATED AWAY OR DISSIPATED IN SOME WAY. With your first at the fourth YOUR IDENTITY KEEPS GETTING FORCED BACK ON YOURSELF. This makes you ask, "Am I really me, or what am I?" With your twelfth at the third YOUR INNER MOTIVATIONS TEND TO COME OUT IN THE OPEN AND BE TALKED ABOUT. This is an indication of insecurity and attempts to reconcile what one inwardly feels with the situation as it seems to be working out. With your eleventh at the second YOUR EARNINGS SEEM TO BE ONLY DREAMS AND HOPES.

THE SPIRIT OF FRIENDSHIP

If his Sun is in your ELEVENTH HOUSE, you have many fond dreams in common. There is a very strong sympathetic bond between you and you should become good friends. This is a position of encouragement. But even the best of friendships does not always last forever. The other person may change and no longer want to see that part of you that he once cherished. Friendships are really designed to lend a helping hand or a sympathetic encouragement AT A TIME OR CONDITION OF NEED. Since we should solve our own needs, in time the purpose for which these friendships arise is no longer active. A law of friendships is that to have a friend you must also be a friend. It has to work both ways. But the feeling of good friendship is a nice, warm, comforting one and most people treasure it as long as possible. It would depend on the condition of your own eleventh house as to the value and importance and duration of meaningful friendships in your life—where they come from and why they go. With your tenth at the twelfth YOUR AMBITIONS MUST SUFFER SOMEWHAT BY BEING PUSHED INTO THE BACKGROUND AND NOT SPOKEN OF OPENLY. With your ninth at the eleventh THERE IS MUCH TALK BETWEEN YOU OF YOUR JOINT IDEAS AND A GENUINE SHARING OF SIMILAR PRINCIPLES (as indeed there is in most close friendships). With your eighth at the tenth THERE IS SOME ENCOURAGEMENT TO BRING FORTH AND EXPLOIT CERTAIN SECRET ASPECTS OF YOURSELF WHICH YOUR FRIENDSHIP ENCOURAGES TO BE LESS SECRET. As will be seen by the secret angle of the tenth at twelfth and the eighth at the tenth, subconscious motivations become more pivotal at the expense of the material goals which one usually aims to follow. One should also have more resolve about not only accepting change but seeking it. With your seventh at the ninth YOU ARE MORE ACUTELY AWARE OF THE PART OTHER PEOPLE PLAY OR CONTRIBUTE TO THE PRINCIPLES YOU BELIEVE IN. With your sixth at the eighth YOU BECOME FAR MORE FLEXIBLE ABOUT THE DUTIES AND OBLIGATIONS YOU ACCEPT AS TO WHETHER THEY ARE RIGHTFULLY OF YOUR OWN CHOOSING. With your fifth at the seventh YOUR SENSE OF PLEASURE AND ENJOYMENT IS DIRECTLY RELATED TO OTHERS AND ONLY ENJOYED IN THEIR COMPANY. With your fourth at the sixth YOU FEEL A HEIGHTENED OBLIGATION TOWARD YOUR SUBJECTIVE SELF, THE CAREFUL MANAGEMENT OF YOUR SECURITY FACTORS AND A DEVOTED LOYALTY TO YOUR HERITAGE. With your third at the fifth YOU BECOME MORE CREATIVE IN YOUR THINKING. With your second at the fourth YOU BECOME MORE CONSERVATIVE WITH YOUR POSSESSIONS. With your first at the third YOU SPEAK MORE FRANKLY, BEING EAGER AND FREE TO VOICE THE REAL YOU. With your twelfth at the second YOUR INNER MOTIVATIONS PROVIDE AN ACTIVE SOURCE OF SUPPLY, NOURISHMENT AND EVEN FINANCIAL PROFIT.

SOMEONE OUT OF THE PAST

If his Sun is in your TWELFTH HOUSE, this is generally an indication of some sort of karmic link with your past. You may indeed feel a very close kinship, but usually any sort of physical intimacy should be avoided, for there is something just a little bit unnatural for you in this position. It is somewhat like having an affair with a close relative. It would seem at times that his ego senses more about you than you are able to understand yourself. This most often leads to a feeling of uneasiness and is vaguely upsetting. It is true that this person may understand you better than you do and this gives him an advantage over you if you acknowledge it. More often there is a tendency not to acknowledge it, in fact deny it. This leads to a certain resentment on his part, which can lead to a certain jerking on the reins just to remind you how well he knows your motivations. This often appears to you as a threat of some kind. In most cases it was meant that way. This person stands prepared to help you in case of acute failure or breakdown on your part, but you may have to get into that state to acknowledge him fully. You may also feel that at times he prefers to see you this way just to justify his insight into your affairs. ANY contact with this person always leaves you upset in some way. With your eleventh at the twelfth YOUR HOPES AND DREAMS ARE CONSIDERABLY DAMPENED, SUBDUED AND DEPRESSED. What essentially in your nature should be out in the open and joyfully expressed is purposely suppressed and put out of mind. With your tenth at the eleventh YOUR KIND OF AMBI-TIONS AND THEIR GENERAL ACCEPTANCE BY OTHERS ARE SOMETHING THAT YOU HAVE IN COMMON. You will find that the general possibility or probability for each of you to achieve your respective goals in life is about the same. If your goal is improbable, unpopular and beset with difficulties, this person feels the same way about his own. This is a very close bond for sympathy. With your ninth at the tenth YOU WILL HAVE TO FIGHT AND WORK HARD TO ESTABLISH YOUR PRINCIPLES. With your eighth at the ninth YOUR REAL PRINCIPLES SEEM TO BE UNPOPULAR AND CONTROVERSIAL AND SOMETHING TO KEEP TO YOUR-SELF. With your seventh at the eighth OTHER PEOPLE SEEM SECRETLY TRYING TO UNDERMINE YOU OR FORCE CHANGES WHICH YOU MAY NOT WANT OR DESIRE. With your sixth at the seventh OTHER PEOPLE SEEM TO DICTATE WHAT YOUR DUTIES SHOULD BE. With your fifth at the sixth THE ONLY PLEASURES YOU SHOULD ALLOW YOURSELF TEND TO BECOME DUTIES AND OBLIGATIONS. With your fourth at the fifth YOU ARE ENCOURAGED TO TAKE RISKS WITH THE FOUNDATIONS OF YOUR HERITAGE—TO ALLOW YOUR EGO TO DOMINATE YOUR PAST. With your third at the fourth YOU ARE ENCOURAGED TO ACT INDEPENDENTLY AND CON-CEIVE A FREE ASSOCIATION BY WHICH YOU ARE TIED TO A PAST TRADITION—IF AT ALL. With your second at the third MUCH OF YOUR THINKING IS CONCERNED WITH INCREAS-ING YOUR SOURCES OF SUPPLY AND MONEY. With your first

at the second YOUR PERSONALITY IS OVERCOME BY MONEY
PROBLEMS AND THE POSSIBLE MEANS TO ESCAPE THEM.

AFTER you have established the basic framework by the FOCUS
OF YOUR HOROSCOPE THROUGH HIS EGO, you may proceed to
expand the comparison further.

A consideration of some importance is the way in which you
respond to the planet ruling his ascendant. It is important because
this is the factor that triggers his personality—TURNS HIM ON and
controls the details of his daily living. How you respond to a planet is
determined by all the factors surrounding the condition of that
planet in your horoscope. How you respond, for example, to Mars is
determined by the location of Mars in your horoscope, the affairs of
your Aries house, and the other planets that are strongly aspected to
Mars. If Mars is on the whole unsatisfactorily conditioned in your
horoscope (which is a judgment of all the factors involved), it is most
unlikely that you could sustain or tolerate any lengthy association
with those with an Aries ascendant.

Of all the other planets in his horoscope (aside from the Sun,
which we have already considered, and the ruler of his ascendant) it
is particularly important how his Saturn affects you. This would
show how he will sit on you to preserve and protect himself. This is a
natural instinct with him which cannot be brushed aside, no matter
what. The important considerations are the close aspects to your Sun
(ego) or Moon (emotions)—especially the conjunction (which will sit
on you), the square (which will force you in line with the dictates of
his Saturn), or the opposition (which will block or oppose you with
all the might of his self-preservation principle).

A close conjunction of his Jupiter on your Sun or Moon will make
him want to help you in spite of himself. Quite aside but an interesting example of this with pets is when your Jupiter falls on its Sun,
you will be kind and indulgent with that animal, even if you may not
particularly like it, or even the species, otherwise. If it is a cat, you
might pet it (or even give it a home) when you generally do not like
cats at all. If you have Taurus or Libra on the sixth house of small
animals and the Venus ruler is angular (in the first, fourth, seventh or
tenth houses), you feel a close kinship with all small animals.

In the astrological theory of MIDPOINTS, which is an entire study
in itself, a particularly sensitive point is the midpoint of your Sun
and Moon. This is measured by taking the exact point equally distant

from each. This could be termed YOUR POINT OF COMPLETE VULNERABILITY INVOLVING YOUR TOTAL POLARITY (EGO AND EMOTIONS). If another person's Sun or Moon falls on this point (or in some systems of astrological thinking, it is equally effective if his Sun or Moon squares or opposes this point), THERE IS PRESENT A DEFINITE CONDITION WHICH COULD CAUSE ONE TO FALL IN LOVE OR FEEL DEEPLY ATTACHED TO ANOTHER. This would be potentially true in spite of all other conditions that would make the relationship unadvisable, impractical, illegal or inevitably disastrous.

As we know, the most unlikely persons tend to fall instantly in love with each other and for the most unlikely reasons. It happens all the time, and when it does, invariably this Sun/Moon midpoint in one has been opportunely set off by the other person's Sun or Moon. We also find very often that each one's Sun or Moon falls in this pattern to the other. This makes for an extremely strong magnetic attraction.

This relationship of Sun or Moon in one person's horoscope to the Sun/Moon midpoint in another's (to whom they are known and proven to be sincerely in love) is a very valuable and reliable way to discover birth position of the Moon in the horoscope when you are not sure of the time of birth. The Moon's motion varies from around 12 to 15 degrees every twenty-four hours. By mathematical calculations you determine the midpoint that is conjunct, square or opposition to the given Sun or Moon in the other, and this suggests the unknown Moon. Then, taking this probable position of the Moon, you can calculate the time of birth. In my professional experience I found this to be very reliable. This is not rectification (by events), which I do not professionally endorse. The key requirement is that there must have been a sincere and compelling magnetic attraction, not just friendship, respect or some other substitute. This is generally present in most marriages no matter how they eventually turn out. At the time there is a total commitment which each acknowledges about the other.

As you might imagine, there are many people whose horoscopes would significantly relate to your own. So, naturally, you have to be brought into actual contact with these individuals in order for these relationships to operate. Certain psychic forces can influence people being brought together in the first place, but what happens after that depends on the mechanics of the horoscope.

What astrology shows us is: Under a given set of conditions certain known factors will react in foreseeable ways and produce anticipated results.

To restate my original position on the comparison of horoscopes, you do not have to trace ALL the intricate relationships that exist between one horoscope and another. These become too complicated and so meaningless.

Of primary concern is how certain key factors, such as the RE-SPECTIVE EGOS, relate to each other. Then all the other factors tend to fall in line by themselves and either cement or dissolve the relationship.

The most favorable relationship that could exist between any two people is to have his sun in a FAVORABLE HOUSE POSITION in your horoscope and also the Sun or Moon of one (or both) falling on the Sun/Moon midpoint of the other.

Chapter 16

THRESHOLDS OF CHANGE

THE 8TH HOUSE

In astrology we look to the conditions of the eighth house to see the possibility and effect of extraordinary changes that might intrude upon and influence the native's life. Extraordinary changes would involve sweeping events by which the native's life is completely and significantly altered in some way. Existing conditions could be completely transformed, and the native would be challenged to begin a new life as a different person. This should in no way be considered as wholly undesirable or always unfortunate. Indeed the reverse may be true. The native may be swept into a new and fortunate situation as the result of overnight good fortune. If tragic events are involved, these may be unfortunate only for others and prove to be a stroke of good fortune for the native. The programming of the eighth-house function tends to take value from one and give to another—or pass emphasis from one situation to another.

The native's capacity to deal effectively with far-sweeping and significant alterations in the primary conditions of his life—whatever it may require—is also shown in the eighth house.

Naturally death, which is a major change (including the native's own death), and the affairs of the dead are also a matter of this house. In astrology (as well as with most religions) death is not considered a total termination but rather a transition from one psychic state to another. There are many kinds of death that may affect the native's life. Important changes often involve a kind of death in which situations and associates undergo such alterations that the old condition has indeed died and a new condition comes to life or takes over.

Since these radical transitions are generally developments that intrude into the picture, unprepared for in the beginning, the talents that are involved for effective adjustment are of an extraordinary nature and call forth hidden reserves and untested depths of fortitude. The native's capacity for meeting such sudden demands cannot be tested in advance, since it is seldom known exactly what will be needed. Usually at such times the sheer physical and material capacities have to be augmented or juiced up by psychic energies, which for short periods of time give almost superhuman strength and endurance. Not all of us can meet such devastating conditions, and many are swept away as the victims of some tragedy. Others, however, rise to unsuspected heights of accomplishment and become heroes or masters of the moment.

It is important to note that the hidden reserve of strength and capability comes from a psychic source which is not available for everyday use. People may have this reserve and yet be unaware of it unless forced into unusual circumstances. One never knows until one has actually met and gone through such an experience what one may or may not be able to do. Most people have more reserve energy than they realize, since we all have some degree of psychic force behind us. Just being born into this life shows that much.

The three psychic houses of the horoscope that deal with subjective matter are the fourth, eighth and twelfth houses, each ruled by one of the WATER signs: Cancer, Scorpio and Pisces, respectively. The true character of these houses (and the tempo of their corresponding signs) is somewhat secret, hidden, intuitive and mysterious. The native is most conscious of the fourth house/Cancer factor because that is HOW HE SEES HIMSELF from the inside, subjectively. He is less conscious of the twelfth house/Pisces factor, which represents his inner motivations and the ultimate value structure of his spiritual realities. He is the least conscious of his eighth house/Scorpio powers, which react on an instinctive (almost animal) level and supply the regenerative and restorative voltage for this psychic plane. Any native may be sensitive to one of these houses, which would give him more awareness of such matters but not necessarily full conscious familiarity. People who are highly keyed to eighth-house matters may be said to enter freely into states of consciousness that go far beyond those enjoyed by ordinary people. Such psychic goings-on are not on a wholly conscious level. It is possible that certain favored people can experience an unusual state of consciousness in which the spirit leaves the physical body and travels around. This is called ASTRAL PROJECTION, meaning to project upon the astral plane of consciousness. Extrasensory perception, clairvoyance and precognition all are variations of eighth-house phenomena which may for certain people play a significant role in their lives.

Any planets that the native may have in the sign of Scorpio partake to some degree of this unusual psychic energy or spirit transference. Also, the house in which Pluto (the natural ruler of Scorpio) falls is keyed for better or worse to some sort of psychic force. It may take psychic force as the only energy that will unhinge and set loose the free-working and desirable conditions the native needs in the affairs of that house where Pluto falls. And the house with Scorpio on the cusp may take all the psychic force the native can muster to cope with the affairs of that house.

If the eighth house is unoccupied, then whatever conditions arise in the native's life of an eighth-house nature are unlikely to be more than the native can handle. The absence of planets shows that the native need not give conscious attention to these matters and whatever occurs in this area will naturally fall in place with no major alterations in his perspective.

The general tempo of the native's eighth-house matters is determined by the sign on the cusp. If that sign is:

ARIES: the native is bound to face during his lifetime some grueling changes which challenge his personal identity but offer an opportunity to realize his self-worth and make a new start. The native will be taxed from time to time to exert every physical effort to offset aggressive situations which threaten to engulf him. Since Aries is ruled by Mars, the native may be drawn into fights which are not of his making, but because of the opportunistic advantage which Mars can offer, he should in some way be able to get an edge on some situation and gain a profit. The native's breaks are somewhat tied to the misfortunes or accidental downfall of others. The native must be on the alert to seize any advantage which sudden opportunity presents. He generally seeks and welcomes change as an opportunity for advantage and personality growth. He may even impetuously provoke sweeping changes just to gain such advantages as arise from taking people unawares. The native's death is likely to take place under conditions of strife and contest, including war and accident.

TAURUS: the native should profit materially from all major changes in his life. Since Taurus is the ideal housekeeper and the eighth house concerns the affairs of the dead, the native is favored for looking after other people's property on a fiduciary basis. This Venus-ruled sign should generally protect the native from all material harm of an eighth-house nature. The native does not seek change and will accept the consequences of such intrusions only after he has evaluated any material advantages which he may aquire. The native's death should be under conditions generally protective, comfortable and attractive.

GEMINI: the native's thoughts tend to naturally reflect on eighth-house affairs as a matter of curiosity and stimulating conversation. He will like to talk about death and gather other people's ideas and opinions on the matter. Generally that which is dealt with on a mental plane (as opposed to a physical, material or spiritual plane) has less personal fear for the native, since he considers it an attitude of mind rather than a physical or spiritual reality. His thoughts are apt to be naïve. He would regard life after death as a family gathering or old-style church picnic where one renews acquaintances and reminisces. Gemini indicates a mental curiosity in these matters but not necessarily depth of insight. The native generally welcomes all change as a variety of mental stimulation, since he already entertains many fantastic ideas. Death is likely to be unspectacular and undramatic— no more than passing from one thought to another or just going to sleep.

CANCER: the presence of the psychic (water) sign on the eighth house suggests a certain psychic penetration of the mysteries of what lies beyond the unseen border, around the bend in time, or precognition of a future event. The native is doubly sensitive about all eighth-house matters. Any kind of death, news or apprehension of death causes tension and anxiety. The native can tune in or out on threatening matters which challenge his daily life. This pattern also suggests spiritual contacts with the spirits of the dead. The native may be mediumistic and receive messages or contacts from sources that are impossible to identify or account for in the regular or normal manner. All this may be more upsetting than comforting to the native, since he is being used as a soundingboard or communication switchboard even against his wishes. Any pronounced eccentricity in this direction will of course set the native apart from people who are not keyed in this manner. This may add to the native's problems, but on the constructive side he is bound to be of some help to others who are eager to obtain the kind of information he is able to supply. Whether they can use what comes through to some advantage is another matter. Undoubtedly at some time in his life the native will feel or sense that he is in touch with something beyond the limits of our ordinary five senses. Whether this helps him (or others) or defeats him in some way depends on other judgments in the horoscope. The native is certainly acutely aware of impending changes (both for himself and others), but whether he accepts this eagerly is something else. He is more apt to be nervous about it and even frightened unless he can tune out when he wishes, as most Cancer conditions should. Death should come suddenly and abruptly, as when a wave subsides or a pulsebeat changes direction—effortlessly, quietly and as naturally as the rhythm of life.

LEO: on the whole this is an unfavorable tempo on matters of the eighth house. The Leo impulse is to control direction and force the situation to justify the ego. The conditions of the eighth house are an inevitability, generally out of the native's control; the psychic forces to be understood at all require insight and spiritual penetration rather than any exploitation of self interest. Consequently, the native's ego is essentially out of tune with whatever conditions of change he meets and the native is obsessed with obstructing these changes or turning the tide of events to benefit himself or others. The native is most apt to be swept aside in the process but not necessarily until after he has made an heroic stand on behalf of some purpose. This stand may in some way help or inspire others, but it is likely to prove fatal eventually to the native. It is generally unfavorable for the spirit of the ego—the principle of the life force—to be closeted in the house of death, where life after death or the transition thereto is more important than any temporal conditions at the moment. The native must somehow struggle with these matters and expend his will in the process. The native actively identifies with change but more from the standpoint of opposing or altering the inevitability rather than riding with the tide and possibly rising above the wreckage of the present. Death is likely to be spontaneous as a consequence of some willful action in which the native is vanquished by a force superior to his ego.

VIRGO: this pattern combines a mental approach with a sense of duty, obligation and service. The native wants to be of help to others in times of extraordinary events which involve sweeping changes and devastating conditions. He is well advised to seek a vocational outlet that would benefit others at such times. He particularly feels a sense of trust in looking after the affairs of the dead, their property or their wishes. The native cannot be said to avoid the consequences or implications of important changes, since he immediately assumes the obligation or duty to pick up and sort out the effects of such change—whatever they may be. Death may be under trying conditions of labor or in helping others meet their daily obligations. It is likely to be plain, unnoticed, undramatic and uncounted—a shift of sand that obliterates as though it never was.

LIBRA: the native invariably sees, not his own, but other people's reactions to change or impending transitions as the primary importance. The native is more conscious of change in other people's lives than he is in his own. This is because he is involved with many others at the time he himself faces significant changes. What happens to him is not happening to him alone but as to one among many others who are also affected at the same time. This suggests large group upheavals such as wars, mass migrations, and common disasters. The important changes in the native's life arise through other people's interests. The native must follow along and make the best of it. He is generally awakened and enthused by the social importance of such occasions. It would not follow that the native looked forward to change because he has little to do with causing it in his life. What he should do after it has happened is to recognize the values resulting from outside contacts which arise at this time. Death would be caused, directly or indirectly, by someone else. The native's bodily functions are not responsible and have no control over his death.

SCORPIO: this pattern places a clamp of secrecy on this area of the native's life which may or may not lead to anything of importance. Whatever experiences or attitudes the native has on eighth-house matters are operative on the instinctive level. He reacts unconsciously, as though he had always been prepared and knew exactly what to do. He does this so naturally that he does not reflect on the consequence or importance of it. The native neither seeks nor avoids change. He tends to take what comes in stride. Death is experienced with the same attitude of inevitability. The spirit or psychic consciousness is apt to depart from the body before the moment of physical death, so material death finds only an empty shell. This suggests unusual states of consciousness prior to death. The native at the time of death will be well prepared and have no fears, since in one sense he has already departed the shell of his body.

SAGITTARIUS: the native tends to regard change, death and whatever lies beyond the ordinary limits of consciousness as a further extension of individual thinking. Change and death to him are a principle of master organization or reorganization where minor differences resolve themselves because each finds its own place in a master scheme. The organization is one of principle like a mathematical equation or a formula in biochemistry or molecular physics. Some people can understand these equations, some cannot. It is not regarded by these natives as important that you understand the specific equation. It is more important that you believe that somewhere in the universe there is an equation that perfectly accounts for every specific instance or pattern. They accept this on faith and are convinced of its desirability. Nothing to the contrary can shake this conviction, which is half material and half spiritual. The native always finds sufficient proof in enough cases, and he firmly believes that any missing proof will be provided in due course. The native on the whole seeks change because he accepts that the difference between what is and what isn't is merely the difference between light and shadow on a master plan which supersedes any private or selfish viewpoint. He dedicates himself to the spiritual rightness of the master plan or fate. He is inclined to be somewhat intolerant of those who do not see the light exactly as he does. He may be spiritually consoling but physically insensitive to the sweep of changes. Death should be pleasant, almost welcome, as a further proof of what he already feels is true. There should be a smile of personal triumph or sense of absolute conviction at the time of death, for the native feels he is passing to greater glory and more magnificent abundance.

CAPRICORN: the native is likely to be highly resistant to change and the implications of the temporal value of his personal efforts. Capricorn is unsuited to seeing any value as more significant than his own, particularly nonmaterial values such as implied in the psychic eighth house. The Capricorn/Saturn tempo is ideal for material solutions in physical situations. It is not well suited for psychic solutions in spiritual experience. In this pattern apparently the native is ill advised to apply anything but material attitudes against the sweep of circumstances. There is some suggestion of difficult circumstances in which the native will be ground down and forced to rebuild his material efforts just to understand the immateriality of their fate. This cannot be an easy lesson to accept because time and time again he may have to start again in a new image or format. Where Capricorn falls in the horoscope tends to be an area where the native eventually wins out but only after many repeated trials and errors. In this case, since death is the reality, the native is fairly assured of a long, tough life in which the body lives on and on—passing almost into a condition of granite or stone before the end finally comes. The native may become a fixture in old age and just as immovable—where only the physical or material shape seems all that remains. He can only accept this inevitability in the light of Saturn as the factor of time, and as such death will not come until the time is right.

AQUARIUS: the native must assume and maintain an attitude of independence (almost indifference) about the implications of eighth-house matters, or else he is liable to become completely lost and disoriented on these matters. He is likely to have some unique and startling opinions about change, transitions, death, spiritual implications, etc. But for him they serve some purpose, since by virtue of the Aquarius/Uranus pattern he is likely to experience some very unusual conditions in this area. The full implication of these eighth-house experiences may not be apparent to others. This pattern suggests the most radical effects of change by which he finds himself on a totally different level—as though by a miracle or intervention of destiny. To the native this must be considered a condition of rare luck which could never have happened in any other way. The native is usually prepared for the wildest kind of change, since he is fortified by seeing far beyond what most people can see. The potential of the future is always more important to the Aquarian attitude than the conditions of the present which, by comparison, are limiting and restrictive. Death should come suddenly, even dramatically, as though by an act of fate. There should also be an impression by the death that hints or implies a vindication of attitudes that the native held, together with a possible link into the future.

PISCES: in this case we have the other psychic (water) sign on this spiritual eighth house which suggests a penetrating depth into the mysteries of this area. This would naturally tend to set the native apart simply because he could feel more and sense more about matters that most people fear. With Leo usually on the ascendant the native is inclined to keep most of these insights to himself, since he is more interested in promoting his personality in a courageous and daring manner. He does, however, inwardly rely on his spiritual faith about psychic forces to give him that daring courage which enables him to push beyond what others would dare. The native's attitudes about all eighth-house matters are highly idealized, and he would count on the inspiration of the moment to face whatever changes are presented by the eighth house. Usually with Pisces these changes would be confined to the background and be well insulated in the subconscious. Inwardly the native will face them, but outwardly it will not show. The native will generally welcome change since it reflects the potential of further insights and a deepening of his inner values, but he will always be less affected by change from outward appearances. Death is apt to involve some sort of mystical experience in which the native gradually drifts farther and farther away. He is unlikely to be conscious of the transition, since all earthly considerations will have faded out of sight and mind.

In meeting the demands of sweeping events which intrude on the native's life, his inner resolve at times of change must come from the qualities of the sign on the eighth house. If that sign is:

ARIES: his inner strength comes from his own courage.

TAURUS: his inner strength comes from the soundness of his material resources.

GEMINI: his inner strength comes from the adaptability of his mental reactions.

CANCER: his inner strength comes from the sensitivity of his intuitive feelings for doing the right thing at the right moment.

LEO: his inner strength comes from the audacity of his presumptions to impress others with his invincibility.

VIRGO: his inner strength comes from his willingness to submit and organize detailed observations, plus an inherent sense of perfection in his solutions.

LIBRA: his inner strength comes from his inclusion of others in any plan for himself.

SCORPIO: his inner strength comes from his ability to go forward alone and brave what lies beyond his experience.

SAGITTARIUS: his strength comes from his faith in the desirability of established codes of behavior—not to justify his own ideas but to vindicate the laws which governed such matters in the past. He does this best because of a living sense of the historical importance of the occasion.

CAPRICORN: his inner strength comes from his dogged determination to go on as if nothing had happened, knowing that his part at least must remain unchanged. He must make a foundation for the future out of efforts of the past.

AQUARIUS: his inner strength comes from his independently conceiving some ingenious attitudes which may be (however eccentric or strange they seem to others) the only solution possible. Nothing from the past will help solve the future of this challenge. Something totally new and visionary is needed to carry the day.

PISCES: his inner strength comes from falling back on unseen values that suddenly make sense. He must carefully observe the spiritual implications and do, not what is immediately expedient, but what will ultimately reflect the real substance of this challenge. A spiritual solution rather than a material solution is needed.

Refer to the section at the end of Chapter 4 for general delineation of the ruler of the sign on the eighth-house cusp.

If the eighth house is occupied by one or more planets, this gives importance to the affairs of that house in the native's overall perspective.

If that planet is the:

SUN: the eighth house reflects the character of the native's destiny. It is only through working with eighth-house conditions that the native can resolve his personal identity and purpose. The native is destined for some momentous changes or significant conditions of change in which he undergoes a major form of rebirth. For more details on this pattern see Chapter 4, "The Character of Your Destiny"—Sun in the eighth house.

MOON: the implications of change and the effect which they have on the native's life become the focus of all his emotions. The native has great insight into such matters, but he also suffers much tension and anxiety over his sensitivity and attunement with drastic events. For more details on this pattern see Chapter 5, "The Focus of Your Emotions"—Moon in the eighth house.

MERCURY: the native's best thinking is directed or centered on issues that other people have neglected as dead or out of vogue or no longer of current value. It is up to the native to bring back to life certain ideas which still have immediate use value or regenerative power in times of necessity. Thoughts may run at times along morbid lines, but the native will find such matters fascinating and profitable.

SATURN: the native's sense of self-preservation is in some way tied to major changes that upset present conditions in a drastic way. The native is advised to sit tight and cling to what others may be throwing away. There is an obsession about a personal guilt for a collective reason. For more details on this pattern see Chapter 7, "Saturn in Your Horoscope"—Saturn in the eighth house.

MARS: the presence of this symbol of energizing force shows much preoccupation with sexual matters and a sense of competition during times of extraordinary events which upset people's lives. The native has talent for acting as a regenerative force on others by juicing up their hidden reserves. He is often welcome as a quick pick-me-up for spirits and attitudes of others who are lost or feel they are being swept aside by circumstances beyond their control. The native becomes involved with dangerous undertakings in which ultimate death seems possible. It is up to the native to keep one step ahead of such actualities.

VENUS: this peace-loving and sentimental force gives protection to the native under trying situations. His sense of love-making and the focus of his affection are directed to a side of life (and the persons therein) that is usually being exploited as a last resort or escape mechanism when one is losing his grip on reality. The demands of the moment have led these people to desperate, violent actions in order to hold on or get going again after something has significantly changed their lives. The native's affections are excited and intensified by such conditions. This pattern is favored for profits and favors from such varied activities as looking after the affairs of the dead, bringing life into emotionally dead conditions (including prostitution and exploitation of pornography), selling or restoring junk, antiques, artifacts, and conducting archaeological exploration.

NEPTUNE: the native has psychic penetration into unusual matters connected with separation of the spirit world from material realities. He is apt to be fooled or deluded by some of his idealizations. But he is also apt to strike rather close to home with some of his visualizations. All eighth-house matters prove a source of inspiration to the native, although he may not be able to communicate these insights to others with much success. The native is prone to use eighth-house potentials as escape from everyday realities. Drugs and other sensory manipulators may be used to induce unusual states of consciousness.

JUPITER: this pattern shows that the native is following certain traditions or codes of behavior that have been tested by others in the past on eighth-house matters. Far from having any fear of eighth-house matters, the native will feel a release and a sense of potential expansion in any pursuit along these lines. Jupiter is generally protective, profitable and lends a sense of moral conviction that whatever happens in the native's life of an eighth-house nature will most certainly turn out for the best. In general the native profits in some way from dead issues, other people's misfortunes and sudden twists of fate.

PLUTO: the native is apt to be drawn into drastic conditions which completely disrupt or transform his life pattern. The situation may be utterly beyond the native's control—such as conditions of war or large-scale tragedy. The native's life may be in considerable danger, but if he is willing to completely let go of the past and strike out in a totally new direction, he may get on top of the situation. The native will be challenged several times to undergo a kind of spiritual rebirth which may be very demanding. This pattern is highly suggestive of a double life on sexual matters or regenerative benefits from matters not suitable for public knowledge.

URANUS: the native can look for the most unexpected conditions of his life to arise from some eighth-house matters. This can more often be a piece of rare luck rather than singular misfortune. To some extent the two could be combined if the native initially considers these intrusions of change as unfortunate but later sees them to have been desirable. The native will always be prepared for an unexpected turn of events, and he will have adopted an independent indifference on the matters since he may feel highly ingenious in dealing with the potentialities of change.

Check Chapter 9 on the significance and importance of any strong aspects between these planets in the eighth house, which by relationship implicates other conditions and persons in the native's eighth-house affairs.

The native is always fortified by the affairs and people ruled by any planet in the eighth house in meeting the sweeping demands of this house. The constructive purpose that his life can take after adjusting to the demands and changes of the eighth house is suggested by the location of the ruler of the eighth cusp.

Chapter 17

TRAVEL AND EDUCATION

THE 9TH HOUSE

Both of these subjects are matters of the ninth house of the horo-scope. In essence the ninth house represents an area—particularly in our higher thinking—that is initially foreign to us because we first have to reach a certain level of understanding and training. We finally come to accept the principles involved by virtue of having arrived at a certain elevation in our development. This brings us in line and drives home a sense of tradition or history of those who have gone before us on the same matter. In our thinking the ninth house repre-sents higher thought and formal education in which our views take shape and JOIN WITH OTHERS IN A CODIFICATION OR RIT-UAL OF THOUGHT. In practice this takes the form of laws, reli-gion, universal principles, abstractions, formulas or equations. It becomes a universal language by which people of all walks and sta-tions in life become as one because they share this conviction of principle. The code so established transcends the individual contribu-tion. Formal education, higher learning, the language or ritual of symbolism and an advanced state of brotherhood all are represented in the intellectual stage of man's development. This is not an area for the untrained, the underdeveloped or the simple physical level of life. It requires a certain report card and entrance credentials for partici-pation and appreciation of what is going on—the lecture being given or the sermon being preached. Persons whose Sun falls in our own ninth house represent our special teachers or appointed guides to initiate us into the mysteries and intellectual solutions in life. The result is always some form of intellectualization which is not exactly a conclusion but an attitude, technique or refined set of mental tools. It supposedly takes just this set of attitudes to venture into foreign areas without feeling lost, defeated or overcome. Rather, the reverse should be true: a feeling of familiarity and being at home, even among strangers, because of a common basis of understanding, regardless of any specifics involved.

Accent on the ninth house takes the individual outside of himself and focuses his point of orientation on matters which no longer require individual proof or personal gratifications. This is true on all houses and signs from Libra and the seventh house through Pisces and the twelfth house. It is somewhat less true for Libra and the seventh because this is the beginning of the native's new orientation and there is much concern with learning to accept this shift in accent from the subjective to the objective plane.

If there are no planets in the ninth house, the matters of this house are not of SPECIAL concern to the native. He may accept them or not, but they represent no problem or conflict. Whatever approach he assumes toward this area is based on an inborn faith which may be rudimentary and naïve or complex and sophisticated depending on the nature of the sign on the cusp. If that sign is:

ARIES: the native has a simple, direct self-identification with the higher principles of thinking. He may in some way be able to make an original contribution in this direction depending on the condition of Mars and other factors in the horoscope. This is not however a virtual necessity because with Libra on his third house his own thoughts lean toward the opinions of others rather than being more forthright and original. He looks in the ninth house (with Aries there) for a commanding leader and courageous teacher who will give him the direction and principal form to follow. The ninth house has more than average meaning for him because the best of his initial efforts to control any factor of his life start with ninth-house principles. The decisive factor is the faith in self-identification by which the native immediately and even impetuously places himself in the line of march which these principles mean to him. He is not only one of the standard-bearers but one of the front-rank militants who are prepared to fight for what they believe in. But what he thinks he believes in is, curiously enough, not necessarily an evolvement of his own thinking. It is more likely the catch-banner of some outstanding leader with a militant ring. Involvement in these causes makes the native feel alive and gives birth to many thoughts that fortify him on his way. This is where the native will feel the most pioneering in spirit and the most self-assured in dedication.

TAURUS: the native is rather more down-to-earth in his principles. He always expects some material benefit, pragmatic proof or emotional gratification, as well as comforts that will sustain him in an attractive and becoming way. The native's higher thoughts all have a material application on which he considerably depends in order to feel warmly affectionate toward others. If his material principles should fail him, it would considerably dampen his affectional nature. He would not even like himself. All his thinking tends to fit together like clockwork or pieces of a gigantic equation with everything in its place, ship-shape and comfortable. The native is unlikely ever to change radically his principles. He may become inwardly upset when something goes wrong in the ninth house, but he will tend to adapt the outer conditions to his principles rather than adjust his principles to reflect more contemporary conditions. The native is fixed and rigid in most of this thinking—particularly those principles that he seems to have been born with. With Scorpio on his third house of individual reflection he is both naturally suspicious of those immediately around him and gifted with a sense of temporal insecurity where everything can be made to reflect something else depending on your motivation. With Taurus on the ninth his own motivations in the area of higher learning are material.

GEMINI: this pattern is almost the opposite from the preceding Taurus picture. The native is adaptive and flexible in principle and very far-ranging and investigative in his thoughts with Sagittarius on his third house. He longs to know more so that he can augment his principles with as many convenient pigeonholes as possible. He aspires to higher learning and reflects a certain brilliance of communication which is very impressive. This pattern is very favored for gifted teachers in higher education. They can be real spellbinders with their students. They would also be easy and pleasing to follow with Libra on their personality image (AC).

CANCER: this sign always gives special insight when dealing with the fluctuating public in its mercurial moods and emotional vogues. The native, however, is more responsive to any possible reactions to and from the public than he is with feeling his own place in the line of march. The place he assumes will be tailored to fit the complexities of what may be in the wind or whatever is uppermost in the public eye at the moment. This may be a profitable trend to tune in on, but it produces a framework of principles that is not exactly what the native believes but rather what he feels he should believe out of protective necessity. With Capricorn on his third house his own thinking is narrow, restrictive, harsh, persistent, inflexible and overly dogmatic. It is certainly not very imaginative or inspirational. This pattern is more favored for editing or publishing of technical and scientific papers or disciplinary admonishments within the law or accepted codes of behavior.

LEO: the native rather creates his own principles which he tailors to suit his ego of the moment. He can champion or endorse programs only if he sees himself in a prominent position in their promotion. The regulating framework, when it comes to guiding principles, is too self-centered, personally motivated, nonobjective and ego-supporting to be treated as universally acceptable or even being halfway right or just. The native may be a leader in some new thought movement, but it is unlikely to be within the established traditions or have universal appeal. It may, however, at the time have a great deal of charisma and personal exploitation value. With Aquarius on the third house the native is inventive and ingenious in the independence of his thinking. Much depends on other factors as to how far he can carry the individuality of this thinking.

VIRGO: this pattern is favored for scientific work in which detail and careful observance of minute specifications is mandatory. There would be much dedication of effort and sense of duty about setting matters straight in all ninth-house affairs. A lifelong interest in higher education is indicated, together with a sense of duty that the native himself should contribute to this work. With Pisces on the third house the native has a gift of magic in arranging his thoughts and perceiving (through intuition) the organizational points that are necessary to carry on the elaborate housekeeping required in the ninth house.

LIBRA: the native looks to other people's principles rather than his own to find the framework around which he strings his beliefs. Paradoxically, with Aries on his third house he has many original and enterprising thoughts, the best of which he slates for social application and testing on others for their reaction value. He has a gift of communication on ninth-house principles, since he relates so naturally to the framework of other people's higher thinking. This is favored for both teaching and publishing and mediating the differences between people through application of the law or set codes of behavior. This is an ideal pattern for a lawyer or upholder of the laws.

SCORPIO: the native's higher thinking drifts in channels not readily accessible or on subjects not suitable for everyday discussion. The native's principles are exceedingly open to change and the potentials of change. In fact they are set up so as to magnify such change, as opposed to the temporal value of any immediate situation. The native sees his work in any ninth-house direction as instrumenting reforms rather than carrying on traditions. He is likely to be a reformer and innovator in this field. With Taurus on the third house his ideas are generally practical and, above all else, disposed to material values.

SAGITTARIUS: naturally, as ruler of the ninth house, this sign is favorably placed, although it does focus the attention on the pie-in-the-sky type of principles. The native is absolutely convinced of the desirability of promoting uplifting movements and preaching about abundance and the potentialities inherent in every situation. With Gemini on the third house there is much exchange of ideas and opinions at the market level of communication, so the native is reasonably aware of what is going on at street level in spite of his high-flown aspirations of what ought to be in principle. What is accepted as guiding principle is essentially accepted on abiding faith and inborn conviction rather than an actual testing and automatic correction for injustices, should they occur along the way.

CAPRICORN: the principles which the native accepts as his own tend to be what are generally acknowledged as sound, sane, workable and proven by time-tested effort and method. Pragmatism (or the criterion that what is true is that which works) is the guide. When something no longer works or verifies its function, then changes may have to be made in the substructure. With Cancer on the third house the native is provided with a built-in antenna for picking up probabilities of proof or reliability of substance. He is deeply and intuitively attuned to picking up current ideas and reactions in the marketplace long before they challenge the effectiveness of his guiding principles. The native's thoughts are more flexible while his principles tend to be soundly consistent. On the whole this is a far more satisfactory pattern than the reverse, with Cancer on the ninth and Capricorn on the third.

AQUARIUS: this is a favorable position for Aquarius because any release of boundaries and extensions of vision are highly productive in the realm of thought, higher principles and universal codes. The native may be considered to belong to a favored clique of principle adherents whose vision is beyond that of ordinary limitations. The degree of genius potential (or eccentricity) is dependent on other factors such as the conditions of Uranus, as ruler of the cusp and its relationship by aspect to other key factors in the horoscope. With Leo on the third house the native is given to expounding his views and opinions, which may or may not be profoundly original. They are, however, certain to be personal and forceful.

PISCES: the native has an unshakable belief in his principles, which are based on higher spiritual laws than those generally used by others in more mundane walks of life. Materiality is seldom a criterion for truth, since the native's beliefs are centered on ultimate spiritual values which transcend all temporal conditions. The native feels no necessity to preach about his beliefs, but he is willing to share them with those who are interested and seek him out. The native conceives of principles as transcending all practical considerations which may or may not fit the situation in which he may be seeking a solution. With Virgo on the third house his thinking is very precise and exacting and a good deal more so than his principles, which tend to remain vague, undefined and always implied as a higher law but never forced to measure up to the actuality.

There is apt to be some subtle contradiction between what the native says or thinks (which is concrete and factual in the third) and what he believes (which is vague and undefined in the ninth).

For general conditions of the key that controls the tempo of ninth-house principles, see the section at the end of Chapter 4, page 83.

If the house is occupied by one or more planets, ninth-house principles become a matter of more conscious concern and direct application. If that planet is the:

SUN: this is of prime importance, as the ninth house becomes the framework around which the native's whole destiny must unfold. His basic integrity and pride of purpose is wholly involved. The Sun indicates a lifelong concern in this matter. For more details on this pattern see Chapter 4, "The Character of Your Destiny"—Sun in the ninth house.

MOON: the native feels emotionally drawn to this area, but whether he is in a position to do much about it or merely lend his emotional sympathies depends on other factors in the horoscope. The native blows hot and cold on what he really believes in, and even then this causes tension and strain in spite of his insights into the principles. For more details on this pattern see Chapter 5, "The Focus of Your Emotions"—Moon in the ninth house.

MERCURY: this is a very favorable position for Mercury, for it puts one's ear in tune with the larger framework of reference and the established principles which prevail over the individuality of thought or more personal or prejudicial opinions.

SATURN: this realistic depressant is unfavorably placed in the ninth house, since it stresses looking backward for correction rather than looking forward for expansion on the principles that guide men's lives. It further suggests that the native has initial difficulty in formulating his principles on a thoroughly realistic basis. Eventually this must be overcome in order for the native to come to terms with his basic sense of self-preservation. Normally speaking, one's sense of self-preservation has more to do with everyday material matters than intellectualized principles or codes of formalized thinking. It is always rather out of step to place this rigid and materialistic reference reminder on such an area as the codes of higher thinking. Failure to do so apparently jeopardizes the native's basic security. For more details on this pattern see Chapter 7, "Saturn in Your Horoscope"—Saturn in the ninth house.

MARS: this impulsive energizer is not well placed in the ninth house where it argues, contests and disputes that which is already established and working rather than pushing the native to originality in his thinking. The native tends to subscribe to principles which forcibly attack other competitive principles or systems of thought. The objective (with Mars) is to gain an advantage (even an unfair one), which is somewhat out of place in this realm of theoretical justice. The native likes to defend aggressively his principles with force and bombastic measures. Reasoning, insight and ingenious penetration all would be more desirable tools than impetuous, physical and sexually intimidating Mars.

VENUS: this is a fortunate placement for Venus because it brings peace rather than disturbing conditions to an area of intellectual achievement and established tradition from the efforts of many minds. The native embraces, rather than opposes, a certain sense of tradition which gives him comfort, and this reflects throughout his higher thinking as a benefic endowment and a more sensitive understanding of what is involved. The native is able to restore a certain loving attention and fond appreciation of certain fundamentals which may have become harsh and meaningless in their present-day arbitrary application. This is especially apparent in dealing with artistic media and creative principles in which the native should especially shine. This pattern is favored for teaching the arts and their relation or function in everyday living.

NEPTUNE: this planet of inspiration is perhaps better placed in the third house of personal application than it is in the ninth house of formalized ritual and established principle. In the ninth it tends to dissolve or ignore boundaries, definitions or guideposts which originally held the principles in position. The purpose for which these principles were formulated is lost track of, covered over or discarded. At best this magic touch can rediscover or bring to light some long-forgotten system which, by its long absence from the realm of man's current thought, is apt to be unwelcome, confusing, distracting and will defraud or tarnish a current belief. The effect and purpose is to suggest something different from or contradictory to what is currently believed. The weight of the matter is ultimately on the side of the Neptunian value, since the Neptunian/Pisces axis relates to our ultimate value structures as opposed to our more temporal institutions. It may, however, cause much anxiety and unrest before this new idealization is accepted and seen in its proper perspective.

JUPITER: the native is blessed with a fortunate way of putting across his important ideas or principles which augment, rather than oppose, the present line of march. What the native is able to contribute tends to prove or substantiate something which is already well established and suggestive of permanent value. Thus the native profits by this and is honored for his efforts, since he is contributing to the apparent abundance, rather than detracting from it. Jupiter always tends to multiply the good that is already there.

PLUTO: this troublemaker in the ninth house is bound to cause friction as it attempts to unseat the opposition. The native senses a real need for drastic overhaul in some of the guiding principles currently accepted as valid. In the conditions where the native feels personally involved he believes that what is established is more of an injustice under present conditions. He is forced into double attitudes (one of which may be acknowledged and the other forced underground). The native definitely sees two sides to something that many people may consider above dispute and irrevocable. Whatever efforts the native may be forced to take on ninth-house matters are apt to attract trouble and resentment and reprisals from the opposition. The causes which the native believes in tend to be the causes of revolution and violent overthrow. Much depends on the aspect relationship of Pluto to see how much of this revolutionary force assumes a personal application in the native's life. It is pretty much bound to show when in the ninth house, since this involves communication and broadcast of all his higher principles. And of course the Pluto qualities are more personalized when aspected to planets that get things done (like the Sun, Mars and Saturn).

URANUS: the perspective of the native's thinking is apt to be upset considerably by sudden intrusions that totally change and disrupt certain things he has always believed. In one sense the native is open-minded and prepared to believe almost anything, provided it just happens to fall in with his own independent, if not to say, unique views and perspectives. The native's principles are anything but consistent and may at times lean toward the far-out, crackpot and outlandishly unconventional. This is not a particularly favorable placement for Uranus, which, if anything, is better placed in the third house of individual thought rather than as a disruptive force in the finalized structures of thinking. In the third, crackpot ideas would get ironed out before challenging the larger principles. In the ninth the disruptive unsettled quality of new boundaries always superseding the present ones tends to disorganize everything—even the genius of new thought.

These key planets in the ninth house which give accent and purpose to ninth-house principles are fortified or restricted by their aspect relationships to other planets. To follow this through, see Chapter 9, "Aspects Between Planets."

Chapter 18

AMBITION, RECOGNITION

AND WORLDLY SUCCESS

THE 10TH HOUSE

Whatever ambition the native has, the amount and kind of recognition he will receive and the degree of worldly success he is likely to enjoy all are shown in the horoscope by the condition of the tenth house.

If the tenth house is unoccupied, none of these matters is of PRIMARY concern to the native. He considers that he has a normal amount of ambition and should stand an even chance to reach a fair amount of success. He is not going to make a big deal about it, one way or the other.

In evaluating the condition of the tenth house, first consider the sign on the cusp. This indicates the type of ambition, recognition or success involved. From Aries through Virgo the ambitions are more personal and are conceived to prove something to the native about himself. If that sign is:

ARIES: the native is aggressively ambitious, with a desire to place his personality before the public, and his success in life will always be dependent on his initiative and enterprise. Much depends on the condition of Mars.

TAURUS: the native is more attracted to the financial side of success and the probable comforts it will bring. The success factor depends a great deal on the fortunate or unfortunate condition of Venus. Having a lucky Venus is decisive. Determining a lucky Venus is a matter of judgment involving all the factors of its condition.

GEMINI: the native wants to be known for his mental talents and style of expression. Having a lucky Mercury is decisive as to the probable outcome of the native's mental ambitions.

CANCER: the native wants to be acknowledged for his loyalty to home values and the rightness of the methods he devises to launch programs. Under Cancer the native is fairly assured of some public attention no matter what he does. Whether fortunate or unfortunate depends on the condition of the Moon.

LEO: the native is ambitious to build up his ego in such a way that he will stand out from the crowd by his compelling individuality. Under Leo the native is sure to make some kind of a mark. Whether it is fortunate or unfortunate depends on the condition of the Sun.

VIRGO: the native wants to dedicate himself to a kind of service that he feels is useful and needed. The desire is less to stand out than to contribute something of value. The degree of importance attached to the responsibilities which the native eventually assumes is indicated by the condition of Mercury.

From Libra through Pisces the ambitions are more objective and are focused on matters outside the native's personal requirements. If that sign is:

LIBRA: the native is more ambitious to see other people recognized in some way. The degree to which these efforts are effective depends on the condition of Venus.

SCORPIO: the native is not sure of just what he wants or how to enter into the game of life. He is generally able to drift along until some extraordinary situation arises which has need of him. This outside event or emergency becomes the focus of his ambitions. Much depends on the condition of Pluto.

SAGITTARIUS: the native is born with strong enthusiastic convictions on certain principles about which he preaches to convert others to these same advantages. Whether others pay attention or his efforts are wasted depends on the condition of Jupiter.

CAPRICORN: the native has deep convictions about the advantages of accepted values, which he persistently and stubbornly pursues. Since more achievements can be credited to persistence than talent, this native is more assured than most that he will adapt to an uphill struggle and eventually receive a just reward. Just how difficult his path may be is shown by the condition of Saturn.

AQUARIUS: the native is naturally drawn to unconventional goals that are generally out of step or ahead of the times. He is most likely to be labeled a nut by most people and a genius by some. Like the Scorpio ambition ruled by Pluto, the outcome for the Aquarian ambition is beyond the native's control, being dependent on the fortuitous alignment of circumstances. A great deal depends on the strength of the native's capacity to act independently, as shown by the condition of Uranus.

PISCES: the native prefers to remain in the background of affairs, doing research or developing a philosophy of ultimate values which will explain the more unfortunate experiences in life. The focus of this interest will be shown by the condition of Neptune.

To determine the angle or focus of influence BY HOUSE shown by the planet that rules the sign on the tenth house, see Chapter 4, page 83.

When considering the tenth house, any planet in the tenth house reveals more of the outcome of this house than the sign on the tenth house. If the tenth house is occupied by one or more planets, the native has some conscious struggle both to formulate his ambitions and to put them across in the eyes of the world. The affairs in other areas and the people represented by those areas ruled by the planets in the tenth house contribute directly to the native's position.

The presence of Uranus or Pluto in the tenth house indicates social conditions over which the native has little or no control but which exert a strong influence over his eventual outcome. The forces of fate and destiny are intimately connected with his outcome. The native can definitely be said to be a person of destiny.

If the tenth house is occupied by the:

SUN: the native's chief purpose is to become recognized for outstanding achievement. The Sun indicates this will be a lifelong struggle. For more details on this pattern see Chapter 4, "The Character of Your Destiny"—Sun in the tenth house.

MOON: this naturally draws the native into direct contact with the public. The focus of his emotions seems directly tied to public issues or interests which force the native before the public eye. For more details on this pattern see Chapter 5, "The Focus of Your Emotions"—Moon in the tenth house.

MERCURY: the native's thinking and style of expression attracts attention because the native is chiefly concerned—mentally—with matters of public interest. The native is mentally ambitious, and something about his position in life is dependent on how he expresses his thoughts or opinions. Writing and personal expression of ideas is favored. See Chapter 8, "Other Planets in Your Horoscope."

SATURN: the native's sense of self-preservation and basic security depends directly on the amount and character of public recognition he can secure. Initially there is a denial of what the native feels he needs most. Later, after much struggle, a way is found to promote himself before the public, but this position is always in danger of falling to defeat because of unrealistic foundations. For more details on this pattern see Chapter 7, "Saturn in Your Horoscope"—Saturn in the tenth house.

MARS: the native must fight for his rightful position. Others will always contest or oppose the native's right to any recognition due him. See Chapter 8.

VENUS: the native will be recognized for some talent for making things beautiful, attractive and pleasing. It pleases the native to create these effects for public attention. This is an indication of moderate or above-average rewards for successful achievement. See Chapter 8.

NEPTUNE: the native has many unusual ideals about his ambitions, which may not be very realistic or suited to practical solutions. The public will regard the native as a dreamer and visionary or essentially unreal and possibly a fraud. In order to achieve his ambitions the native must resort to a touch of magic. See Chapter 8.

JUPITER: the native is usually favored with some kind of success and a title, whether or not he is particularly deserving in the eyes of some. The native will tend to be somewhat over-recognized or over-compensated in terms of his worth. The abundance which Jupiter bestows in the tenth house is invariably out of proportion to anything that was earned by most standards. See Chapter 8.

PLUTO: the native is drawn into revolutionary changes and social conditions that either sweep him into or out of prominence. The forces which bring these conditions about are somewhat beyond the native's control. See Chapter 8.

URANUS: the native will be labeled eccentric (or possibly by some a genius) for some extremely independent position. His rise or fall will happen suddenly and to some extent be beyond the native's control, intention or fault. See Chapter 8.

Since much for the outcome of the tenth house depends on the condition of not only its ruler but also planets in the house, we look to Chapter 9, "Aspects Between Planets," for those factors that strengthen or weaken their position.

Chapter 19

THE MEANING OF FRIENDSHIPS

THE 11TH HOUSE

The capacity and need for friendships, as well as the inclination to share one's fondest wishes with others, all are shown in the horoscope by the condition of the eleventh house. People who have a strong eleventh house need to find others of similar sympathies with whom to share themselves and give mutual encouragement on an impersonal basis. The eleventh house is not the area of intimate or interpersonal relationships but rather the gathering together of groups of like intent who desire to express their feelings collectively.

Whenever things are pooled into a common denominator, there is a corresponding loss of individuality in favor of the collective ideal. To some people this is a loss; to others a gain.

It is unlikely that highly individualized types will readily submit their fondest hopes and wishes—which are generally but not always a private matter—to a collective leveling process where the good of all is favored over individual benefits.

Almost everyone at one time or another needs the sympathetic encouragement of friendships. It is well to remember that to have and hold a friend, one must be or earn a friend. It seems to be a fact that friendships seldom outlive the purpose that brought the individuals together in the first place. In a few rare cases friendships endure throughout a lifetime, but we are perhaps dealing with a relationship that is more than just a friendship. For further details on this relationship between friends see comments in Chapter 15, "The Spirit of Friendship." This shows the effect of friendships on our perspectives.

If there are no planets in the eleventh house, then friendships come and go in the normal course of events. There is no special consideration necessary or major alteration in the native's perspective because of friendships or collective issues. Such friendships as the native acquires are for the sole purpose shown by the location of the planet that rules the eleventh house.

If the sign on the eleventh house is:

ARIES: Friendships are rather important to the native, even if he has no planets in the eleventh house, because it is through friendly contact and group participation that the native comes to sense his identity and to see himself as he really is. Friendly interaction with others (not just impersonal contacts with the public, which are shown in the seventh house) seems to give the native a sense of purpose. Without this interaction the native is inclined to sink into a glob of sameness, where nothing seems to differentiate itself. Always look to the Mars house to see how this heightened sense of identity is utilized or forced into constructive purpose.

TAURUS: Friendships are considered a material advantage and a source of comfort and addition to the general attractiveness of one's surroundings. A practical angle enters into all friendly relationships, and friends are measured by the gratification and attractive contribution they can make to or receive from the native. All close friendly relationships must meet the test of physical attractiveness, down-to-earth reality and source of comfort and satisfaction derived. For the focus of this need, look to the location of Venus in the horoscope.

GEMINI: one's friends are generally chosen on their talent for mental stimulation. There is much lively interchange between the native and his friends. Depth is not favored as much as versatility and variety. One's friends all would appear especially talented and persuasive in salesmanship. For the use of this stimulation see the key that Mercury provides.

CANCER: the native would be very sensitive and protective about his friends. This is an indication of many friends, all of whom have some subjective association for the native. This position is favorable for friendships with women, and a wide sector of the public would at times be considered on a quasi-friendship basis (like the fans of a celebrity). The native would have moods and periods with his friends when the scene would be too much and he would have to turn off or blow up. Friends create tension, but the native generally puts up with it. The location of the moon highlights the insight and emotional value which the native gathers from his friends.

LEO: this is more favorable for friendships with men or strong personality types who tend to dominate those around them. Flattery and putting on a big show are more important than substance or durability. One seeks friends as a source of entertainment or purely for pleasure or as an excuse for extending the influence of one's ego. Responsibilities connected with such relationships would be out of place. The native and his friends all would try to outdo one another. The location of the Sun shows where this friendly support of the ego is needed.

VIRGO: this is favorable for friends among conscientious and critically oriented people who take their duties very seriously. The sometimes overly serious intent and the fussiness over details, obligations and duties are usually out of place with good friends. There is much criticism given and received. The location of Mercury will show how this detailed knowledge gained from friends can be made useful.

LIBRA: this is probably the most favorable sign for extensive social relationships and friendships among talented and artistic people. The native always shows concern for the other person's viewpoint and is generally unselfish and most desirous to give and receive pleasure in social groups. The location of Venus will show the specific benefit which the native may expect from all these extensive social contacts.

SCORPIO: this is not a fruitful sign for friendships, as the native and those he chooses as close friends are secretive about their intent toward each other. The strongest bond between such relationships is a naïve curiosity about the other's personal and intimate affairs. There is always in these relationships a sexual undertone, whether acknowledged on the surface or not. The force of circumstances creates strong, intense relationships but also sweeps them aside when times change. There is always a certain intensity of feeling and a heightened sense of urgency with these alliances, as though trying to catch the last bus. Look for the location of Pluto in the horoscope to see the real meaning or intention of these people in your life.

SAGITTARIUS: this is very favorable for friendships, especially among those who share the same conviction of principles or code of ethics. There is a warm comradely spirit, always jolly, sometimes naïve, full of optimistic cheer but which can be out of touch and out of place with other considerations. It is sometimes difficult (under Sagittarius) to pick up new friends when those of the old school tie have wandered off because the slogans and catchwords that seemed so meaningful then may seem insincere with another generation. The native will prefer old friends who are tried and true. Charity and tolerance are not nearly as evident when two different codes of laws of behavior are involved (under Sagittarius). The purpose is generally to bolster each other's sense of righteous faith. Look for the position of Jupiter to see why this material proof of one's principles is necessary.

CAPRICORN: this is not a favorable sign for friendships in general. It is difficult to make friends, although, once made, they are often retained longer than friendships formed under other signs. There may be a "till death do us part" connotation. The native is naturally drawn to older, more mature types, and they in turn are more prepared to see the native in a charitable light. Friendships may generally be more gratifying in later years after each friend has had some test of character and proof of durability and financial success. The native, in spite of his slowness to open up to friends, will always value the association because it ties in with some aspect of his instinct for self-preservation. Always look for the location of Saturn to see how mature relationships with others can indeed contribute to the native's emotional and financial security.

AQUARIUS: this is a very favorable sign for friendships with all types of people, who all, however, will seem to have some distinguishing quality, if only their eccentricity. They all are bound to be unique in the native's eye. There is a mutual spirit of tolerance, broad-minded and uncritical, which is right for conditions of close friendship. One should not have to defend oneself or one's principles among those selected as friends. These relationships are subject to unexpected developments, sudden beginnings, endings or twists of interests. All parties maintain a certain independence of attitude and self-sufficiency upon which others should not intrude. The location of Uranus will more clearly show the value and purpose of these interesting involvements.

PISCES: this is a favorable sign for warm relationships when in close contact, but out of sight is out of conscious mind. The image is more important than the reality, and friendships can be formed by what each imagines or idealizes the other to be—not what he really is. If this relationship should turn out differently from expected, then each goes his way with no recriminations or backward glances. A friend remembered can be more pleasing than his actual presence, which may be jarring or incongruous with the qualities for which the native likes him. The sentiment of friendship slips in and out of the conscious mind at the native's will or inclination. What is sought in friendship is a source of inspiration or a key that unlocks what one already has within himself. Once the key has been used, it tends to be forgotten but not without appreciation. The location of Neptune in the horoscope will show the importance or utilization of the inspiration one receives from special friends.

For more details on how to read the focus of friendship through the location of the ruler of the cusp, see the section at the end of Chapter 4, page 83.

If the eleventh house is accented by one or more planets, particularly key planets like the Sun, Moon, Mars or Saturn, then the affairs of that house take on added dimensions in the native's daily life.

If that planet is the:

SUN: then of course the native's whole resolve is through joining with others of sympathetic intent for a collective purpose. The native is unable to work out his destiny without joining with others. The Sun in the eleventh house shows that this is a lifelong involvement which may concern many groups and many types of affiliation. For more details on this pattern see Chapter 4, "The Character of Your Destiny"—Sun in the eleventh house.

MOON: the native is moody about his friends and their relationship to him. He is sometimes overly enthusiastic and sometimes resentful. They invariably make him nervous with their demands, but he creates tension with them as well. The native is somewhat inclined to regard the public as friendly in an unselective way. With almost everybody he adopts a deceptively warm and intimate manner that does not mean what it suggests. The Moon in the eleventh house is indicative of many friendships with women and sensitive personalities. The native is not consistent, running both hot and cold in his close relationships. For more details on this pattern see Chapter 5, "The Focus of Your Emotions"—Moon in the eleventh house.

MERCURY: the native's friends are important for stimulating his thinking and influencing his style of communication, since he unconsciously tries to mimic others. There is much friendly mental exchange between friends which is important to the native.

SATURN: in order to develop his sense of self-preservation, the native must actively cultivate the collective value of group psychology. The native is initially reluctant to dedicate himself wholly to group associations, but eventually he comes to see the desirability for him of such affiliations. This pattern is favorable for lasting friendships, since the native feels the necessity to cling for dear life. It is not so favorable for sudden or casual relationships, which have no serious purpose in the native's life. The friendships formed could hardly be called social or even essentially pleasurable. The native tends to make a business out of group relationships which for him is mandatory. It is only through friendships that the native is able to grasp the fundamentals of reality. For more details on this pattern see Chapter 7, "Saturn in Your Horoscope."

MARS: this pattern indicates tempestuous relationships, with friends, sudden arguments, disagreements and always a certain amount of competition, whether acknowledged as such or not. Once the native or the friend senses that he has in some way won the best of a situation, then his thoughts and interests turn elsewhere for fresh fields of active competition. With Mars there is always some subtle suggestion of sexual possibilities entering into the relationship, whether or not this seems out of place. Most often this just passes off in spirited resistance or heated exchange of words. There is a tendency for each to irritate the other, which forces the other to take adjusting or protective measures. The native considers it an honor if he likes you well enough to give you an argument. If he didn't care about the value of your resistance, he wouldn't bother to rise to the occasion with his competitive spirit.

VENUS: this is very favorable for warm, kindly and rewarding relationships with many friends. Each supports and complements the other in an affectionate way that suggests real sentiment. The native is a good friend and has good friends. These friendships generally have more substance than other friendships because there is a sense of deep compatibility. The native and his friends are ideal for each other. If harm should come to the native, it would never be through a friend.

NEPTUNE: this is favorable for unusual inspiration given or received from friends but is not so favorable for lasting, durable or very real friendships. The strength of ties may be more in the imagination than in reality. These relationships are apt to appear and dissolve overnight for the vaguest reasons or no reasons at all. Each tends to imagine the other in his own frame of reference, whose image may be only a ghostly resemblance to the actuality. The native tends to see in others what he wants to see and ignore what does not suit him. There is a high degree of deception, purposeful or accidental, involved on both sides. Each fools the other, but this doesn't get in the way while the friendship is going on. In fact it may heighten the imagined desirability because what the one doesn't make up, the other assumes anyway. It is always best to wear a mask when dealing with these relationships. It is never advisable to reveal oneself— especially with one's friends. There is apt to be more sharing of secrets than everyday factual matters or concrete realities.

JUPITER: the native profits from friendships in a rewarding way. The native seeks the affluent and successful members of society as friends, and the native also assumes such an impressive air when dealing with his friends. Optimism, faith and cheering the old-school tradition in a jovial manner is indicated. The sense of relationship arises from a common belief in principles or codes of behavior rather than a similarity of personal identities of a more intimate nature. The native needs his friends in order to prove some point. When found and reciprocated, it makes him feel expansive and justified and confirms that all is right in his world. He in turn does the same for them, so they stand or fall together.

PLUTO: this pattern is unfavorable for social relationships, except when they share a sense of revolutionary reaction against society or social orders. This may produce a spirit of comradely feeling, which exists only as long as they are marching along together through some significant change. The native's friends turn him on to more violent efforts for instrumenting changes or provoking social adjustments. This may remain only a topic of social exchange between close associates unless Pluto is keyed to primary elements of the native's character (such as planets that get things done like the Sun, Mars or Saturn). Always look to the location of the Scorpio house to see what substance there is in the reactionary attitude he shares with others. One naturally picks one's friends from those who are somewhat dedicated to rebellion.

URANUS: this pattern indicates unusual and eccentric friends, as well as unusual circumstances involved in these relationships. The native also is eccentric in his selection of friends. Uranus at its best generates some spark of genius potential. In this case that part of the native's character shown by the Aquarius house is given a collective focus through associations with similarly unusual people. The native would appear to have an edge in some way on his friends, and they gravitate to him for very special reasons. He sparks up their life in a way that no one else can. In matters of friendship the native is well advised to maintain a completely independent attitude, which may appear as erratic or eccentric to others but never to those who qualify as his close friends. The native's friends have an unexpected effect on him which relates in some way to the affairs of his Aquarius house.

Chapter 20

THE BRIGHT SIDE OF DESPAIR

THE 12TH HOUSE

Most of us at some time or other are forced to deal with some aspect of ultimate reality on a completely personal basis—that is, what it means to us individually. Just how we meet this test is shown by the condition of the twelfth house.

The twelfth house of the horoscope has been spoken of many times in this book as the area of ultimate values and the concern for those who during life's struggle have fallen by the wayside. The interest is in the problems of apparent failure, loneliness, rejection and the feeling of despair. This area of life's experience is of special importance and conscious concern only to those who have prominent planets in the twelfth house or are prominently keyed in some way to Pisces/Neptune, the natural sign and natural ruler of the twelfth house.

If you have no planets in the twelfth house, then the matters of this house do not figure in your daily life. It does not necessarily mean that you are not conscious of inner values or subconscious motivations, but you can accept these factors with no hangup. In general you can accept and face what must be done when such inner values are put to the test. Whatever sign appears on your twelfth house, your subconscious values support the affairs and people in your life shown by the location of the ruler of your twelfth house.

As already discussed, our ambitions are identified in the tenth house along with the judgment that others will generally pass on us in the form of our reputations.

The eleventh house suggests in unexpected ways and means that the judgment in the tenth house is only the material answer and not the final valuation, which is found in the twelfth house.

Not everyone, fortunately, in life is dramatically confronted with this final step. Many people indeed pass through life facing only the material consequences of their conscious ambitions and the reputation that this entails. Not everyone has to take one step further and face the social, philosophic and spiritual consequences of life. But if they do, this is shown in the twelfth house.

The sign on the cusp of the twelfth house shows the general tempo of inner spiritual matters in the native's life. If the sign is:

ARIES: the native meets all twelfth-house matters with supreme self-confidence, since it provides the native with the ideal situation to show the individuality of his effort and at the same time give him a deeper sense of personal worth. He brings much original enterprise to bear on any and all twelfth-house matters. All his actions show concern and interest in these matters and he will fight first for these values. With Taurus on the ascendant the results will always be realistic and practical.

TAURUS: The Taurus attitude is one of practical bookkeeping to ensure maximum comforts and attractive conditions. On the twelfth house the native is bound to have a healthy, straightforward, down-to-earth, dependable attitude toward all inner values just as though they were obviously evident. He is most unlikely to bypass them or forget them, since to him they are a sound source of practical satisfaction and add depth to any material situations. With Gemini on the ascendant you may be sure the native gives everything a good once-over.

GEMINI: The hidden values are a matter of mental curiosity, as well as a fascinating subject for even casual conversation. The native talks and thinks about these subconscious motivations. He is bound to have some original and refreshing opinions and to keep other people's interest alive in all these matters. With Cancer on the ascendant the native is very much aware of all matters of public interest, and the hidden motivations seem even more apparent on the mental level.

CANCER: The native is inclined on occasion to become deeply troubled by unfortunate conditions and inner frustrations but at the same time will keep his feelings to himself. With Leo on the ascendant the native indulges in much outward display of his importance, which somewhat belies the deep sensitivity of his inner nature, however secret. Fortunately for the native with Cancer on the twelfth house he can tune out when conditions are more than he can meet or accept. But the public always has a back door on his motivations, and he adjusts to their wishes more than might be apparent. The "ideal king" does have sympathetic antennae for those in the background.

LEO: the native assumes a certain egotistical prerogative with regard to his inner motivations and/or subjective values about which he feels proud and expansive. He is inclined to make a show or eager display of such important matters whenever any opportunity to expand creatively presents itself. Naturally the values which the native wholeheartedly embraces are such that they relate perfectly to the requirements of his ego. The native would be singularly untroubled or even curious about such values as others might feel important but which he was unable to relate to his own life. With Virgo on the ascendant, even though the native feels this inner strength behind him, he is still inclined to defer to others in everyday matters or to be shyly hesitant about too open a display of his inner motivations.

VIRGO: the native has a real desire to serve and physically help those who are less fortunate. Where Virgo falls always shows a practical involvement that encourages the native to assume responsibilities and obligations of labor to get a necessary job done. With Libra on the ascendant the native is well aware of the other fellow in every situation.

LIBRA: the native is somewhat inclined to regard misfortune as being the other person's fault and unlikely to happen to himself. With predatory Scorpio on the ascendant this feeling is encouraged for selfish reasons. The Libra attitude on the twelfth house also tends to pass the buck or turn the other cheek when the cards are down. There is also a tendency, even on spiritual matters, to make expediency the rule. Libra on the twelfth house is not as favorable for getting to the root of the trouble or particularly for seeking the solution on a personal level. He may, however, be willing to go into the matter if joined by a group.

SCORPIO: the native is given to unusual insights and has extensive hidden talents for dealing with all trying twelfth-house conditions. With Sagittarius on the ascendant he is bound to bring expansive hope to all situations that need good cheer and optimism. Scorpio on the twelfth gives added depth with which to penetrate these difficulties beyond which might ordinarily be expected from this outgoing native.

SAGITTARIUS: The native has a natural richness of spirit and an abundance of personal faith but not necessarily the practical familiarity to deal with the more difficult causes of distress. With Capricorn on the ascendant the native is naturally sold on self-discipline and a material orientation that tends to equate all problems with material mismanagement. This results in a certain spiritual poverty, which is covered up by a naïve enthusiasm about twelfth-house matters. This native is well equipped to deal with material adjustments but ill equipped to deal with all life's problems—particularly the deeper ones.

CAPRICORN: This native finds sounder solutions for twelfth-house matters than the preceding pattern because the discipline and dogged determination are turned inward on the native's inner resources rather than outward on everyday matters. With Aquarius on the ascendant the native is given to dreams of fancy and independent imagination which are surprisingly fortified by certain practical inner resolve. However since Capricorn severely limits the material to be considered and places all that selected for consideration on a practical basis, the native's spiritual preoccupations with the world are considerably limited. This undoubtedly gives the native more freedom to indulge his potential for individual genius (indicated by Aquarius on the ascendant).

AQUARIUS: The native is drawn only to those situations and persons who exhibit some outstanding and unique quality about their spiritual condition. He is highly selective and independent about where he tunes in or what he is willing to let penetrate his inner sympathies. With Pisces on the ascendant his head is in the clouds, so he can pass right by most of the ordinary cases in favor of some special mission to which he feels divinely guided. The Aquarius attitude is independent, selective and specialized.

PISCES: strangely enough, the Pisces sensitivity on its own house is more detached and clinically dispassionate than one might imagine. This undoubtedly fits one better for a more overall and comprehensive perspective on the ills and heartbreaks of life, but it doesn't exactly give the one in need the warmth and understanding he might want. The Pisces attitude is entirely spiritual and idealized, so if you don't catch the image, you may miss the whole point. There is rather a minimum of physical attention in favor of the pie in the sky, which is exactly the criticism of most present-day religious organizations. With Aries on the ascendant the native is given to a "me first" attitude in most things which, as he sees it, puts spirituality right where it belongs—up in the sky for Sunday contemplation only.

For further reference on the native's capacity to face twelfth-house reality one should look for the house position of the ruler of the cusp. This shows the purpose in life for which any twelfth-house knowledge is mandatory. For details on this see the section at the end of Chapter 4, page 83.

If the twelfth house contains one or more planets, an awareness of this spiritual implication becomes a matter of some personal concern. Just how much concern depends on which planets fall in this area. If that planet is the:

SUN: this is most important, for it shows that the character of the native's destiny would unfold only in the pattern of twelfth-house interests and solutions. The Sun shows a lifelong struggle on this problem. For more details on this pattern see Chapter 4, "The Character of Your Destiny"—Sun in the twelfth house.

MOON: the native is emotionally drawn to the background in order to reflect and more deeply feel the spiritual implications of our daily life. The native feels a burden of sadness and is emotionally drawn to all those who are in need of protection, help, understanding, compassion and forgiveness. The native has insights and revelations and a peculiar sensitivity about the needs of certain misunderstood individuals or segments of society. This can create much tension within the native, and he has many changes of attitudes and moods on these matters. For more details on this pattern see Chapter 5, "The Focus of Your Emotions"—Moon in the twelfth house.

MERCURY: the native's thinking is naturally drawn to all matters connected with the unfortunate conditions and the reasons or solutions for them. The best thinking is that of a subconscious nature, which plumbs for hidden depths and mysterious implications.

SATURN: the native's sense of self-preservation centers on solutions to unfortunate conditions through inner fortitude. This is a difficult problem to solve and an unfortunate placement for Saturn, which works best on practical problems through material solutions rather than spiritual attitudes. In this case his material solutions can be solved only by spiritual attitudes. The native needs to develop a fundamental sense of reality about subconscious motivations. For more details on this pattern see Chapter 7, "Saturn in Your Horoscope"—Saturn in the twelfth house.

MARS: the native's natural pattern for initiating action and ex-erting pressure is directed away from open and direct confrontation in favor of indirect, behind-the-scenes activity which suggests in-trigue, plots, and subterfuge. The native is most alive, physical and dynamic when engaged in underground matters or dealing with per-sons whose lives have relegated them to the background. One is sexually attracted to unfortunates. Compassion arouses sexual feel-ings.

VENUS: the native's sense of romance is attracted to those condi-tions and persons who perhaps through no fault of their own, have been neglected or passed over by others. The native is able to create happiness and receive a sense of gratification from those in need. The native is drawn to matters of spiritual beauty in preference to more everyday definitions of comfort and gratification. One's sense of beauty is directed toward the unreal and the idealized image or the empathy that one can project into suggestive situations.

NEPTUNE: the native enjoys an unusual source of inspiration from matters that would depress most people. The native sees not the unfortunate outer conditions but the wondrous inner potential, which to him transforms even the most difficult situations or per-sons. Inner contemplation is very important to this native, and he has almost a divine way of seeing beyond ordinary conditions, especially those that are hopelessly frustrating to others.

JUPITER: the native possesses a richness of spirit that brings op-timism, hope and avowed faith to matters which would defeat most people. The native privately receives benefits or material help from those who sense the value of his contributions in matters of spiritual importance. This helps sustain his sense of faith that he is justified in banking on this nonmaterial aspect of life. His faith is indeed proved again and again in material blessings.

PLUTO: the native tends to become involved or swept into signifi-cant social conditions which bring about devastating changes in the native's inner life. He becomes deeply conscious of vast significant factors which at first tend to overwhelm his inner resources but in the end only extend the boundaries to include far more than he ever dreamed possible. The manifestations of change are initially inward and subconscious but eventually of course are bound to be reflected in all other departments of the native's life. The necessity to face difficult and trying situations brings to light hidden and unsuspected depths in the native's character.

URANUS: the native is subject to erratic and unexpected exposure to hidden value structures in situations and persons under unfortunate and trying conditions. The native is likely to be brought face-to-face with situations that may in some ways be utterly beyond his supposed capacities for meeting such emergencies. The extent to which the native is prepared for this depends on the conditions of Uranus, the Aquarius house, and the relationship with other key planets. Uranus always introduces the unexpected, which may or may not momentarily defeat the native according to his predisposition. In this pattern the unexpected presents itself in the area least likely to be seen or most difficult to judge or solve by means other than spiritual values.

With planets in the twelfth house one should also note the house that they rule, for these give hidden support and fortitude for acquiring twelfth-house values.

Any planets in the twelfth house are forced into function by planets that they aspect by hard angles. They are encouraged by planets through soft angles. See Chapter 9, "Aspects Between Planets."

Chapter 21

DEVELOPMENTS AND

PREDICTIVE TRENDS

IN THE HOROSCOPE

There is an absolute rule in astrological interpretation: NOTHING WILL EVER OCCUR IN THE NATIVE'S LIFE THAT WAS NOT PROMISED OR DENIED IN THE NATAL HOROSCOPE.

Therefore any predictive trends become a matter of timing these natal promises. If two planets are relatively unrelated at birth, then the importance of any future contact (by progression or transit aspect) is comparatively nil.

The question is often asked if the horoscope changes in any way. The answer is yes, but only very slightly. This is called PROGRESSION. It is based on the concept that one day in the native's life in some way reflects a year later.

For example, if the native was born on June 4, 1926, the planet's position at the same time on June 5, 1926, would reflect the native's progressed horoscope one year later. June 24, 1926, would reflect his life twenty years later.

The angles or structure of the horoscope do not change, although some astrologers like to experiment with this when, for example, the native moves from one location to another. This may cast a new perspective on certain factors of the horoscope, but it in no way should be considered a replacement of the natal condition. Basically only the planets move forward or backward through the houses by this progression.

This movement of one day per year does not account for as much change as one might suppose. Some planets hardly move at all throughout an entire life-span. Only the Moon, Mercury, Mars and Venus move fast enough to make much difference. The most important change would occur if a planet changed house. This could happen with any planet because it may be almost ready to change houses at the time of birth. The position at birth predominates in reading the horoscope. Some qualification may be allowed as a time development but only as an addition to the basic interpretation.

A common rule or attitude, but not universally accepted by all astrologers, is: The promise is given at birth, the progression SETS THE STAGE, and the current transit TIMES THE ACTUAL EVENT. Thus all three indicators would be present at the time of the event.

A word of caution is in order at this point about the meaning of events as foreshadowed by the horoscope. Astrological interpretation reveals the MEANING OF THE EVENTS. It does not specify the EXACT FACTS OF THE EVENTS. An astrologer through intuitive powers may chance on the facts of the event, but this is a coincidence. It does not come from astrological factors ALONE. This is important because one should be perfectly clear and honest as to what he expects from astrology.

As stated elsewhere, astrology is a symbolic language and it reflects the attunement and intuitive rapport of the interpreter to filter the message that is structured in the horoscope. It is not an absolute matter. There is no exact cold-fact interpretation that is irrevocably detailed to the exclusion of certain other possibilities. The value lies in what it suggests to those who are studying the matter. And this suggestive potential should in no way be ignored or discredited because PSYCHIC POWERS DEPEND ON SUCH CHANNELS OF SUGGESTIBILITY.

It is my studied opinion that current transits, as they relate to the natal horoscope, are the most important predictive element in timing the horoscope. And the transits of the planet Saturn, as outlined in Chapter 7, far outweigh the value of any other planetary movement in the horoscope.

Chapter 22

ASTROLOGICAL ANALYSIS

WHEN YOU DO NOT HAVE

THE TIME OF BIRTH

The question often arises: What can you do, if anything, when you don't have the correct time of birth?

Since the earth moves on its axis one degree every four minutes, the time of birth must be known as close as possible or serious errors will result in setting up the birth map—the wrong signs will appear on the houses and planets will fall in the wrong house. Any horoscope that is set up for a time other than the TRUE MOMENT OF BIRTH is entirely speculative.

The most speculative art in all astrological procedures is a practice called RECTIFICATION. This is a procedure used to approximate the true moment of birth by rectification of a horoscope to tie certain known EVENTS to hypothetical patterns. The error in rectification is based on the controversial assumption that specific events (to the exclusion of other specific events) CAN ALWAYS BE DEDUCED FROM A FIXED PLANETARY PATTERN. This is simply not so and has in fact been proved false by reputable astrological research.

There is no specific event which can be absolutely tied to an exclusive planetary pattern. Since the individual horoscope constitutes a uniquely personal planetary pattern, it cannot be deduced what the effect—say, the death of a parent or the birth of a child or the loss of one's partner—should be in that native's life UNTIL YOU HAVE THE TRUE BIRTH HOROSCOPE. You cannot PREDETERMINE or generalize what that effect should be and then construct a probable horoscope around that event (or even series of events) to fit one's rationalization. Rationalization as such (or logic or any other form of patterned thinking) has no place in astrological knowledge. ASTROLOGICAL KNOWLEDGE IS AN INTUITIVE AWARENESS OF A DIVINE PATTERN THAT EXISTS AND IS TRUE FOR THE SPECIFIC NATIVE. You can't twist horoscopes around to fit some fondly held theory or beautiful equation like the molecular content of water.

The death of a parent, for example, affects the native's life in any number of different ways. Aside from the emotional attachment that the native may or may not acknowledge, the effect of that death on the life pattern is in no way a standard reaction. It is extremely presumptive on anyone's part WITHOUT THE TRUE BIRTH HOROSCOPE to suppose blindly what this effect SHOULD BE. But let us assume for illustration that one has somehow correctly presumed what this event should be. That still doesn't mean that one can make an equally valid assumption as to the effect of another event (say, the birth of a child) and so on.

The procedure of rectification tries to arrive at a horoscope that will seem to satisfy the greatest number of event patterns from a long list of actual events. Therefore its adherents say the weight of probability lies in favor of one horoscope over another. The fallacy of rectification is well illustrated in the classic story concerning all the speculative horoscopes produced and defended with the utmost conviction for the late Winston Churchill. Apparently no one was ever able to obtain his true birth time until after his death, when it was published among his private notes and papers. And it so happened that the true birth horoscope turned out to be considerably different from all the favorites considered to be the most probable because they suited his life as others considered it should be.

This is not to deny that someone by intuition might chance on the correct horoscope. But this results from something besides astrological factors alone.

A solar horoscope is often used by astrologers when no exact birth time is known. One variation of this method is to consider zero degrees of the Sun sign to be on the ascendant and zero degrees of all the other signs around the map in their natural order, or to consider the degrees of the Sun sign at its noon position on the day of birth as the ascendant and the same degrees of all the other signs around the map in their natural order.

A solar horoscope can be very interesting (just like the Sun-sign readings or Sun/Moon polarity readings, which are even more interesting) BUT THEY MUST NOT BE MISTAKEN OR ASSUMED TO HAVE THE SAME IMPORTANCE AS A TRUE BIRTH HOROSCOPE.

An American astrologer of considerable importance and brilliance, Edward L. Johndro, discovered what he considered to be an even more satisfactory horoscope, which is set up on what is called the arcs of right ascension instead of the base sidereal time factor and therefore needs only the noon position on the day of birth. His work in this direction is very sound and persuasive, and perhaps this is a valid horoscope from some other point of view. But again, this should not be confused or blindly substituted for a true birth horoscope. The type of horoscope we have been talking about in this book is THE HOROSCOPE FROM THE POINT OF VIEW OF THE NATIVE AS THE CENTRAL REFERENCE OR FOCUS OF ATTENTION.

What I have called the true birth horoscope shows THIS FOCUS OF ATTENTION THROUGH WHICH ALL THE NATIVE'S ASTROLOGICAL QUALITIES MANIFEST THEMSELVES.

When we do not have the exact time of birth, it is exactly THIS FOCUS that is missing. This would include the character of the destiny, the focus of the emotions, the image of the personality and all the other manifestations of the life pattern.

If one clearly remembers at all times that the FOCUS IS MISSING, one can still deduce a great deal about the NATIVE'S GENERAL CHARACTER and some probability as to his BASIC BEHAVIOR RESPONSES, by reference to what I would call a NATURAL WHEEL. A natural wheel would be the placement of the planets in a horoscope wheel (not map) with Aries, the natural first house sign, on the ascendant, Taurus on the second house, and so on.

The value is to reestablish the basic relationship that signs and planets have to their respective house functions. This is something which is taken for granted but in practice is often overlooked or disregarded when building the basic framework for astrological analysis.

The most important meanings that any sign symbolizes have direct reference to the function of the house to which it is related in the natural order of rulerships. And the same thing can be said about the meanings of the force symbolized by the planets. They are, again, directly related to the function of the houses to which they are related by sign.

If anyone will carefully review all that is in his mind with relation to the meaning of any sign or any planet, he should realize that about 90 percent (or more) of this meaning comes from its relationship to a specific house area of the horoscope. IT IS THROUGH THE HOUSES THAT SIGNS AND PLANETS ARE IDENTIFIED AND RELATE TO EACH OTHER.

If we set up a natural wheel, this places our planets in their natural habitat according to the sign under which they happened to fall when we were born. Their basic character remains the same. Mars is the energizer no matter where it falls. This placement of Mars in the natural wheel shows THE TEMPO OR QUALITY that Mars will assume for us as we act out our personal patterns. Without the true birth horoscope it cannot, however, show the focus through which Mars will act to carry on its functions.

For example: PLANETS IN ARIES HAVE FIRST-HOUSE REFERENCE. The native will utilize that particular planetary force as part of his personality pattern or as though it had such reference. He will give it individuality, aggressive development, offensive use as a tool to gain his immediate objectives, and conscious attention as a basis for self-worth. The basic qualities which this planet represents can be developed further as a special talent, and at the same time the native provides some wholly fresh, new approach to the matter.

PLANETS IN TAURUS HAVE SECOND-HOUSE REFERENCE. There is a monetary value or supply possibility connected with the native's use of this quality. It should mean money for him in some way. The native considers it of material value worth maintaining in good working condition as a source of comfort and gratification. As part of the native's makeup it is definitely AN ASSET.

PLANETS IN GEMINI HAVE THIRD-HOUSE REFERENCE. The value is mental as a source of effective stimulation or aid in communication or free exchange of the native's opinions in the marketplace. This quality has exchange value or conversion status and can be utilized to improve all relationships and contacts in the immediate environment and as a means for the native to sell his thoughts or convert them into something he can use.

PLANETS IN CANCER HAVE FOURTH-HOUSE REFERENCE. The values tend to be subjective and bear close relationship to something connected with the native's emotional security, sense of home, or relationship to his background or heritage. A full awareness of their importance to him and his unqualified acceptance of these qualities as basic to his makeup are demanded of the native in any programs he may formulate. These qualities have public appeal for the native and can be used to attract the public by utilization of their potential at just the right time. These qualities are to be pushed not because the personal ego desires their utilization but because of a propitious timing between the native and others around him.

PLANETS IN LEO HAVE FIFTH-HOUSE REFERENCE. The values have creative potential and can, if properly used, become a source of pleasure and speculative gain. One has to approach these matters with a certain courageous daring and imperious unconcern about their probable outcome. It would not do for the native to be niggardly or bashful about their display. This is an item to push and, if anything, overcapitalize. With qualities in Leo one has to assume the authority, whether he has earned it or not.

PLANETS IN VIRGO HAVE SIXTH-HOUSE REFERENCE. The values are tied to duties and obligations. The native has to cultivate this quality with effort and diligence and carefully fit it into the overall programs with complete awareness for all the other considerations that might be involved. Discipline, taking orders, fitting in, and fully accepting responsibility all are involved with any of these matters in Virgo.

PLANETS IN LIBRA HAVE SEVENTH-HOUSE REFERENCE. The values are social, competitive and dependent on others for their introduction into our lives or the course of their direction. These qualities are keys with which one might gain the cooperation of others or stir up their competitive spirit so that they oppose us in some way. The privilege of calling the shots falls to others—not to ourselves with any qualities in Libra.

PLANETS IN SCORPIO HAVE EIGHTH-HOUSE REFERENCE. These values are hidden resources of which we may have need during extraordinary situations which tax all our resources. These are the qualities that we have at our disposal in times of crisis or in preparing for or adjusting to such sweeping changes as may suddenly affect our lives or intrude upon our daily living. This is the fortitude with which we face death, tragedy and the demands for rebirth or starting over in a totally new direction. These are factors in our makeup that have regenerative powers. They recharge our batteries and juice up our spirits.

PLANETS IN SAGITTARIUS HAVE NINTH-HOUSE REFERENCE. These values are those of the higher mind that have been coded or formalized by others who have gone before us and view certain principles just as we do. These qualities are not something that we can personally change, since they hinge on whole structures of belief which we are predisposed to accept like religion or law. We may optimistically pursue them in their present format, but we are unprepared to change them to reflect momentary considerations. These are permanent beliefs that we wholeheartedly support.

PLANETS IN CAPRICORN HAVE TENTH-HOUSE REFERENCE. These values are matters of practical concern which we tend to see in the line of duty and what is expected or demanded of us by those in authority or exalted position. We may feel forced to accept certain conditions as though they were the final judgment of others on the matter. In this area we must shape up or get out. Our reputation is directly related to how others feel we should act, and we seldom question their right to this authority over us.

PLANETS IN AQUARIUS HAVE ELEVENTH-HOUSE REFERENCE. These values should be products of the independence of our thinking, for in privacy we are surely entitled to our own wishes and hopes. These qualities are cherished and shared with special friends who share our sympathies. Because of our creative independence on these matters, we are granted some eccentricity of behavior, which we take for granted and rightly so. There is a potential for some degree of genius in this direction, but whether or not it effectively gets off the ground depends on many other factors. It may only drive us nuts.

PLANETS IN PISCES HAVE TWELFTH-HOUSE REFERENCE. These values are capable of producing peace and inner composure in spite of any other factors that may be dragging us down or casting us into despair. These qualities have a great source of inspirational value which, if believed in, can sufficiently lift up our spirits and transform all ills to which we have fallen heir. These are the true rays of hope which will guide us in times of darkness, when all else may seem lost or hopeless. This is what we must turn to as a final source of salvation and confirmation of the ultimate values in our lives.

PLANETS IN SIGNS GIVE US TALENTS IN THE QUALITIES OF THAT SIGN.

From reading the foregoing list of planets in signs, you may conclude from knowing your own planet locations that you have no talents in some areas and may become apprehensive. If you have no planets in certain signs, it means that you do not need those special talents to face what will be required of you.

This is not to say that after you have your true birth horoscope and find planets in house areas other than those for which you have talents you do not have the proper tools for that job. You may not have the normal, regular tools for that job, but in your case your application calls for the tools you have been given.

For example, if you have no planets in Gemini, the normal sign of communication, you do not have the normal talents for communication. But, let us say, in your horoscope you have Mars in the third house. The tools you will need to handle the functions of the third house of communication are, then, not the regular ones that would be planets in Gemini but a special one, which in this case is Mars with a first-house reference. Or you may have planets (or assets) in Gemini, but they are needed elsewhere—say, in your seventh-house demands with others.

In approaching astrological analysis when you do not have the focus of application given by the exact birth time, we next consider the aspects formed between any of the planets. The noon position (as given in the *Ephemeris*) is sufficient for all planets except the Moon, which moves approximately one degree every two hours. It is generally unsafe to hazard any definite speculations about the Moon's aspects unless the birth time is known.

However, reference is made to page 281 under the comparison of horoscopes where a very useful key is suggested not only for determining the Moon's probable position but for arriving at the approximate time of birth without rectification. This is a speculative theory well worth looking into.

A word of advice about the importance of aspects, particularly to those learning astrology. For all practical purposes you should disregard all minor aspects and concentrate solely on the five major aspects. I will go a step further and strongly recommend that in initial horoscope interpretation you use only the three hard-angle aspects of conjunction, square and opposition. These are the aspects that force the native to action. The conjunction irrevocably COUPLES, the square FORCES, and the opposition BLOCKS the independent possibility of one planet acting without the other. Both must be considered in the same action, for better or worse.

The soft-angle aspects, the sextile and the trine, are far less effective in their operation for affecting the native's character. They have more to do with the fortunate and less frictional activities, which the native may from time to time engage in WHEN HE FEELS LIKE IT and when he is not being forced into things by the conditions of compelling reality. The soft-angle aspects mainly encourage (but in no way compel) each other to act. The effect of the sextile and the trine are almost the same, only the trine is said to be luckier because it requires even less effort than the sextile to go into operation.

Also it is recommended that you allow only 3° in variation from exact to determine whether two planets are in effective contact. Later you may wish to extend this orb of allowance to account for complexities which enter the picture, but do not allow yourself this latitude in the beginning or you will muddle up the picture and get off on the wrong foot. You will generally find that if you restrict yourself in the above manner, your attention will be drawn to the really important factors and you will avoid the confusion of trying to synthesize something beyond your comprehension.

Above all, do not include an aspect by allowing a greater orb of allowance just because you hate to lose possible contact with a favorable combination that you would like to have. This is a frequent indulgence of all students of astrology, who want to see the best and leave out that which is less favorable. A detailed discussion of the nature of aspects is found in Chapter 9, "Aspects Between Planets."

Once you have established the general character of your makeup— that is, the planetary forces at your disposal with their qualifying limitations and special refinements, shown by the aspects—then you can determine exactly which quality under certain conditions or use might be considered an asset and which a liability.

Once you know your assets and liabilities, you can determine the PROBABLE OUTCOME for yourself if you use certain qualities in certain situations. According to your specific situation, if you are pushing the right quality in the right place, you are working with an asset.

For example, if you have Mars in Libra, you inevitably stir people up against you, so it is mandatory to be prepared to either outsmart them or beat them in competition, for that is surely what will result when dealing with others in general. Now if you are thinking about a job situation or how to handle your routine responsibilities (both of which are a sixth-house matter), you should not try to use the Mars approach in handling people, as it will only result in the above-mentioned consequences—in this case a liability. You should instead utilize any Virgo qualities you have or something else that would be closer to the demands of the sixth house. Then you would be working with your assets.

If you have Venus in Libra, you have a social asset in dealing with others and winning them over to your position or interest. This would be an asset for you in dealing with the boss (a tenth-house matter) or influencing friends (an eleventh-house matter) or any function involving others.

If you have Mercury in Aries, you are generally frank, outspoken, opinionated and aggressively critical. This would be a definite liability to use in the beginning of any tenth-house career matters involving your boss or those in top authority. It is unlikely that they would be overjoyed to hear your views and biting criticisms no matter how true they may be. In this case you should avoid communication except on matters of routine nature. But by the same token, what would be a liability in tenth-house matters would certainly be an asset in fifth-house creative efforts.

A word of comment about analysis, astrological or otherwise. Analysis that involves LOOKING BENEATH THE SURFACE TO FIND THE INNER AND TOTAL MAN is a talent. Not everyone can do this. Most people only see what is on the surface or believe what is reflected by this surface image.

In astrology approximately only one-twelfth of the horoscope (the area of the first house) deals with what is seen on the surface. The other eleven-twelfths deal with the total person. Now, some gifted individuals can intuitively sense things about other people—without astrology or anything else. To them surface actions are only reflections of this inner man, which is the total person. There is a concept in psychology about this called the Gestalt school of pattern behavior. Individuals who are keyed to pattern recognition need to experience only a fragment of a recognizable pattern to be aware of the total pattern, even though they have not yet experienced the total pattern in the other person.

It is well to mention this whenever you attempt the depth analysis of public figures. One must remember that many of the things discussed are not what the average person sees or knows from just the public image. Everyone seems to forget that he is in total different and much more than what he seems on the surface, but he neglects to extend this possibility to others whom he may be trying to analyze or understand.

CRCS PUBLICATIONS

CRCS PUBLICATIONS publishes high quality books that focus upon the modernization and reformulation of astrology. We specialize in pioneering works dealing with astrological psychology and the synthesis of astrology with counseling and the healing arts. CRCS books utilize the insights of astrology in a practical, constructive way as a tool for self-knowledge and increased awareness.

ASTROLOGY, PSYCHOLOGY & THE FOUR ELEMENTS: An Energy Approach to Astrology & Its Use in the Counseling Arts by Stephen Arroyo .... $7.95 Paperback; $14.95 Hardcover

An international best-seller, this book deals with the relation of astrology to modern psychology and with the use of astrology as a practical method of understanding one's attunement to universal forces. Clearly shows how to approach astrology with a real understanding of the energies involved. Awarded the British Astrological Assn's. Astrology Prize. A classic translated into 8 languages.

ASTROLOGY AND THE MODERN PSYCHE: An Astrologer Looks at Depth Psychology by Dane Rudhyar .... 182 pages, Paperback $5.95

Deals with Depth-Psychology's pioneers with special emphasis on Jung's concepts related to astrology. Chapters on: Psychodrama, Psychosynthesis, Sex Factors in Personality, the Astrologer's Role as Consultant.

ASTROLOGY, KARMA, & TRANSFORMATION: The Inner Dimensions of the Birth-Chart by Stephen Arroyo .... 264 pages, $9.95 Paperback; $17.95 Deluxe Sewn Hardcover

An insightful book on the use of astrology as a tool for spiritual and psychological growth, seen in the light of the theory of karma and the urge toward self-transformation. International best-seller.

CYCLES OF BECOMING: The Planetary Pattern of Growth by Alexander Ruperti .... 6 x 9 Paperback, 274 pages, $9.95

The first complete treatment of transits from a humanistic and holistic perspective. All important planetary cycles are correlated with the essential phases of psychological development. A pioneering work!

AN ASTROLOGICAL GUIDE TO SELF-AWARENESS by Donna Cunningham, M.S.W. .... 210 pages, Paperback $6.95

Written in a lively style by a social worker who uses astrology in counseling, this book includes chapters on transits, houses, interpreting aspects, etc. A popular book translated into 3 languages.

RELATIONSHIPS & LIFE CYCLES: Modern Dimensions of Astrology by Stephen Arroyo .... 228 pages, Paperback $7.95

A collection of articles and workshops on: natal chart indicators of one's capacity and need for relationship; techniques of chart comparison; using transits practically; counseling; and the use of the houses in chart comparison.

REINCARNATION THROUGH THE ZODIAC by Joan Hodgson ..... Paperback $5.50

A study of the signs of the zodiac from a spiritual perspective, based upon the development of different phases of consciousness through reincarnation. First published in England as *Wisdom in the Stars*.

LOOKING AT ASTROLOGY by Liz Greene .... 8½ x 11, $5.95

A beautiful, full-color children's book for ages 6-13. Illustrated by the author, this is the best explanation of astrology for children and was highly recommended by *School Library Journal*. It emphasizes a healthy self-acceptance and a realistic understanding of others. A beautiful gift for children or for your local library.

A SPIRITUAL APPROACH TO ASTROLOGY by Myrna Lofthus ... Paperback $12.50

A complete astrology textbook from a karmic viewpoint, with an especially valuable 130-page section on karmic interpretations of all aspects, including the Ascendant & M.C. A huge 444-page, highly original work.

THE ASTROLOGER'S GUIDE TO COUNSELING: Astrology's Role in the Helping Professions by Bernard Rosenblum, M.D. .... Paperback $7.95

Establishes astrological counseling as a valid, valuable, and legitimate helping profession, which can also be beneficially used in conjunction with other therapeutic and healing arts.

THE JUPITER/SATURN CONFERENCE LECTURES (*Lectures on Modern Astrology Series*) by Stephen Arroyo & Liz Greene .... Paperback $8.95

Transcribed from lectures given under the 1981 Jupiter/Saturn Conjunction, talks included deal with myth, chart synthesis, relationships, & Jungian psychology related to astrology.

THE OUTER PLANETS & THEIR CYCLES: The Astrology of the Collective (*Lectures on Modern Astrology Series*) by Liz Greene .... Paperback $7.95

Deals with the individual's attunement to the outer planets as well as with significant historical and generational trends that correlate to these planetary cycles.

CHILD SIGNS: Understanding Your Child Through Astrology by Dodie & Allan Edmands 150 pages, 12 photos of children .... Paperback $6.95

An in-depth treatment of a child's developmental psychology from an astrological viewpoint. Recommended by *Library Journal*, this book helps parents understand and appreciate their children more fully. Nice gift!

DYNAMICS OF ASPECT ANALYSIS: New Perceptions in Astrology by Bil Tierney. Groundbreaking new work! .... 288 pages, Paperback $8.95

The most in-depth treatment of aspects and aspect patterns available, including both major and minor configurations. Also includes retrogrades, unaspected planets & more!

ASTROLOGY FOR THE NEW AGE: An Intuitive Approach by Marcus Allen .... Paperback $5.95

A highly original work with an uplifting quality. Emphasizes self-acceptance and tuning in to your own birth chart with a positive attitude. Helps one create his or her own interpretation. Ready now.

THE PRACTICE & PROFESSION OF ASTROLOGY: Rebuilding Our Lost Connections with the Cosmos by Stephen Arroyo .... late 1984, Paperback $7.95

A challenging, often controversial treatment of astrology's place in modern society and of astrological counseling as both a legitimate profession and a healing process.

HEALTH-BUILDING: The Conscious Art of Living Well by Dr. Randolph Stone, D.C., D.O. Approx. 150 pages, Paperback
A complete health regimen for people of all ages by an internationally renowned doctor who specialized in problem cases. Includes instructions for vegetarian/purifying diets and energizing exercises for vitality and beauty. Illustrated with drawings & photographs.

POLARITY THERAPY: The Complete Collected Works by the Founder of the System, Dr. Randolph Stone, D.O., D.C. (In 2 volumes, 8½ x 11),
The original books on this revolutionary healing art available for the first time in trade editions. Fully illustrated with charts & diagrams. Sewn paperbacks, over 500 total pages.

A JOURNEY THROUGH THE BIRTH CHART: Using Astrology on Your Life Path by Joanne Wickenburg...168 pages, Paperback $7.95
Gives the reader the tools to put the pieces of the birth chart together for self-understanding and encourages creative interpretation of charts by helping the reader to think through the endless combinations of astrological symbols. Clearly guides the reader like no other book.

THE ASTROLOGY OF SELF-DISCOVERY: An In-Depth Exploration of the Potentials Revealed in Your Birth Chart by Tracy Marks.......288 pages, Paperback.................................$8.95
A guide for utilizing astrology to aid self-development, resolve inner conflicts, discover and fulfill one's life purpose, and realize one's potential. Emphasizes the Moon and its nodes, Neptune, Pluto, & the outer planet transits. An important & brilliantly original new work!

THE PLANETS & HUMAN BEHAVIOR by Jeff Mayo...180 pp, Paperback $7.95
A pioneering exploration of the symbolism of the planets, blending their modern psychological significance with their ancient mythological meanings. Includes many tips on interpretation!

ASTROLOGY IN MODERN LANGUAGE by Richard B. Vaughan...340 pp, $9.95
An in-depth interpretation of the birth chart focusing on the houses and their ruling planets-- including the Ascendant and its ruler. A unique, strikingly original work! (paperback)

THE ART OF CHART INTERPRETATION: A Step-by-Step Method of Analyzing, Synthesizing & Understanding the Birth Chart...by Tracy Marks Paperback $7.95
A guide to determining the most important features of a birth chart. A must for students!

THE SPIRAL OF LIFE: Unlocking Your Potential With Astrology..... by Joanne Wickenburg & Virginia Meyer...paperback.........$7.95
Covering all astrological factors, this book shows how understanding the birth pattern is an exciting path towards increased self-awareness and purposeful living.

HOW TO HANDLE YOUR T-SQUARE by Tracy Marks...(new edition)..$10.95
The meaning of the T-Square, its focal planets, aspects to the rest of the chart, and its effect in chart comparisons, transits and progressions. A perennial best seller! (paperback)

NUMBERS AS SYMBOLS OF SELF-DISCOVERY by Richard B. Vaughan......336 pages, Paperback.................................$7.95
A how-to book on personal analysis & forcasting your future through Numerology. His examples include the number patterns of a thousand famous personalities.

For more complete information on our books, a complete booklist, or to order any of the above publications, WRITE TO:

CRCS Publications
Post Office Box 1460
Sebastopol, California 95473
U.S.A.